WILL SHORTZ'S BEST BRAIN BUSTERS

Will Shortz's

BY WILL SHORTZ

 Published in the United States by Times Books, a division of Random House, Inc., New York, and simultaneously in Canada by Random House of Canada Limited, Toronto. All of the Brain Busters that appear in this work were previously published in *Games* magazine.

Library of Congress Cataloging-in-Publication Data

Shortz, Will
Games magazine presents Will Shortz's best brain busters / by Will Shortz.
p. cm.
ISBN 0-8129-1952-1
1. Puzzles. I. Title.
GV1493.S567 1991
793.73—dc20 91-26535

Manufactured in the United States of America

CONTENTS

CONTENTS

INTRODUCTION

A British puzzlemaker once wrote that a career in puzzles leads slowly, but inevitably, to insanity.

So far, after 25 years of professional puzzlemaking, I have not reached that point. At least I don't think so.

You might think, judging from the difficulty of some of my puzzles, that I'm trying to drive *you* insane. This is not true. My goal is to whack you on the side of the head, twist your brain in a novel way, make you see language—and the world—in a new light. But in the end, I do want you to finish my puzzles, and to feel the satisfaction of having accepted their challenge and succeeding.

This book contains some 150 of my best puzzles, all originally published in GAMES magazine or one of its sister publications (GAMES Special Edition or The Four-Star Puzzler) between 1979 and the present. The formats of most of the puzzles are either original or based on original ideas. Some of the repeated formats, like The Spiral, Petal Pushers, and Left and Right puzzles, are borrowed from foreign publications, but in most cases I was the first person to present them to American solvers.

I'd like to thank everyone at GAMES who over the years improved these puzzles by suggesting changes in the clues or the directions, or in other ways. Special thanks go to Mike Shenk, who tests all my puzzles before publication. I owe Mark Danna a debt of gratitude for his expertise and care in preparing the manuscript for publication.

Now it's time to get busy. And if these puzzles drive all of us insane, let's at least have a ball on the way!

Will Shortz

PUZZLETOWN ZOO

Sixteen four-footed animals are located in the west wing of the Puzzletown Zoo. Their names have all been hidden in the novel, space-saving directory below. How many of them can you find? Each name can be found in a series of consecutive squares connected horizontally, vertically, or diagonally. For example, the word GOAT can be spelled beginning with the letter G in the top row, then moving down to the O, right to the A, and diagonally up to the T. In spelling a word, do not stand on a letter (as the M in LEMMING) before going on. You may, however, reuse a letter later in a word. Only the general names of animals are used—not, for example, names of male or female varieties. **ANSWERS, PAGE 116**

Y D G C T
S E O A R
K N H M E
G U I O L

1. ______ 5. ______ 9. ______ 13. ______

2. ______ 6. ______ 10. ______ 14. ______

3. ______ 7. ______ 11. ______ 15. ______

4. ______ 8. ______ 12. ______ 16. ______

LEFT AND RIGHT #1

There are only two directions to this puzzle—left and right. Each answer is a six-letter word, which is to be entered in the grid one letter per square according to the numbers. Half the answers will read from left to right, as in the example, SUMMIT (1–2). Half will read from right to left, as in the answer to 2–3, which begins TIM-. Work in both directions to complete the puzzle.

ANSWER, PAGE 116

CLUES

1–2 Meeting of leaders
2–3 Lumberjack's cry
3–4 Provides evidence against
4–5 House of King James I
5–6 Emotional shock
6–7 Charm
7–8 Bank employee
8–9 Put down again, as tiles
9–10 Crown
10–11 "Greatest hits" pastiche
11–12 Cried out, as a dog
12–13 Expel from the country
13–14 Fighting forces
14–15 To the victor go these
15–16 Splinter
16–17 Book or movie critique
17–18 German "republic"
18–19 Put through without discussion
19–20 Attic window
20–21 Stay
21–22 Vitamin B_3
22–23 French woman's name
23–24 Leaves via ladder?
24–25 Kind of tank
25–26 Lemon's relative
26–27 Europe's northernmost NATO member
27–28 Expressed boredom
28–29 Pertaining to canines?
29–30 The second of two
30–31 Part of the eye
31–32 "20 Questions" category
32–33 Gave birth, as a sheep
33–34 Trash
34–35 Brightest star
35–36 Courting man
36–37 Spoiled
37–38 Below

MARKET SLICES

These days you never know exactly what's in your favorite products at the store. You have to read the labels carefully. The same goes for the products' names. Below are 16 words taken from well-known commercial logos. How many of the products can you identify? For example, the word LOG in #1 is from KELLOGG'S.

ANSWERS, PAGE 116

1. log	**2.** RACE	**3.** ills
4. chic	**5.** OGRES	**6.** MUCK
7. FEAT	**8.** harm	**9.** pica
10. RING	**11.** rill	**12.** wee
13. SHE	**14.** bell	**15.** alle
16. ride	**17.** rān	**18.** HEAT

THE SPIRAL #1

This puzzle turns in two directions. The spiral's Inward clues yield a sequence of words to be entered counterclockwise in the spaces from 1 to 100. The Outward clues yield a different set of words to be entered clockwise from 100 back to 1. Fill in the answers, one letter per space, according to the numbers beside the clues. Keep track of which way you're going, and have many happy returns.

ANSWER, PAGE 116

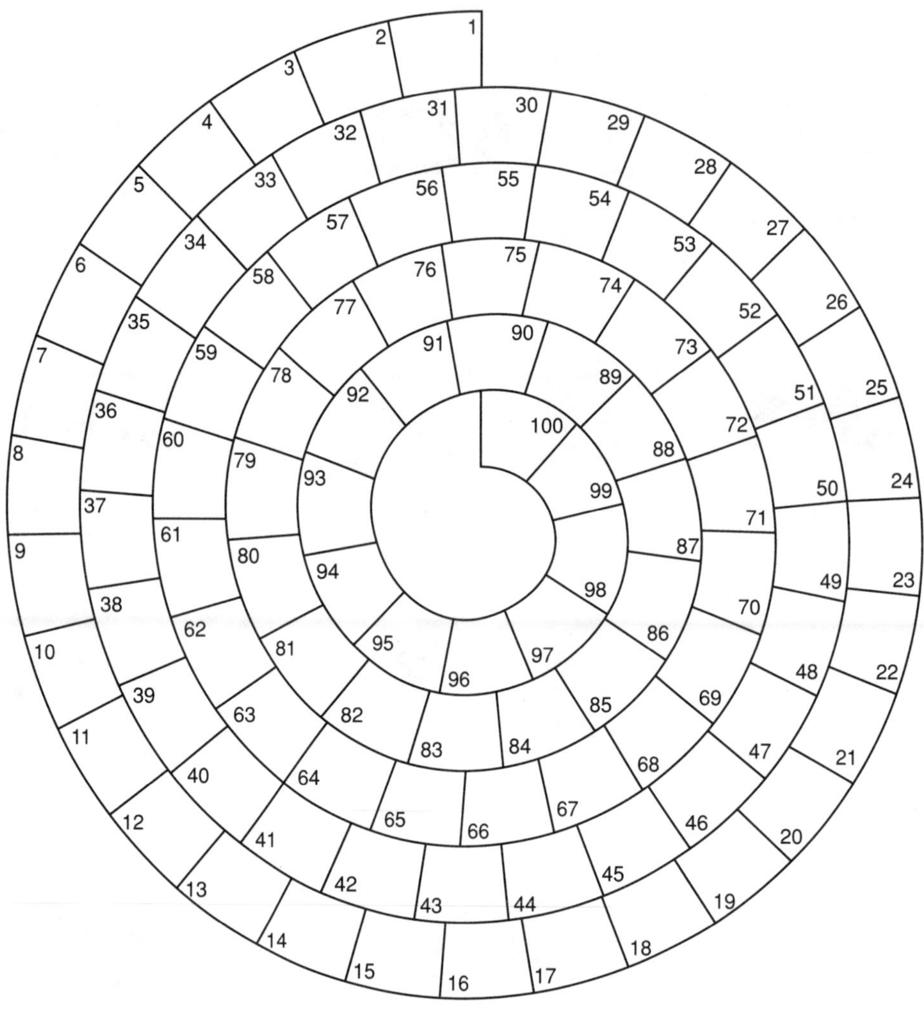

INWARD

1-8 Prominent persons
9-14 Said "no"
15-22 Pertaining to some blood channels
23-30 Gargantuan
31-36 Step or extension, for example
37-44 Tape cartridge
45-50 Military raid
51-55 *Zorro, the Gay* ___
56-60 Late
61-66 Drunk's sound
67-73 More than a couple
74-80 Part of the ç in "façade"
81-85 Snake poison
86-91 Outer tooth layer
92-100 On occasion

OUTWARD

100-95 Jew, e.g.
94-89 Arab, perhaps
88-82 The windflower
81-77 Frankie of the Four Seasons
76-70 Announce, as one's candidacy
69-62 Explorer Amerigo
61-54 Chemically combined with water
53-48 Even though
47-40 Flowerlike ornaments
39-34 Holy
33-28 J.R.'s series
27-24 Composition for one
23-18 Actress Ina
17-11 Part of the purchase price of a new car (hyph.)
10-6 1950s auto fiasco
5-1 Conductor's stick

TWO BY TWO

You might call this a word search puzzle for a rainy day. Hidden in the ark below are the names of 45 animals—concealed, naturally, in twos. That is, each name must be divided into pairs of letters (AA/RD/VA/RK, for example) before being located in the grid. Answers appear forward, backward, up, down, and diagonally; the first has been circled as an example. Finding the others won't take you 40 days and 40 nights, but that (gird yourself) is a matter of Noah count.

ANSWER, PAGE 116

~~AARDVARK~~	CHIMPANZEE	GOPHER	LION	RHINOCEROS
ALPACA	CHINCHILLA	HARE	LYNX	SQUIRREL
ANTEATER	CHIPMUNK	HEDGEHOG	MINK	TORTOISE
ANTELOPE	COUGAR	HIPPOPOTAMUS	MONGOOSE	WALRUS
BABOON	COYOTE	IBEX	MONKEY	WEASEL
BADGER	DORMOUSE	IMPALA	OCELOT	WILDEBEEST
BEAR	ELEPHANT	JACKAL	PLATYPUS	WOLF
BEAVER	ERMINE	JAGUAR	RABBIT	WOMBAT
BOBCAT	GOAT	KANGAROO	REINDEER	ZEBU

AN WA LR US HE DT WE NX

HE ER AV BE YW DG EN LY AS TI

AN TE LO PE NU AR EH CA NT ON EL OA

HI YO NT UG OT OG LA PA IM EP

TO HE CO AR LF KT WO IL AL HA

ST EE EB LD WI RT AN DT BA WO WO CK CH NT RE OF AL LF

AN BA BO ON LI LE OI DG SH MB JA IB EX IN IT EL WH ZE

TE BC ER EI HI ER SE NI AT GU OO DE BB CH RR BU

ST AT OS HE PP BR RK OO EA AR ER RA IP IM UI TH

OF ER LI OP FE VA GO NG FR OM MU GE PA SQ

NE OC EL OT SI RD KA PH MO NK EY SS NZ EV

IN EN AM VE AA GO RS ER MI NE EF EE

RH IF US YP AT PL TE DO RM OU SE EN

ON WITH THEIR HEADS!

It looks like the day after the French Revolution, what with these 20 lonesome bodies each trying to get a head. But what you actually see is merely an extreme example of identity crisis. These split personalities just don't have their heads screwed on right. Can you do the honors and reunite each with his own? (We'll give you a head start by noting that head B, with the tongue out, matches body 1, with the ice cream cone.)

ANSWERS, PAGE 116

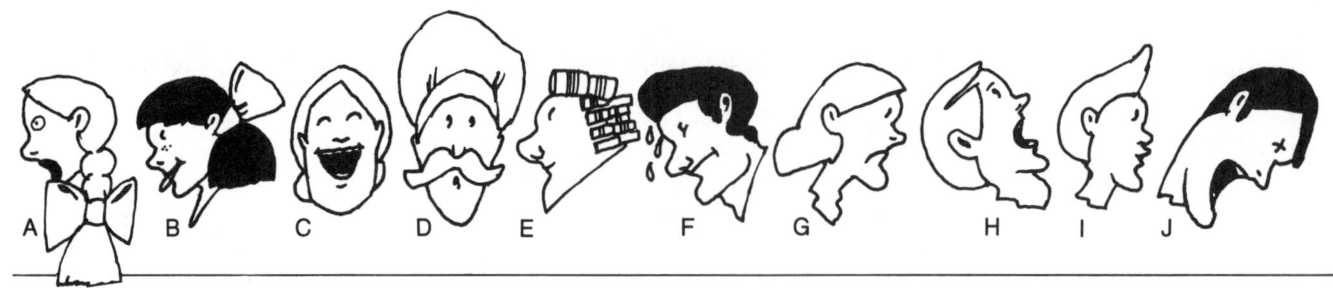

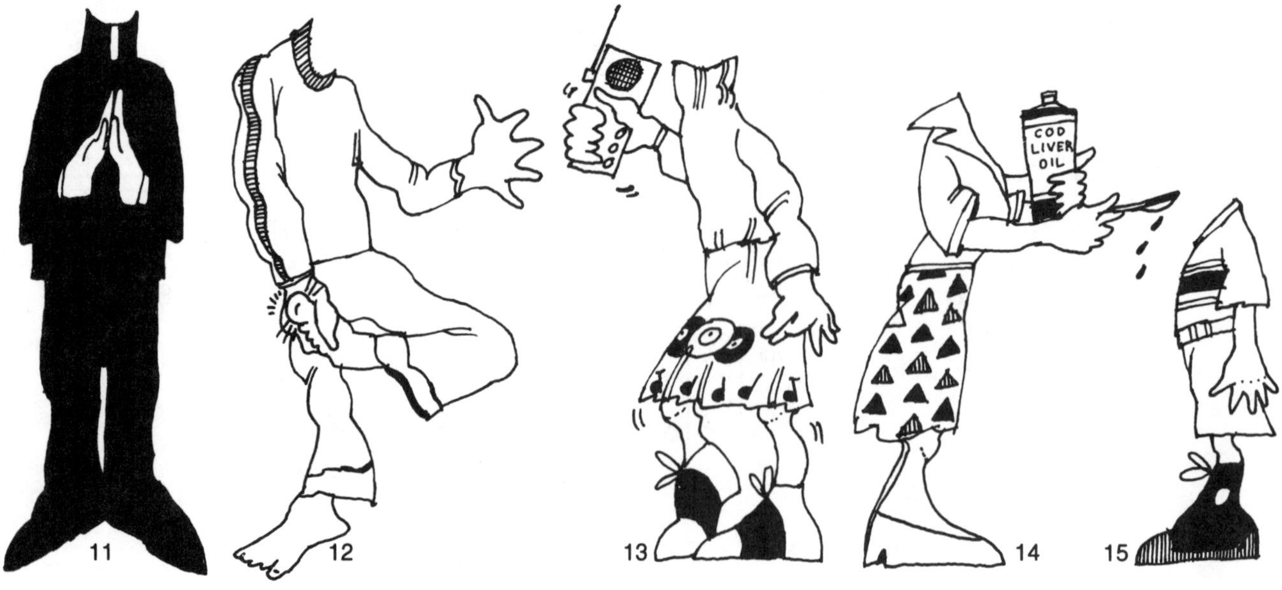

ON WITH THEIR HEADS!

6 7 8 9 10

16 17 18 19 20

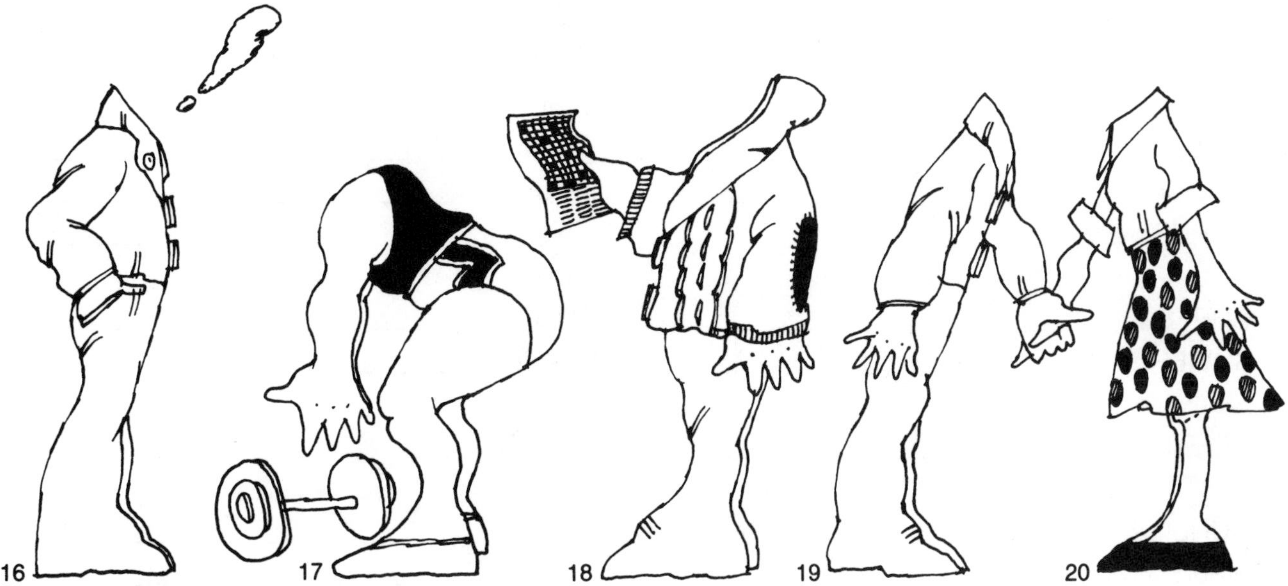

ANGIE LLOYD

BY THE ARROWS

All answer words in this puzzle begin in the numbered squares on the left side of the grid. Answers to the Across clues are to be entered across the grid, one letter per square. Answers to the By the Arrows clues start across but then bend in the middle and proceed diagonally down, as indicated by the dashed markers. Follow these pointers in working from both sets of clues to complete the puzzle.

ANSWER, PAGE 116

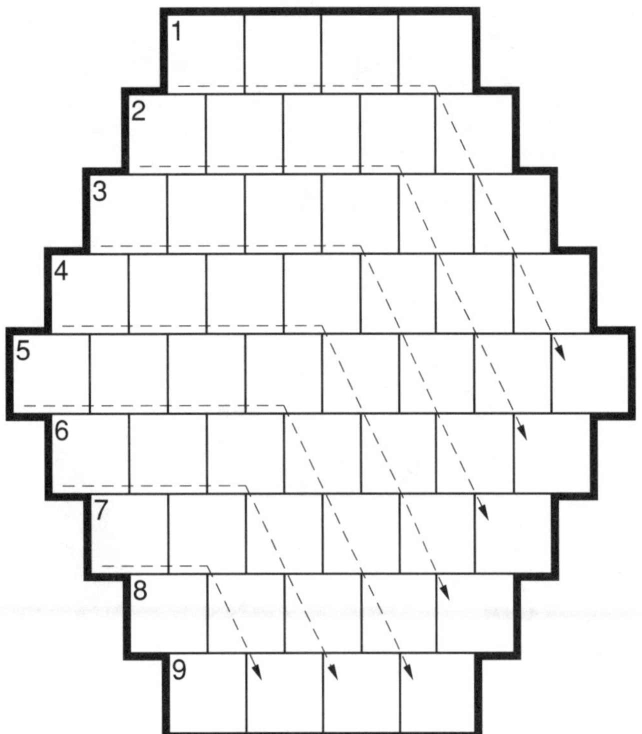

ACROSS

1 Cigarette: Sl.
2 Come to a point
3 Muckraking piece
4 Permanently unites
5 Gang thugs
6 "Petty" or "grand" theft
7 Not in the open
8 Former AFL-CIO head
9 Twiddling one's thumbs

BY THE ARROWS

1 Provide support
2 Pictorial rug
3 The 3 in 2^3
4 Eerie Halloween setting
5 Site of frantic activity (2 wds.)
6 Stage before pupal
7 Female student

TWIST-A-RHYME

Rearrange the letters of the four words in each set to form four new words that rhyme. For example, given the words BEARD, HERDS, DAIS, and ADDER, you would anagram them to spell BREAD, SHRED, SAID and DREAD.

ANSWERS, PAGE 116

1. ONSET __________
   NEWS __________
   WRONG __________
   HORNET __________

2. CURES __________
   SOWER __________
   SEVER __________
   STEER __________

3. DUNE __________
   WELD __________
   CURED __________
   TWEEDS __________

4. SINGER __________
   ASPEN __________
   VINES __________
   SPINAL __________

5. RANGED __________
   ENLARDS __________
   DACRON __________
   DARNED __________

6. BUSIER __________
   SOLE __________
   HOSES __________
   WIVES __________

BULL'S-EYE 20 QUESTIONS #1

Here's a test of your word "marksmanship." The answer to each of the 20 questions in the puzzle is one of the 26 words in the bull's-eye target. Each answer scores a "hit," which you may cross off in the target since no answer word is used more than once. When all the clues have been answered, the six unused words can be arranged to form a comment by the writer and educator Paul Goodman.

ANSWERS, PAGE 116

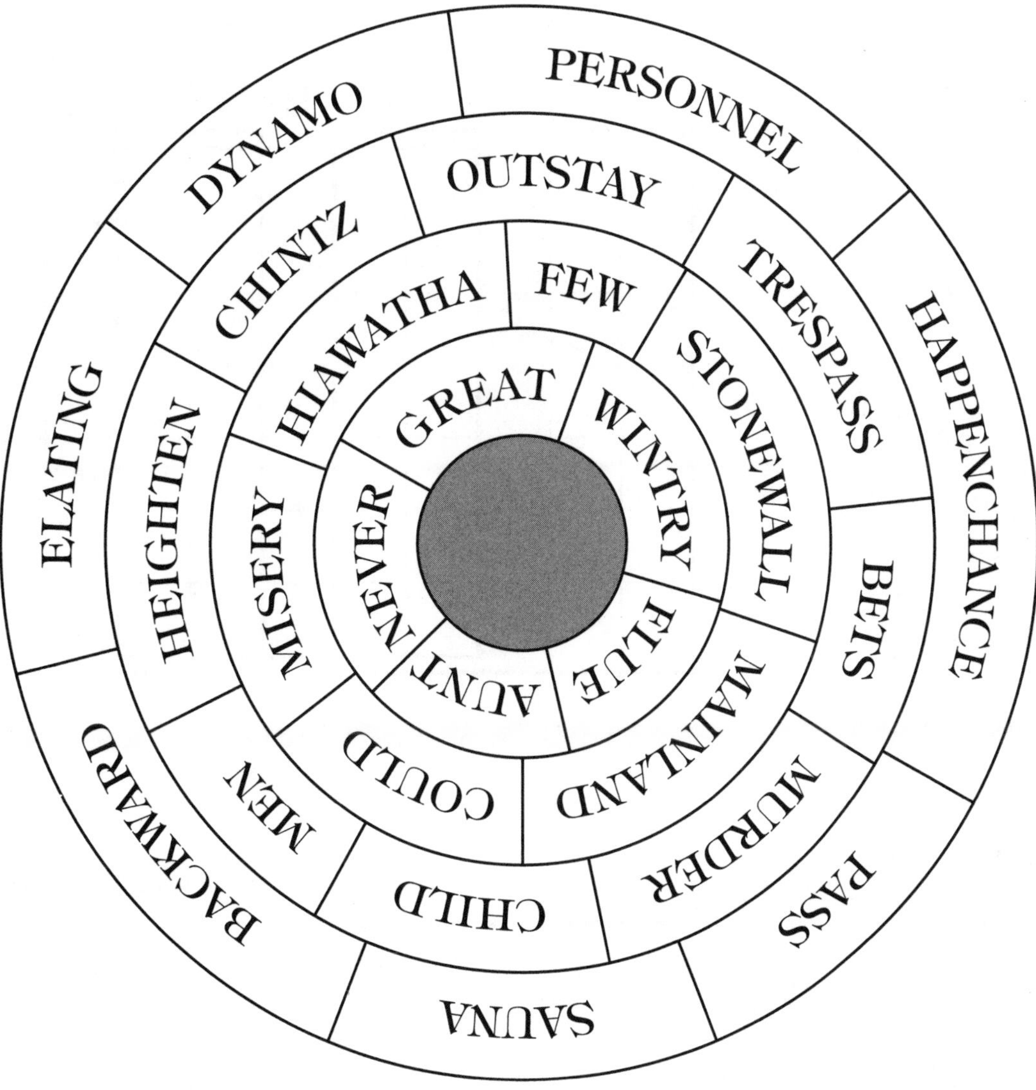

WHICH WORD ...

1. contains two numbers spelled within its letters?
2. would spell the name of a fish if you interchanged its first and last letters?
3. sounds like Pig Latin for a word meaning "fat"?
4. is an anagram of a day of the week?
5. would become its own opposite if you dropped its first letter?
6. spells a colorful liquor backward?
7. would sound like a state name if you accented it on the second syllable?
8. would spell a new word if you omitted one w?
9. has a smaller word meaning "resort" inside another word meaning "lock of hair"?
10. is pluralized by adding three letters?
11. has all its letters in alphabetical order?
12. is composed solely of letters that look the same when reflected in a mirror?
13. would spell the title of a popular movie if you dropped the first and last letters?
14. would spell a new word if you changed all the A's either to T's or to K's?
15. would spell two new *unrelated* words if divided in the middle?
16. has two familiar homophones (words pronounced alike, but different in spelling and meaning)?
17. has each of its letters in it appearing exactly twice?
18. would spell a new word meaning "jelly" if you moved its last letter to the front?
19. can be divided into consecutive state abbreviations?
20. is mentioned somewhere within these 20 questions?

LINK ACROSTICS #1

To solve these puzzles, answer the clues for three five-letter words reading across each line. The last two letters of the words in box A are the first two letters of those in box B, and the last two letters of the words in box B are the first two letters of those in box C. For example, if the clues in the first line were "Miss Garbo," "Piece of furniture," and "Exit," you would fill in GRE(TA)B(LE)AVE. When each puzzle is done, three additional related words will read down the shaded columns.

ANSWERS, PAGE 116

1. JUST DESSERTS

A.
1 Large parrot
2 Actress Merman
3 Arm-hand joint
4 Building addition
5 Alpha's opposite
6 Imitation gems
7 Skin

B.
1 Terrible
2 Run off to get hitched
3 "Turkey in the ____"
4 Newsboy's cry
5 Excessively showy
6 Extra inning
7 Cut, as wool

C.
1 Painful sore
2 Garden bloom
3 Roused from slumber
4 Gathered, as leaves
5 Expiring
6 "Grand" larceny
7 Firebug's crime

A B C

1
2
3
4
5
6
7

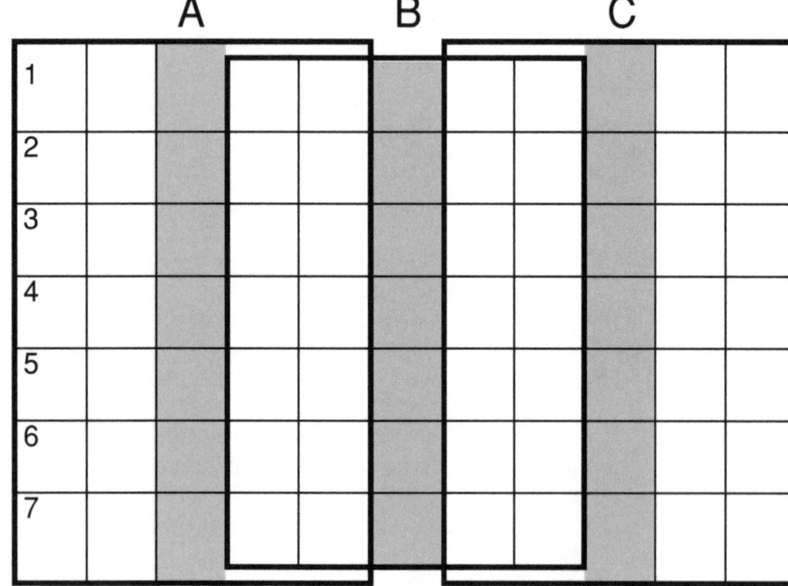

2. THEY NEED THEIR SPACE

A.
1 Indian statesman
2 "Humble" dwelling
3 Blue, as the sky
4 Like some French vowels
5 Woodworking tool
6 Any dog
7 Coup d'etat group

B.
1 Cuban dance
2 Condescend (to)
3 Varnish ingredient
4 Columnist Stewart
5 Burglary
6 Mormon Tabernacle ____
7 *Last ____ in Paris*

C.
1 Morning sizzler
2 Leprechaun
3 Kind of tube
4 Pertaining to the eye
5 Play a banjo
6 Twist of humor
7 "Gee whillikers"

SQUARE ROUTES #1

Square Routes is a word game within a puzzle. Each clue consists of three words that can precede or follow a fourth word to complete a compound word or a familiar two-word phrase. For example, the clue words LIST, BOOT, and HOLE would lead to the answer BLACK (to complete BLACKLIST, BOOTBLACK, and BLACK HOLE). To solve, first answer as many clues as you can. Then enter each answer in the grid, beginning in the square corresponding to the clue number and proceeding in any horizontal, vertical, or diagonal direction. (The direction can be determined by logic and by the crossing letters of other answers.) Work back and forth between grid and clues to finish. When you're done, every square in the grid will be filled, and at least half the letters of each word will be crossed by other answers.

WORD LIST, PAGE 128 **ANSWER, PAGE 117**

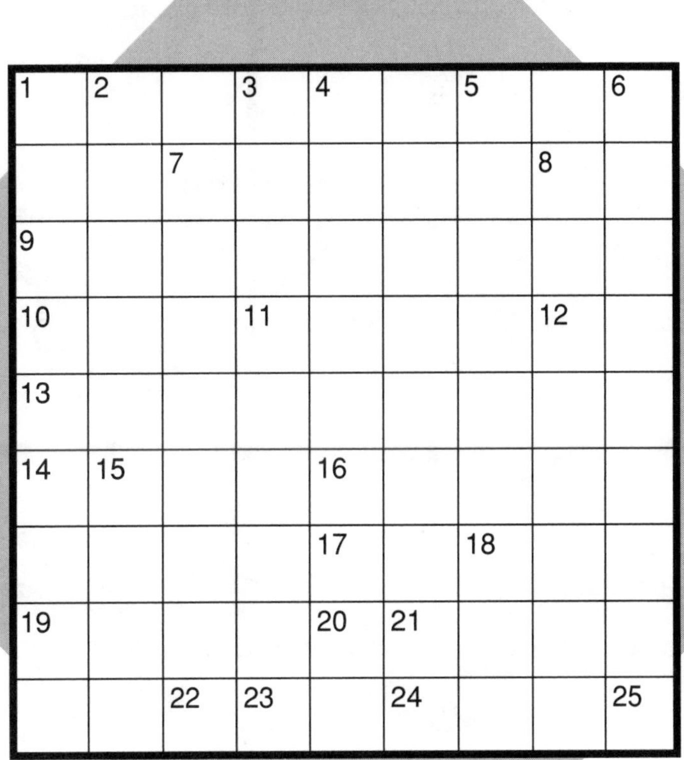

1	2		3	4		5		6
		7					8	
9								
10			11				12	
13								
14	15			16				
				17		18		
19				20	21			
		22	23		24			25

CLUES

1	Booby	Cross	Back
2	Cracker	Fail	Guard
3	Sword	Jelly	Story
4	Worm	Mother	Quake
5	Boot	Peg	Pulling
6	Single	Nail	Cards
7	Approval	Electric	Wet
8	Stock	Foreign	Student
9	Glow	There	Noon
10	Brain	Cloth	White
11	Person	High	Rocking
12	Hunger	Zone	Wildcat
13	Picture	Main	Work
14	Track	Rat	Relations
15	Gold	Double	Bearer
16	Good	Mare	Crawler
17	Safety	Cushion	Rolling
18	Chain	Plank	Busters
19	Balls	Eaten	Gypsy
20	Screen	Stack	Holy
21	Patent	Cabinet	Man
22	Sport	Eye	Lens
23	Indian	School	Time
24	Beach	Bound	Pulled
25	Mind	Room	Lip

3-D WORD HUNT #1

In the three-dimensional block of letters below, how many five-letter words can you find? A word may start at any letter, but must proceed along balls that are consecutively connected by straight lines. For example, the word BIRCH starts at the B in the upper right corner, moves left to the I, down to the R, forward to the C, and left to the H. In forming a word you may return to a letter and use it twice (like the D in BIDED), but you may not stand on a letter and use it twice before proceeding (like the O in CROON). Only uncapitalized, unhyphenated English words are allowed. A score of 18 or more words is good; 26 is excellent. Our answer shows 38 relatively common and 6 less common words. **ANSWERS, PAGE 117**

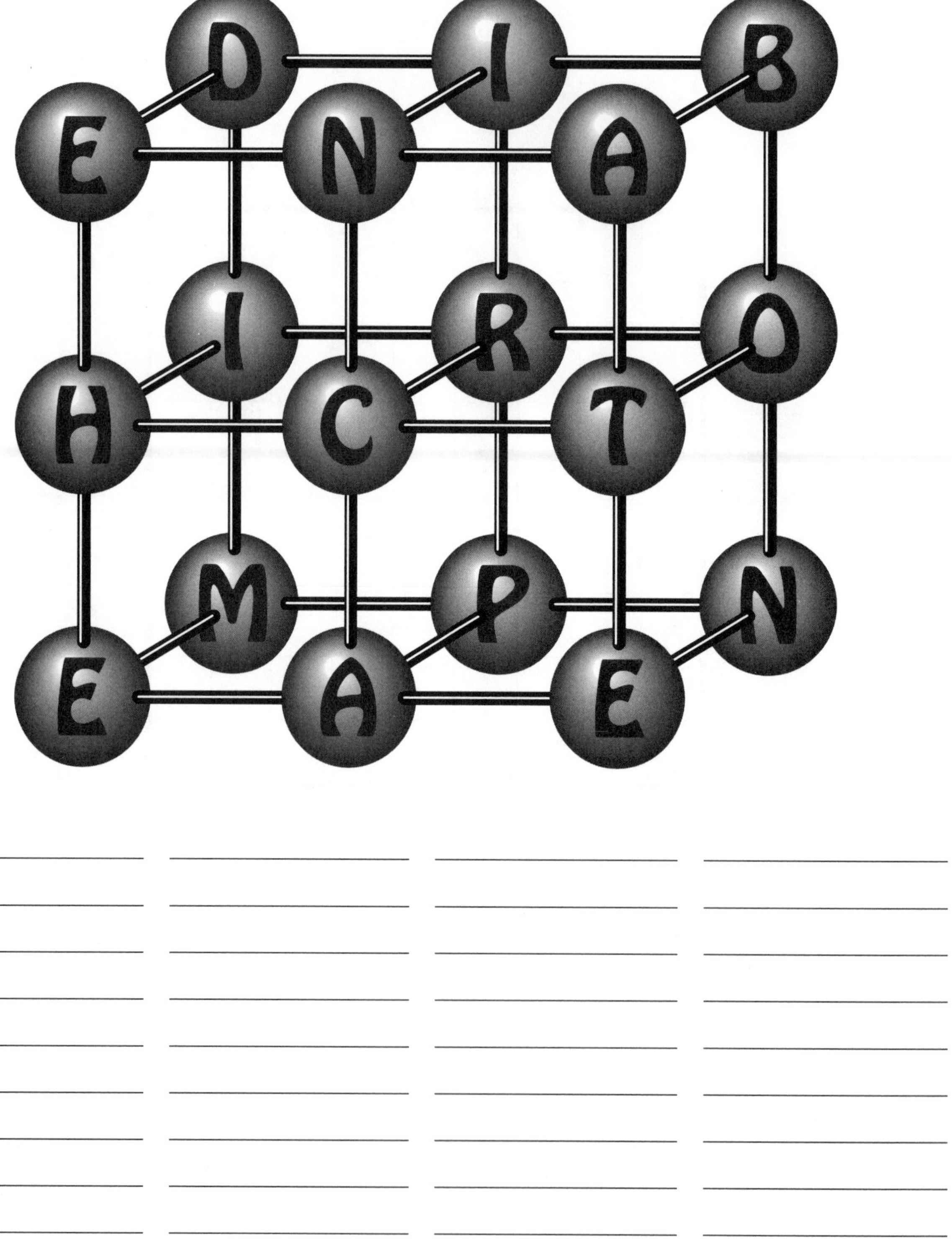

AT THE SCENE OF THE CRIME

How good a witness are you? Study this picture carefully for up to three minutes ... then turn the page for questioning. Once you turn, you will be relying solely on your memory of what you have seen.

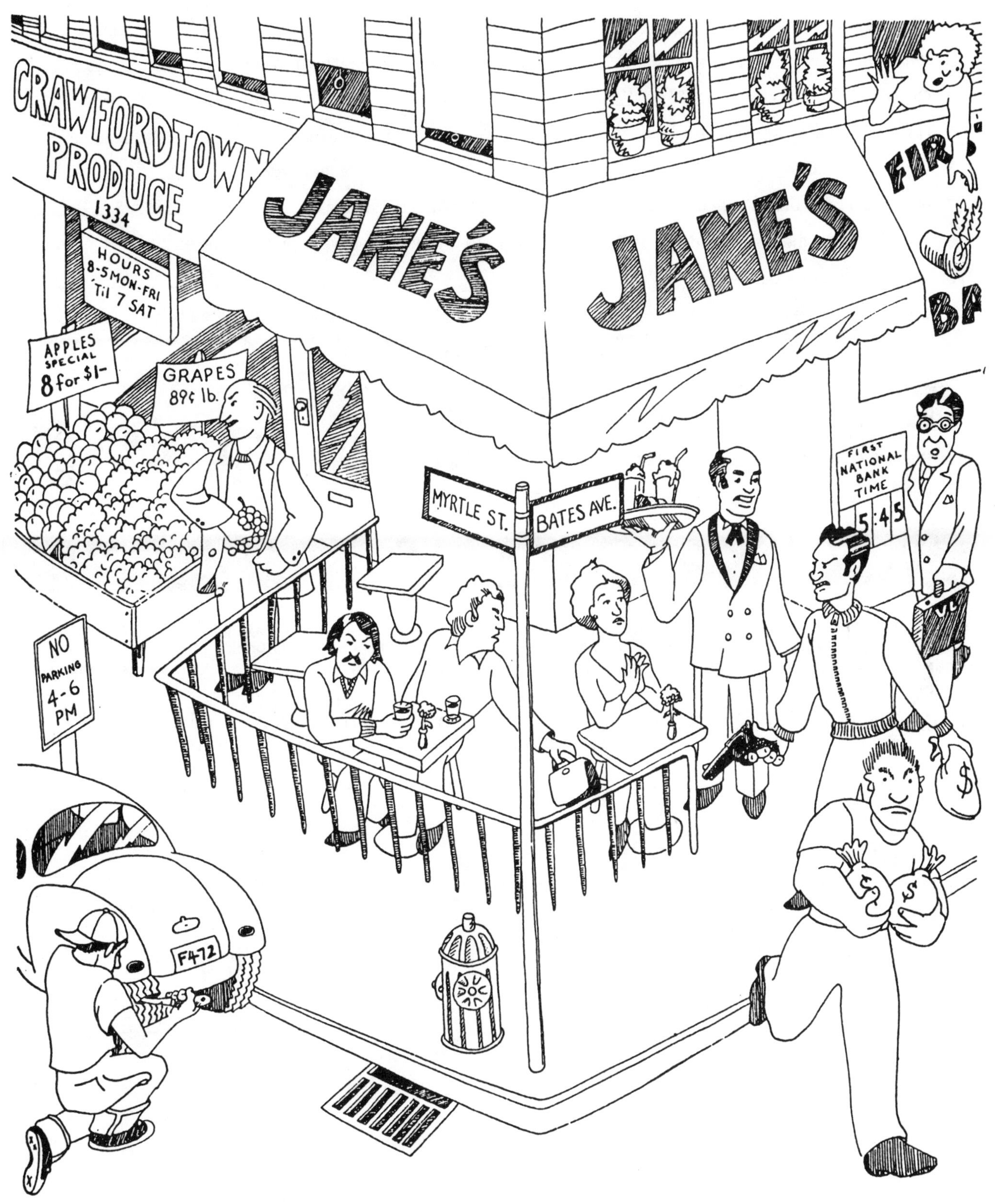

STEVEN PARTON

AT THE SCENE OF THE CRIME (PART 2)

In the rather busy street scene on the previous page, you were witness to one robbery, four misdemeanors, and an approaching calamity. The police would like your firsthand account of what happened, so please report the facts and events to the best of your memory.

ANSWERS AND RATINGS, PAGE 117

1. What time was it by the bank clock? ______________
2. What day of the week was it? ______________
3. What was the name of the outdoor café? ______________
4. On what street was its entrance? ______________
5. How many thieves were staging the holdup? ______________
6. Were they armed? ______________
7. How many bags of loot were they carrying? ______________
8. Was the thief in the street wearing a hat? ______________
9. How many people, besides you and the holdup men, were at the scene of the robbery? ______________
10. What were the initials of the man in the business suit? ______________
11. What immediate danger was he in? ______________
12. Was the onlooker from the second floor a man or woman? ______________
13. What store was next door to the café? ______________
14. On what street was its entrance? ______________
15. What was the shopper stealing? ______________
16. What was the license number of the car parked in front of the store? ______________
17. Why was it illegally parked? ______________
18. What part of the car was being vandalized? ______________
19. What offense was being committed against the lady diner? ______________
20. Was there a police phone at the corner? ______________

Bonus:

21. Please identify the holdup men from this lineup:

a. b. c. d. e.

SWAP SHOP

In each pair of words below, swap a letter in the first word with a different letter in the second word to form two new common, uncapitalized words. Circle the letters that are switched. In the example, the G in ANGLE has been exchanged with the K in STAKE to make ANKLE and STAGE.

ANSWERS, PAGE 117

Ex.	A N (G) L E	S T A (K) E
1.	M O U T H	S T O R Y
2.	E N A C T	T O X I C
3.	I R A T E	O G L E D
4.	R E A C H	S T O V E
5.	A L I E N	P R O N G
6.	I N F E R	G R A N T
7.	B L I N D	S P O O L
8.	G U I L D	T E N S E
9.	B U L G E	S H A D E
10.	S W O O P	B A N D Y
11.	R O U G E	P H O N Y
12.	Q U O T E	S T A I N
13.	L I G H T	Q U I E T
14.	M A J O R	N U D G E
15.	S W E E T	P L A T E
16.	F L U K E	S T U N K
17.	W O U L D	S H O R T

CROSS-O #1

Hidden in each box on this page are five words—four related objects or names, plus a fifth that identifies what the other four have in common. Each word is divided into five parts and concealed sequentially from left to right in consecutive columns.

For example, one of the names in box #1 is FLORIDA, with the letter F in the first column, LO in the second, R in the third, ID in the fourth, and A in the fifth. The category, STATE, is similarly concealed in left-to-right fashion. Now see if you can find the three remaining states. Then try the other boxes on your own. You may cross out squares as you solve, because each will be used only once.

ANSWERS, PAGE 117

S	R	X	T	A
F	A	R	AI	ON
O	E	W	G	E
T	LO	A	ID	S
H	T	E	A	I

1. STATE

FLORIDA ______

______ ______

A	OU	B	K	T
E	O	K	O	E
J	U	L	N	ER
SH	N	C	L	LE
KN	L	I	D	W

2. ______

______ ______

______ ______

D	N	D	R	S
V	U	A	E	RA
MI	D	N	N	A
A	E	R	U	SS
GO	I	E	O	VA

3. ______

______ ______

______ ______

P	N	A	T	G
C	R	SH	A	T
GE	T	S	N	N
PA	U	ER	O	ER
G	ER	T	IN	L

4. ______

______ ______

______ ______

S	AP	M	IK	O
O	I	R	C	G
P	T	I	E	ER
G	RE	N	N	E
NU	P	GA	G	A

5. ______

______ ______

______ ______

FO	G	O	U	S
V	B	M	I	Y
G	LA	B	OU	NE
E	O	AZ	E	E
MA	R	G	N	R

6. ______

______ ______

______ ______

BE	IC	T	OL	T
S	O	N	N	R
N	A	U	AR	S
P	R	I	E	D
L	E	H	I	AS

7. ______

______ ______

______ ______

B	UR	N	W	S
CO	U	O	E	RD
P	A	F	U	GE
T	R	L	T	N
ST	L	D	FO	E

8. ______

______ ______

______ ______

PETAL PUSHERS #1

This magic flower blooms only when you recite the mystical incantation of 32 six-letter words. You can discover these special words with the help of the flower petals and the two sets of clues. Answer the clues and enter the words inward from the tips of the petals to the heart of the blossom (one letter in each space). Half the words proceed clockwise from the numbers; the other half counterclockwise. When you are done, take off your shoes, chant the words three times under a full moon, and all the magic properties of the flower will be yours.

ANSWER, PAGE 117

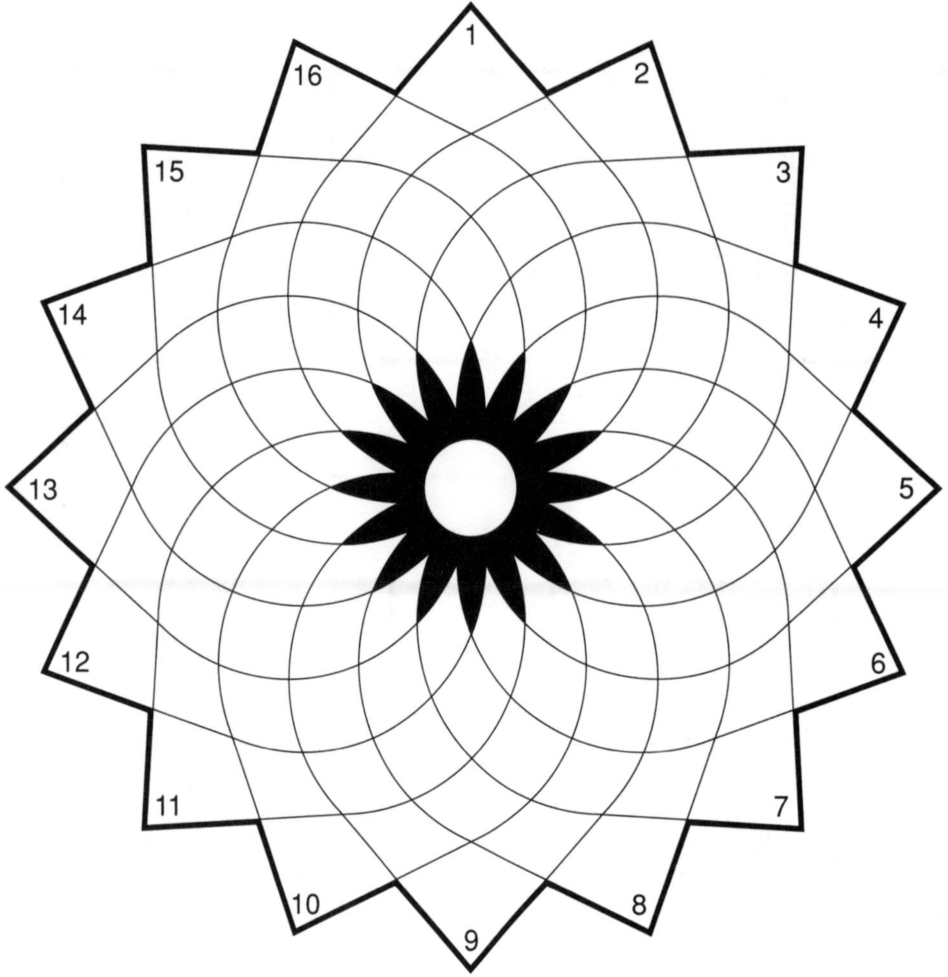

CLOCKWISE

1 Barnum's circus partner
2 California beach resort
3 Australian relative of the opossum
4 Most loyal
5 Central hall of an ancient Roman house
6 Rushed forward
7 Household servant
8 Heroine of *The Merchant of Venice*
9 Infant's toy
10 Spraying
11 Repudiation
12 Folk song
13 Tangled, as hair
14 Perceived
15 Comedian in the king's court
16 Washington's ____ International Airport

COUNTERCLOCKWISE

1 Cleared the table, as a waiter
2 Ice cream drink
3 Cried loudly
4 Bell ringer
5 Military forces
6 Short and squat
7 Governmental unit
8 Stickler for tradition
9 Cheap and inferior liquor
10 Home of the Globetrotters
11 "Sign on the ____ line"
12 Rouse
13 Kind of envelope
14 Salty
15 Traveler's woe
16 Kind of floss

LINK-LETTERS

In Link-Letters, the whole is greater than the sum of the parts. The answer to each clue on the left side of the puzzle grid goes in the squares to the left of the first black bar. The answer to each clue on the right goes in the squares to the right of the second black bar. Then one letter—the "link-letter"—goes in the square in the middle to complete a single word across the line. For example, if the clues for a line in the grid were, respectively, "choose" and "lyric poem," you would write ELECT in the left squares and ODE in the right squares, and fill in R in the middle to complete ELECTRODE. When you have finished a puzzle, the central letters will spell a seven-letter word reading down.

ANSWERS, PAGE 117

1. It Has Three Parts

Left	Right
Sumter or Knox, e.g.	____ of way
Beanie	Metropolis
Penniless	"Act your ____!"
$1,000	Not this or that
Piece of china	House of twigs
Period with a tail?	Doe or buck
Sharpen, as a knife	Toothy item

2. A Dollar a Kiss?

Left	Right
Use a broom	Seizes
The witching time	Exist
Huff and puff	"Crazy" birds
Brings to the ground	Imitate
Word from a ghost	Coat with metal
Heifer's mate	____ can
Half gainer, e.g.	Opposite of "lady"

3. Beauty Spot

Left	Right
Go into	Ascend
Broken arm holder	Earns a profit
____ and tonic	Sandwich meat
On fire	Political meeting
Golf standard	____ Rushmore
Donna Summer music	Bedouin's home
Large water ducts	500 sheets

HONEYCOMBS

Each answer is a six-letter word to be entered around the appropriate number in the honeycomb, beginning at the triangle indicated by the short line and proceeding one letter per space. An answer may read clockwise or counterclockwise—the direction in each case is for you to determine. As a small solving aid, we'll tell you that all 26 letters of the alphabet are used at least once in each completed honeycomb.

ANSWERS, PAGE 118

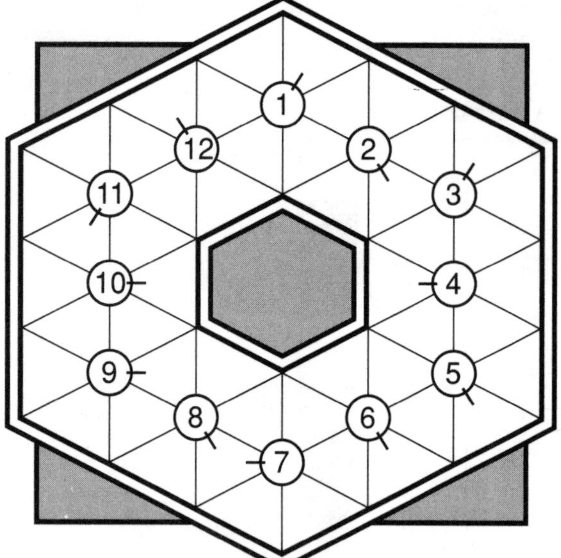

PUZZLE 1

1. Kind of ring or glove
2. Tarzan's domain
3. Discard
4. Beginner
5. Great, in '60s slang
6. Ice-cold
7. Tire-changing aid
8. Employee
9. Legitimate
10. Arab temple
11. Modernize
12. Grid of numbers

PUZZLE 2

1. ___ alarm (clock feature)
2. On fire
3. Southwest Indian or his home
4. Satisfy, as thirst
5. Pay by card
6. Senility
7. ___ Territory (1861-89)
8. Wild dog
9. California desert
10. Check, as facts
11. Pro- or con-, e.g.
12. Any word in this grid

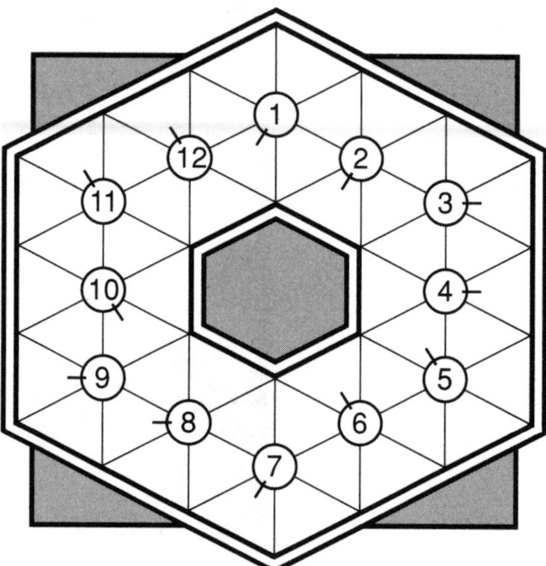

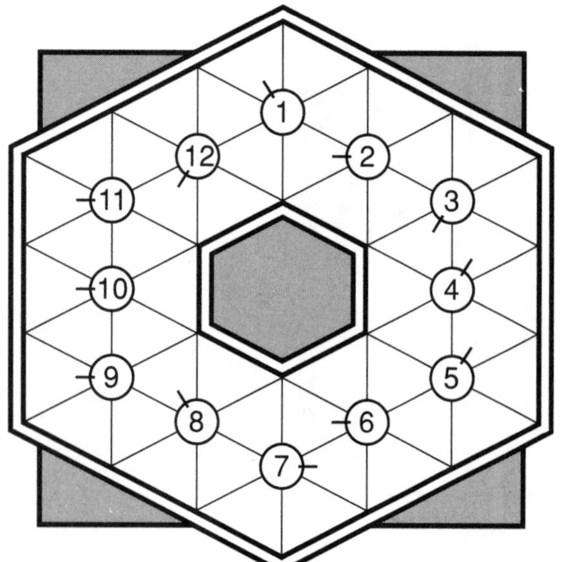

PUZZLE 3

1. Irritating
2. Site of frozen assets?
3. Israeli language
4. Capricious humor
5. Sit uncomfortably
6. Look up to
7. Glittery showmanship
8. Places for mushrooms?
9. Reddish quartz
10. The heart, jocularly
11. Farmer's truck
12. Bruce Lee skill

PICTUREGRAM

Picture this: a crossword with a hidden illustration. When filled in, each row (1-12 Across) and column (A-L Down) in the grid will contain two or three successive words that answer the clues below. Fill in the words in the same order as their clues, one after the other, and one letter per square. (For example, if the clues to a row were "Opposite of hot," "First digit," and "Trousers," you would write in the 12 successive letters COLDONEPANTS.) In the completed grid, every square is used once across and once down.

To form the illustration, do not enter the letters L, U, and V in the grid—instead, substitute the symbols shown below for these three letters, wherever they would normally appear. When you're done, *voilà!*—an illustration we hope you'll just love.

ANSWER, PAGE 117

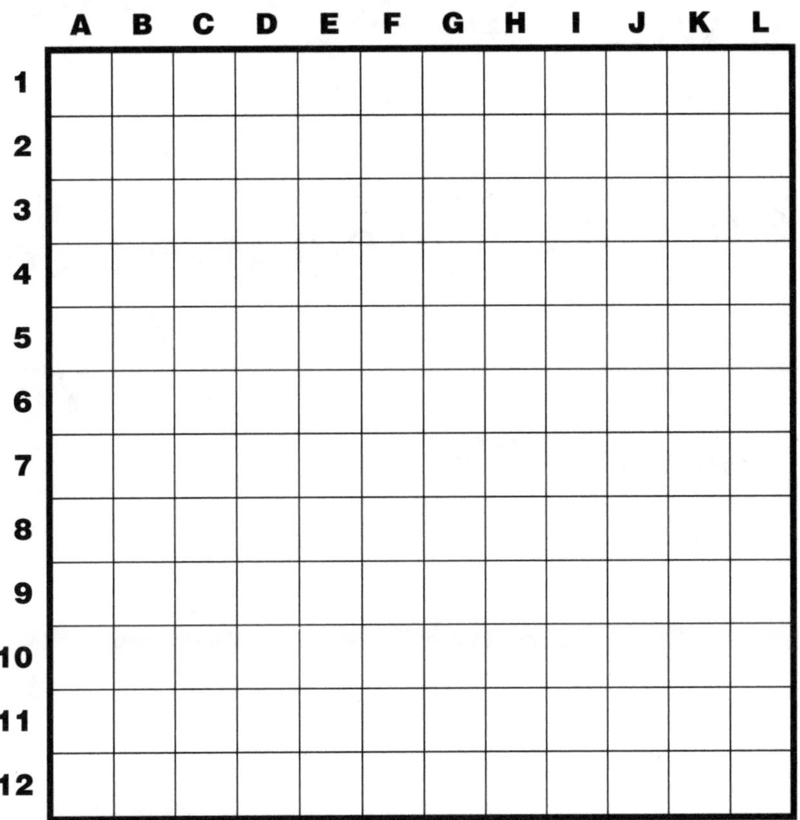

L =   U =   V =

ACROSS

1 a Military combat
b Rackets
2 a Comedian ___ Silvers
b "The clink," in Britain
c Superstar
3 a Make angry
b Diamond ___
c Stuck
4 a Bullfight cheer
b Greek triangle
c Part of the forelimb
5 a Electrician's tool
b Famed Greek
6 a Hit, say, of the '50s
b Hogwash
c Young fellow
7 a Comforts
b Shore dinner fare
8 a Anonymous John
b Lois of the *Daily Planet*
c Future ewes
9 a Outcome
b Make one's residence
10 a Water: Fr.
b Roger Bannister's run
c Giant of Greek myth
11 a Right a wrong
b Lusters
12 a Sheep with fine wool
b Record's opposite

DOWN

A a Fitting
b Late, late show?
B a Feeling of terror
b Card game
c Roof's edge
C a Scrabble piece
b Lay off workers
c Litigant
D a ___ du Diable (Devil's Island)
b Agnus ___
c Reunion gatherers
E a Watch flirtatiously
b ___ room
c Put in a row
F a Tips to be filed
b Stooped
c First sign of August?
G a Nick of *48 HRS.*
b Unavailing
H a Gymnast Korbut
b Strip
I a Fortunate: 2 wds.
b With more frills
J a Aretha Franklin's music
b Andean worker
c Afternoon reception
K a Word after break or get
b Metrical foot
c Whips
L a Melancholy
b Totals
c Judgment

PAPER CLIPS

Have you been paying attention when you read the daily newspaper? Really paying attention? Then try this. From what section or everyday feature of the paper has each of the lines below been clipped?

ANSWERS, PAGE 117

1 with wife **Christie Brinkley** is now be

3 and sank six consecutive free

4 one hea

5 (4) **Slim Cooking**

6 Yes, the city

7 partly cloudy tonight. Low 21 in the

8 6 Bubbablubchip

11 **11 Lendl et al.**

10 **—Stumped in Dothan, Ala.**

12 Knits

13 **8:05—WQXR—**Symphony Hall.

14 molding foreman.

17 **Da**

16 Republican and 90% for Bush, whose

PAPER CLIPS

2

HUH? WHERE IS IT? I KNOW

renovat-

on the third club and continue with a

elters are inadequate. Are ridden with

Pierce 5 8 6 15-1

9

Futuristic ideas appeal to you. Pi-

ere are often black, often worn with deep,

15

FMC

have at least

1711 25 —1½

18

Vietnam (R). 1:20, 4, 7:20,

657

Play-4: 0536

WRY SANDWICHES #1

Rearrange the letters of each word on the left below, and add two or three letters in the middle, to form a seven-letter word answering the clue on the right. The words on the left are the outside letters, or "bread," of the seven-letter "sandwich." The letters you add are the "filler" and will appear consecutively in the shaded squares inside. For example, given the word ASTER and the clue "Weird," you would answer STRANGE, with the letters NG appearing in the shaded squares. When a puzzle is completed, read the shaded letters in order, line by line, to spell a daffynition of the puzzle's title. **ANSWERS, PAGE 118**

1. QUADRUPLETS

Word	Clue
FINCH	Sheer fabric
MOIST	Bahamas' leading industry
PENT	Put in cipher
RYES	Doctor's needle
ERIN	Same old everyday thing
SNIPE	Greek E
RATIO	Bank employee

2. SKYWRITING

Word	Clue
HUMPS	Auto wreck (hyph.)
TECS	Man in a lineup
GIVEN	"Good ___!"
BARON	Expand
DONG	Gift from heaven
CANE	Water flask
RISE	On the level

3. HUSH MONEY

Word	Clue
CREPT	Flawless
TILTS	He doesn't do what's right!
GETS	Closet's use
ACTOR	Circus performer
LAMA	Immeasurably deep
METER	Unwanted houseguest?
NAVE	VFW member

QUIET, PLEASE!

Shhh! The town librarian requests silence first and foremost. It's not merely a coincidence that the library scene below contains so many things whose names start with silent letters. For example, there's the gnome in front of the librarian's desk. How many more "silent" things can you find? Only one form of an answer is allowed—thus, wrestler or wrestling, but not both. A score of 12 or more is good; 16 is excellent. Our answer lists 22 items.

ANSWERS, PAGE 117

FREDERICK WINKOWSKI

HALF AND HALF #1

The unusual twist of this puzzle is that the definitions of the answers have been replaced by *hints*. Each clue consists of three words that in some way relate to the answer, but that may or may not contain a synonym of it. For example, in the first clue, "Cards," "London," and "Overpass" all suggest the answer BRIDGE without defining it.

Each answer, like BRIDGE, is a six-letter word. To put it in the diagram, divide it in the middle and enter it downward, the first half in the squares designated by the first number of the clue, the second half in the squares designated by the second number. Every word half appears in two or more answers, so every answer will help with at least one other.

Note: For an extra challenge, before you begin, you might cover up the third column of hints and try to solve the puzzle with just the first two. (You can always peek later, if you need to!)

ANSWER, PAGE 118

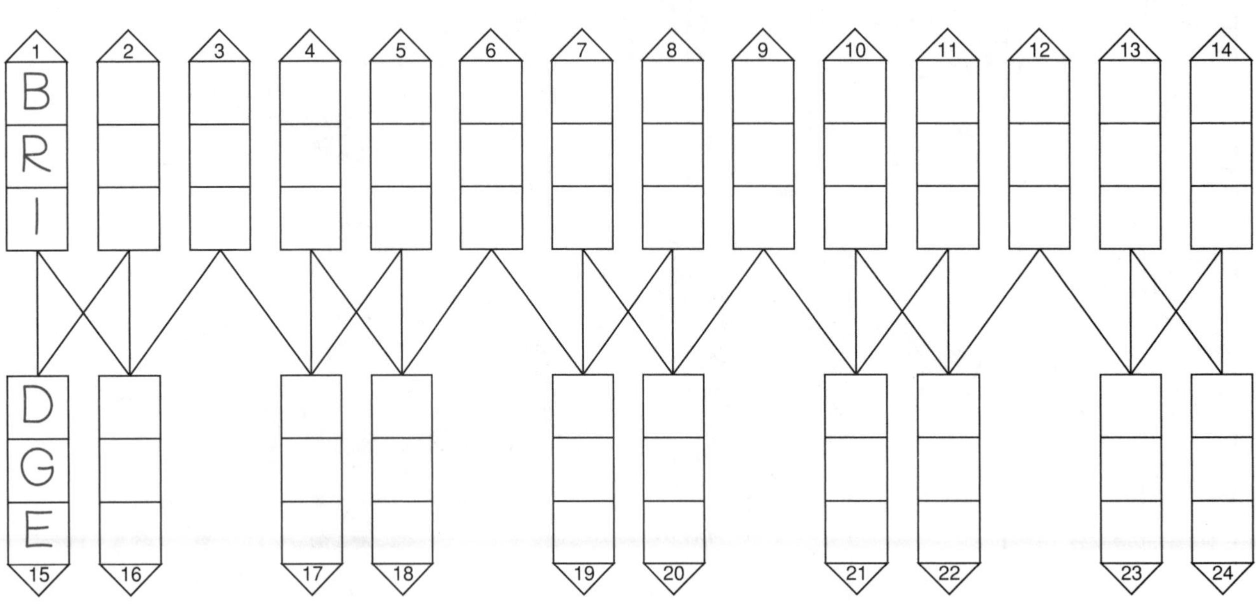

1–15	Cards	London	Overpass
1–16	Intelligent	Sparkling	Sunny
2–15	Snacks	Raid	Icebox
2–16	Goosebumps	Halloween	Scare
3–16	Paid	Goods	Purchased
3–17	Basketball	Check	Evict
4–17	DeGaulle	Riviera	Country
4–18	Constitution	Author	Artist
5–17	Charles	Throne	Heir
5–18	Schoolbook	Reading	Early
6–18	Nail	Carpenter	Pound
6–19	Dane	Shakespeare	Village
7–19	Plug	Electrical	Store
7–20	Picnic	Excursion	Pleasure
8–19	Sole	Boneless	Meat
8–20	Cabinet	Secretarial	Arranging
9–20	Wound	Jack-in-the-box	Season
9–21	Goblin	Drink	Fairy
10–21	Extremist	Religious	Iranian
10–22	Bashful	Most	Timidest
11–21	Party	RSVP	Ask
11–22	Stocks	Money	Purchase
12–22	Collar	Police	Nab
12–23	Airport	Reach	Come
13–23	Local	Indian	Indigenous
13–24	Preserve	Mother	Wildlife
14–23	Leaf	Salad	Vegetable
14–24	Last	Tolerate	Survive

WORDS AND NUMBERS

Hidden in this letter grid are the 50 words listed below. They may appear in any direction—horizontally, vertically, or diagonally, forwards or backwards—but always in a straight line. You will not find the words, however, exactly as they are printed. Each word contains the *sound* of one or more numbers, and we have substituted these numbers for their corresponding letters in the grid. AFFORD, for example, will appear in the grid as AF4D, and ASININE will appear ASI9. One word has been looped for you as a start.

ANSWERS, PAGE 119

```
1 E Y P R E 1 O D L O F 5 O G 1 N U K L L 7
K C U M I 2 A E 5 J E B A F 4 D P L A Z I N
D 4 E 4 D T C Y P D S H S U G 2 T 8 2 W C 2
I N Q L M N C 1/2 E 2 2 V I O D C N N S V O S
S E E U E U E H L U B R 9 8 M E A 4 E 9 1 D
U O N P 2 B L M 4 N O C 8 H R E O R X I S A
O J 6 D A M R 8 S K P F G P L A 1 W 1 U G Y
R H I R S T R 8 4 W A R D C A O N X O Q A 4
D C S T 1 U C H Y I 8 N U 8 O G I A U W 2 E
1 O D E R L O I N F F 1 Z O W T E V 8 E P N
E N 8 N A 7 D 2 U 2 O L O Z R O L G R M W 6
W 1 H S Q U E L T N R O 9 6 E D O E G O 8 Z
7 O 6 D I P 2 S I U O A A P 8 1 H 1 R S O E
4 T I 2 D E M S 9 E B N C S W L 5 G U 3 H T
```

AFFORD
ASININE
BEHALF
BENIGN
CANINE
CARTOON
CELEBRATE
CLASSICS
CONFORM
CONTENT
ENFORCE
EXTENUATE
FIVEFOLD
FORENSICS
~~FORMULATE~~
FORTITUDE
GATEWAY
GEODESICS
GRATEFUL
GUTHRIE
HERETOFORE
HOLE-IN-ONE
HUNDREDWEIGHT
LEAN-TO
OBTUSE
ONCE
PETUNIA
PITCHFORK
PRENATAL
PRETEND
QUININE
SEVEN-UP
SIXPENCE
SOMEONE
STENCIL
STRAIGHTFORWARD
STUPID
TENDERLOIN
TENNIS
THREESOME
TOODLE-OO
TUESDAY
TUTU
UNWON
UP-TO-DATE
VERMILION
WAITER
WEIGHTY
WONDROUS
ZETA

EQUATION ANALYSIS TEST #1

This test does not measure your intelligence, your fluency with words, and certainly not your mathematical ability. It will, however, give you some gauge of your mental flexibility and creativity. Since we developed the test, we've found few people who could solve more than half the 24 questions on the first try. Many, however, reported getting answers long after the test had been set aside—particularly at unexpected moments when their minds were relaxed; and some reported solving all the questions over a period of several days. Take this as your personal challenge.

Instructions: Each equation below contains the initials of words that will make it correct. Find the missing words. For example, *26 = L. of the A.* would be *26 = Letters of the Alphabet.*

ANSWERS, PAGE 118

a. 26 = L. of the A. ___Letters of the Alphabet___

b. 7 = W. of the A.W. ______

c. 1,001 = A.N. ______

d. 12 = S. of the Z. ______

e. 54 = C. in a D. (with the J.) ______

f. 9 = P. in the S.S. ______

g. 88 = P.K. ______

h. 13 = S. on the A.F. ______

i. 32 = D.F. at which W.F. ______

j. 18 = H. on a G.C. ______

k. 90 = D. in a R.A. ______

l. 200 = D. for P.G. in M. ______

m. 8 = S. on a S.S. ______

n. 3 = B.M. (S.H.T.R.!) ______

o. 4 = Q. in a G. ______

p. 24 = H. in a D. ______

q. 1 = W. on a U. ______

r. 5 = D. in a Z. C. ______

s. 57 = H.V. ______

t. 11 = P. on a F.T. ______

u. 1,000 = W. that a P. is W. ______

v. 29 = D. in F. in a L.Y. ______

w. 64 = S. on a C. ______

x. 40 = D. and N. of the G.F. ______

OH, OH!

What do the 66 words and phrases below have in common? Answer: Their only vowel is the letter O. That peculiarity is what makes this crisscross puzzle more of a challenge than you might expect. Fit the words in the grid, reading across and down, to complete the interlocking pattern. The four GAMES editors who tested the puzzle required less than a minute to identify the first word across in the grid (13 letters) and from 8 to 35 minutes to fill in the rest.

ANSWER, PAGE 118

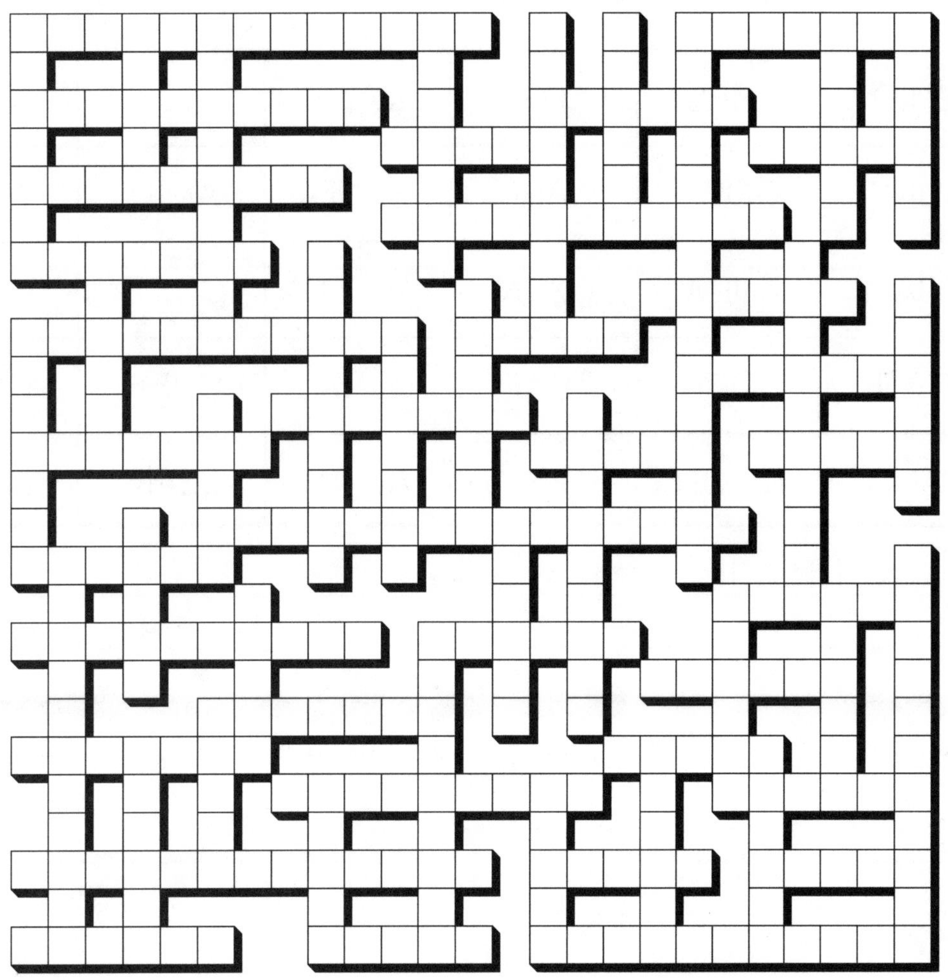

Five Letters

BOOST
DOGGO
FROND
GHOST
GODOT
MODOC
ON/OFF
ORLON
ORSON
ROBOT
SCOWL
SHOOT
SNOOK
THROW
TONTO
TOOTH

Six Letters

BONGOS
CONDOR
COTTON
DONORS
F TROOP
GODSON
HOLD ON
HOTDOG
JOLSON
NONCOM
ODD LOT
ODDS-ON
OXFORD
PHOTOS
PONCHO
ROCOCO
SCHOOL
TOMTOM
TORPOR

Seven Letters

BOG DOWN
COMPORT
FOXTROT
KNOW-HOW
MORMONS
MOROCCO
O'CONNOR
OSHKOSH
OSMONDS
POTSHOT
SOCK HOP
WOODLOT

Nine Letters

DON KNOTTS
FOOL'S GOLD
FRONT DOOR
HOT TO TROT
JOHN BROWN
POT OF GOLD
TOLL BOOTH

Ten Letters

CHLOROFORM
FOOTSTOOLS
VOODOO DOLL

Eleven Letters

CROSS OF GOLD
DOCTOR SPOCK
KNOCK ON WOOD
MORK FROM ORK
WORD FOR WORD

Thirteen Letters

COTTON BLOSSOM
SONG OF SOLOMON

Fifteen Letters

FROM TOP TO BOTTOM
WORLD OF TOMORROW

UNITED NATIONS

Like the U.N. General Assembly on a typical day, the puzzle below contains a tangle of countries. Hidden among the letters of the six words in each row of the grid are the names of three countries, each containing six letters. The countries are spelled out left to right, one letter per word. For example, BRAZIL is found in the first row by taking the B in the first word, the R in the second, the A in the third, etc. (Two more countries are also concealed in the first row.) You may cross off letters as you proceed, because no letter in the grid is used more than once. One letter in each word will remain when you're done. Can you locate all 15 countries?

ANSWERS, PAGE 118

1	BRIG	ERRS	RAGE	DAZE	LICE	TELL
2	JUNK	GOUT	WARN	SAND	AMID	WANT
3	SCAM	ANEW	OXEN	PAID	CODE	LOAN
4	FACT	YOUR	TRAP	RINK	CURE	DYES
5	PANG	MOON	GIRL	AVOW	LEAN	LADY

1. BRAZIL
______
______

2. ______
______
______

3. ______
______
______

4. ______
______
______

5. ______
______
______

MIND YOUR P'S AND Q'S

We don't know why, but a lot of words starting with the letter P seem to have synonyms starting with the letter Q. For example—**p**roficient/**q**ualified, **p**roblematic/**q**uestionable, **p**hony/**q**uack. Twelve more "p" words are given as your "q's" below. How many of the corresponding synonyms, all beginning with the letter Q, can you supply?

ANSWERS, PAGE 118

1. Peculiar ______
2. Prompt ______
3. Prey ______
4. Peaceful ______
5. Plume ______
6. Predicament ______
7. Pentad ______
8. Pursuit ______
9. Pugnacious ______
10. Partridge ______
11. Ponytail ______
12. Patchwork ______

DIG THIS!

ACROSS

1 Ruler before the Ayatollah
5 He raised Cain
9 Actress Bernhardt and others
15 "Floppy" record
19 Boxing finale
20 Tabula ___
21 Stage test
22 Dash
23 Collector's ___
24 "You said it!"
25 House of William III
26 Fodder figure
27 Itch to be spent
31 Western range
34 Cock-a-doodle-dooed
35 Voyeur's station
36 Have a lively imagination
37 Korean troops
38 Accelerated particle
42 Comedian Louis and actress Carrie
43 "___ Only Just Begun"
44 Subdue
45 Feature of many card games
49 Asian penin.
50 Whittled
52 Marry
53 Vertebra: Prefix
54 Hide from the police
55 Dream: Prefix
56 Ledger write-off
58 Yet
59 Re-establish
61 Odin's wolf
62 Boxing champ defeated by Ali
64 Bestseller of 1971
69 Dark rock
70 Racing's 500
71 Veronica's boyfriend
72 Brit. award
73 Aptitudes
76 Dandruff bit
77 Health hangout
80 Ship of 1492
82 Mexican liquor, kin of tequila
83 Tax dodges
84 Viet ___
85 Kitchen suffix
86 "Bitter" humor
87 Weeds
88 Singer Marvin
89 Honoree of a July 26 feast
91 "King" Cole and others
92 Already claimed, with "for"
94 Animal protection grp.
97 Tuft of hair
98 Health food, for some
99 Misfit
105 Change colors
106 Strip
107 Sacred bird of Egypt
108 Card holdings
112 "All ___" (court order)
113 Owing money
114 Quaver, e.g.
115 The O in B&O
116 Aeolian poems
117 Prickles
118 Angry, with "off"
119 China's ___ of Four

ANSWER, PAGE 119

DOWN

1 Take to the slopes
2 Old ___ (out-of-date)
3 Senate "yes"
4 Mean fellers
5 Noah's "port"
6 Condemns
7 Sailing
8 Round street object
9 Sticks' partner
10 Pierce ___
11 Pat Nixon's maiden name
12 First-class
13 Bear clinches
14 "___ on it!"
15 Plunges
16 "___ Ike" ('50s campaign slogan)
17 Tapioca ingredient
18 Wood defect
28 Remains here?
29 Peeved
30 Juice: Prefix
31 Earth depression
32 "I'm ___" (1977 song hit)
33 Godlike, in a way
37 Brush-up course
38 Expert
39 Cry at a bookie's?
40 Bone: Prefix
41 1979 Disney sci-fi film
43 Take by force
44 Stone pit
46 Belt material, perhaps
47 Word before "Gesundheit!"
48 Mistaken
50 Meteor metal
51 Czar Nicholas's daughter
56 Hippie attire
57 Church gifts
60 Highest note
61 With tenderness
63 Capuchin monkey
64 Steak
65 Something to break or wear
66 Stroke of luck?
67 Heavenly headgear
68 "Natural" game
74 Forsaken, old-style
75 Town on the Thames
76 Clue for Holmes, perhaps
78 Check casher
79 Change
81 Shakespeare's Lord of Tyre: Var.
83 Capital of Tibet
88 Do completely
90 Cigarette stat
91 Quick round of golf
92 Felt
93 Walk softly
94 Houston player
95 Seafood delicacy
96 Pucker, as the lips
97 Expand
98 Honeymoon ___
100 Blue-pencil
101 Phnom-___
102 Within: Prefix
103 Loose, earthy deposit
104 Modern hautbois
109 Word before "Gotcha!"
110 French diarist Anaïs
111 Frankfurter, for short

THE TREASURE OF SILVER ISLAND

Chests of silver lie buried at seven locations on this island. Can you find them?

The 300-year-old map of Silver Island, above, shows the Caribbean mining colony as it looked in its heyday. Located along a major shipping route of the Spanish Main, it was once a major producer and exporter of silver ore. Its wealth and location, however, made the island a frequent target of pirates. And so, to prevent their silver from falling into the wrong hands, the miners, according to legend, buried some of the metal at seven locations around the isle.

We recently launched a puzzleistically scientific search of Silver Island to see if there was any truth to the legend, and, lo and behold, we hit pay dirt. You can, too, with the following clues:

1. All the information you need to find the buried treasure is neatly condensed on this single sheet of paper.
2. The treasure is buried in exactly seven holes on the island.
3. The puzzle tests, in turn, your observation and solving ability.
4. The solution does not involve any guesswork. It's completely on the square.
5. Look for signs of digging. Clues will lead you to the exact location of the treasure.
6. If you're totally puzzled, take a break. Go try some other puzzles nearby, and then come back to Silver Island.

ANSWER, PAGE 119

HOWARD LEWIS

"B" HIVE #1

When this puzzle is completed, 30 six-letter words will swarm in circular fashion around the numbers in the beehive. To solve, answer the clues (which all start with the letter B, naturally) and enter each answer word around the corresponding number in the grid. Each answer will begin in the space indicated by the arrow and will proceed clockwise or counterclockwise—the direction is for you to determine. As a small solving hint, we'll tell you that each of the 26 letters of the alphabet will be found at least once in the completed hive.

ANSWER, PAGE 119

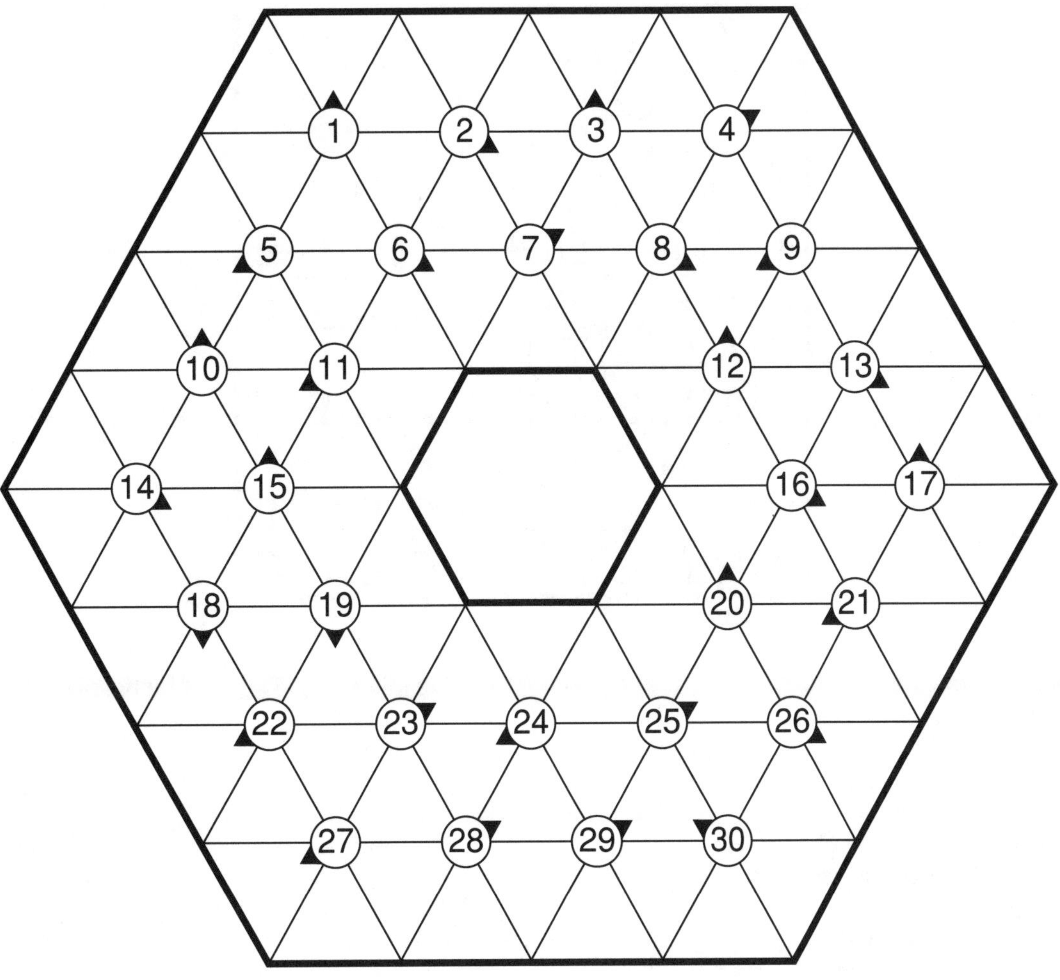

1 "Bounty" spokesperson Nancy
2 Breathe out
3 Brain layer
4 Business meeting necessity
5 Belmont rider
6 Blowing hot and cold
7 British candy
8 *Becket* co-star Sir Richard
9 Bad trip
10 Broadway's Papp
11 Belonging to a club
12 Busted
13 Being less wealthy
14 Breeze
15 Base stuff
16 Bird in a clock
17 Billiard table feature
18 Burroughs character
19 Balkan sea
20 Bringing back to health
21 Big disturbance
22 Baby
23 Browsed, as through a book
24 Blather
25 Beckon
26 Belonging to them
27 Bother, as with bugs
28 Brought up
29 Bitter harangue
30 Begin to bite

PUNS AND TWISTS

Put a single word in each blank below in order to complete the sentence in a punny way. (The number in parentheses after the sentence tells you the number of letters in the word.) Then find the word in the grid, moving from square to square horizontally and vertically, but not diagonally, and shade it in. One letter in each word will fall in an empty square; fill it in as you go. The first answer has been done as an example. When the puzzle is finished, every letter in the grid will be used exactly once, and the 14 letters you filled in, reading line by line from top to bottom, will spell a familiar song title.

ANSWER, PAGE 119

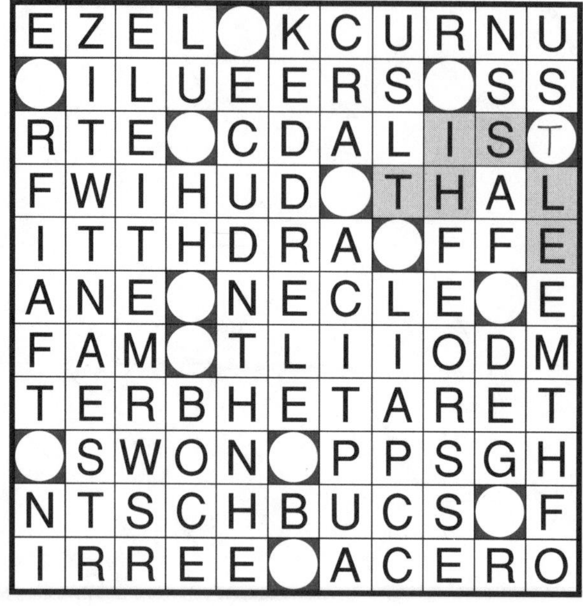

1. If he thinks he can fool me, THISTLE fix him! (7)
2. Is your biology class before or ___________? (9)
3. The dishonest hardware store owner will try to ___________ switches that don't work. (9)
4. The gossip couldn't ___________ mouth long enough to take a bite of food. (7)
5. Fresh-picked corn at the farmers' stand costs only a ___________. (9)
6. A square is a perfect ___________ figure. (11)
7. ___________ are very important for these toddlers, so don't wake them up! (8)
8. After the boxer's embarrassing defeat, doesn't his idle ___________ a bit hollow? (9)
9. Last night ___________ a few of the oats the stableboy gave her. (9)
10. Many Southerners speak ___________. (11)
11. Do you like your spare ribs ___________ lean? (6)
12. The double-talking politician has been known to ___________ he was three years old. (7)
13. The father borrowed his ___________ to pull the house trailer. (9)
14. Uncle catches wild birds in nets, and just as quickly ___________ them. (10)

LETTER CARRIERS

Think of a two-letter abbreviation suggested by each clue below and enter it, without changing the letter order, in the two blanks at the side. You'll end up with a common five-letter word (unrelated to the clue). For example, given the clue, "Letter carrier's base" and letters _ H _ NE, you would fill in the abbreviation P.O. to complete the word PHONE. See if you can finish the following 12 Letter Carriers posthaste.

ANSWERS, PAGE 118

1.	C E _ _ R	Prosecutor
2.	_ A R _ H	Show host
3.	_ I M I _	Six-pointer
4.	S _ O _ E	Home entertainer
5.	P _ _ U E	Brains rating
6.	C H _ _ K	World body
7.	C _ U M _	Record
8.	C _ _ E L	Morning
9.	S _ R U _	Trucker's "ears"
10.	_ A _ O R	Quayle, for one
11.	_ _ E A L	Kind of bracelet
12.	_ U _ H Y	Afterthought

RHYME AND REASON #1

Each clue below consists of a regular definition in which, as a special hint, one of the words rhymes with the answer. For example, the first clue, "Tube to draw drink through," is answered by STRAW, which rhymes with "draw." If you drop one of the letters in the answer word and rearrange those that remain, you'll spell one of the words in the diagram. For example, by dropping the T in STRAW and anagramming the rest, you get WARS, found in the third row of the grid. (The clue numbers have nothing to do with the locations of the answers.) Cross off that word and write the extra letter beneath it. When all 28 clues have been solved in this manner, the letters written in the grid will spell, in order, a couplet by Ogden Nash.

ANSWER, PAGE 119

ARCH	DINER	EACH	RUNTS	WARD	ACME	SIGHT
BOUT	RAKE	ENGRAIN	SHORE	DARES	ROILS	SPLICE
~~WARS~~	CRYER	GRAB	WILT	BIER	JERK	TUSK
T						
WORE	TENORS	PAIL	HARE	SLIDE	WATERS	NOSE

CLUES

1. Tube to draw drink through
2. Mammal with humps
3. Smelled like a skunk
4. Place for an athlete's letter
5. Person who'll lend a hand
6. Writing utensils
7. Figures done on skates
8. Valentine art
9. Bed cover
10. Planet with a pattern of rings
11. Large boat
12. Dropped a note (to)
13. Whirl
14. Have misgivings about
15. Wild card in poker
16. Coarse, as the voice
17. Reason for court-martial
18. Place to stash goods
19. Take a ___ (rest)
20. Where a coat of arms is revealed
21. Having a burning desire
22. Say word like "y'all"
23. Woman beside a groom
24. Where to sit
25. Sleeper's roar
26. Whaler, for one
27. Flat terrain
28. Very sweet red fruit

KREUZWORTRÄTSEL

Achtung! You are looking at a crossword puzzle similar to the ones in Germany. Where we place black squares, German puzzlemakers place their clues, so that the entire puzzle is contained in a grid. Just follow the arrows to enter your answers. Our words are English, but some answers, like those to the eight illustrated clues, have a German flavor. When the

Des Moines state		Three-ring affair	Golf peg		City on the Rhine	Family ___	Vipers	Highlander	A drug		Egg factory	Former German party		News broadcasters		Diving sound		Italian port	Sha of tc billir
Eight: Prefix					Flavors	40						Enough						Autumn beer fair	
Breaded veal cutlet	24															Lasso			
					Historical time						Verdi opera					Gives approval			
Actress Black	Laterally		Rock star John	Gusto		21		7	Month before Sept.		Making a snarl	Meanie	Red vegetables			Perfume			
Mideast canal								German highway									Cereal		
Ocean getaway			10					Treatment									Illegal payment		
Famous storyteller		Cabbage dish						Family									Peas' home		Turn on th swit
					___ Charles		Sea animal		She's honored in May	Procure		28							
Beatles' "Penny ___"				2	Source					Kin of the orange		Symbol for iron		Plains Indian	Colder	Preposition			Mob scen
Singleton			Musical theme									15	School for tots		31				
			"That ___ nice!"					Perform	Lacking vigor		38					Confederate general	Thailand, once		
			37		Giving up							Might	OPEC concern				Graves		
Smiling	Remove one's grip		Tax agcy.	Nothing					Cap		Hold up		Lawn intruder					Harbor boat	
Author Leon		13						Admired man	6				"___ you glad?"						Hin-dran
Drug agent: Slang								In a line		34			Incline				German sub		
Flow plentifully				20				Rome's river									Flash of light		
			Command to a dog		Waste receptacle			Owns	Vietnam city		To-do		12				Endures	Formerly	
Skill		*Mona ___*			Waistbands							Pub drinks		Early Peruvian	Stadium cheers				
Detectives								You: German		Hoglike animal	19					You and me		Gobble up	
					Opposite of SW		A slow mover						Ill feeling						
Swimmer Mark	Outline of a play									Former German body				22					
Temperature scale									41		Health resorts					Secretary: Slang			

grid is completely filled in, write in the margin or onto a separate sheet of paper, in order, the letters in the 43 numbered squares; you will have a thought from Nietzsche.

ANSWER, PAGE 120

Smoked | Writer Ephron | Stylish | Fuzzy fruit | Pert with girls | Grazing ground | Form of "to be" | Vagrant | Illinois city | "To your health!" | One of the decks | Drag

3 | Send off heat | School avg. | City of sin

Arizona Indian | 30 | Lavender | Wrong | 9

"The Red" | 39 | Battle reminders | *King* ___ | Song for one

Shooting star | 14 | Con-fusion | German beer hall

Show ___ | Big name in chess | Hitchcock movie | Bullfight cheer | Land of bullfights | 25 | 42 | Mythical bird

Druggist's weight

Norse chieftain | 26 | Faucet word | Obvious

Slippery | Grind, as the teeth | Sales pitch | Reply from a canyon

Hospital vehicle | Self-esteem | 11 | *Deutsch* | Forever | Opposite of 'taint | Go in | Metal mined | Each

New: Prefix | *Scarlet Letter* heroine | Select

Mars, for one | 36 | Heavy string | 1 | Sorrowful | ___ cent

Very much in love | 16 | Fair-haired | Bridge hand | Wooden leg?

18 | French/Belgian river | 4 | Geologic time | Whole | Chimney black

By oneself | Cuts prices

Word of rejection | Article | Roman fiddler

Place to study | Morning bells | 27 | Visage | Swindle | Wild dance | Actor De Niro | Helix

32 | Twirl | Hole cover-up | Art style | German beer | 33 | 35

Crafty | German exclamation | Hairstyle | Upon | Genuine

"Hiss!" | Pull along | Zuyder ___ | Fathers | Your and my | Part of a bridle | 29

___ En-lai | Goof

23 | Cats' prey | House-wife

Cluckers | Give it a shot | 8 | Tough meat | 43

DAVID KING

THE SPIRAL #2

This puzzle turns in two directions. The spiral's Inward clues yield a sequence of words to be entered counterclockwise in the spaces from 1 to 100. The Outward clues yield a different set of words to be entered clockwise from 100 back to 1. Fill in the answers, one letter per space, according to the numbers beside the clues. Make sure you know when to go back or forth, or you'll be going back and forth.

ANSWER, PAGE 120

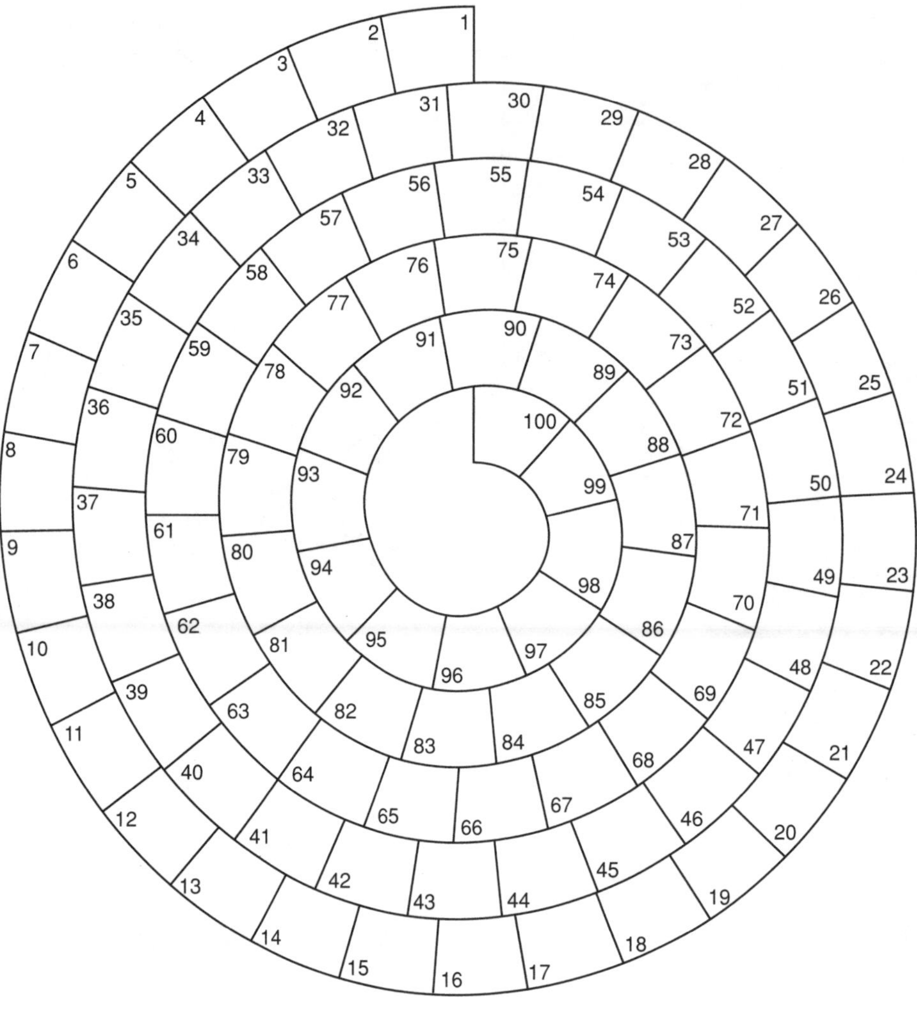

INWARD

1–7 Shortstop or third baseman, e.g.
8–14 Dirty, run-down building
15–22 Hyatt competitor
23–27 Primitive calculators
28–34 What Ivan or Nicholas ruled over
35–41 Health setback
42–46 Perfectly clear
47–55 Sale item at the clothier
56–62 Voting "nay"
63–67 Artless
68–72 "She loves me, she loves me not" flower
73–78 Los ___, New Mexico
79–89 Surpassed in competition
90–94 Belly button
95–100 Atlantic City resort

OUTWARD

100–93 "Pro" or "nounce," in "pronounce"
92–85 Backup singer for Martha in '60s pop
84–77 Musical prodigy
76–69 Its capital is Kuala Lumpur
68–61 Nonconformists
60–54 Honeymooners' mecca
53–49 German-made pistol
48–40 Twits
39–33 Sicily's capital
32–26 Like emergency measures
25–18 Slaughterhouse
17–11 Fortification elevation
10–5 ___ and feathered
4–1 Explorer Ericson

PROVERBS AND CONVERBS

We say great minds run in the same channel. We *also* say fools think alike. It all depends on your point of view.

Each proverb or saying below has a familiar proverb contradictory in meaning hidden in the grid above it. Start in the upper left-hand square of each grid and proceed square by square (horizontally or vertically, but not diagonally) to spell the answer. Do not cross your path or enter a single square twice. Not all the letters in any grid will be used.

ANSWERS, PAGE 119

1

A	B	S	O	N	D
M	E	E	F	R	E
A	C	N	W	I	N
K	U	P	O	R	G
E	S	C	H	E	T
L	T	H	E	A	R

"Out of sight, out of mind."

2

A	L	L	W	R	Y
D	N	R	O	A	K
N	A	K	Y	M	E
O	P	L	A	U	S
L	U	D	A	K	J
L	B	O	Y	C	A

"Keep your nose to the grindstone."

3

Y	N	A	N	T	T
O	U	C	R	U	E
D	L	O	H	C	A
D	O	N	A	L	S
N	G	V	A	C	K
E	W	T	R	I	E

"It's never to late to learn."

4

T	O	P	C	O	O
E	O	L	Y	R	K
H	M	A	N	S	S
T	A	M	E	P	O
O	R	B	L	C	I
N	D	E	H	T	L

"Many hands make light work."

5

C	O	N	K	I	T
U	S	A	Y	L	L
R	A	I	T	C	E
I	O	S	B	T	D
N	G	R	E	H	W
E	T	A	C	O	M

"Seek, and ye shall find."

6

N	O	T	A	G	G
A	I	H	I	O	N
G	N	E	N	P	I
V	O	D	U	T	H
E	U	R	L	Y	T
N	T	E	D	N	O

"Fools rush in where angels fear to tread."

7

Y	U	C	K	E	I
O	P	R	A	X	T
U	Q	T	T	E	W
C	A	N	R	G	I
L	M	I	Y	H	T
O	W	N	O	U	Z

"A penny saved is a penny earned."

8

N	I	M	R	O	D
A	C	E	D	L	E
S	O	G	U	Y	T
T	R	I	F	S	S
Y	A	N	O	L	A
M	E	I	S	H	Y

"Do unto others as you would have others do unto you."

9

H	A	T	S	I	S
E	W	H	L	O	E
F	M	O	T	S	T
N	C	H	E	S	A
E	U	F	R	I	T
R	D	T	E	Z	Y

"Look before you leap."

CAN YOU THINK UNDER PRESSURE?

This test measures your ability to follow directions and think clearly under pressure. It is said that people who score well make good teachers, computer technicians, and masochists. You have exactly six minutes to read and answer the following questions. Have a pencil ready, and a clock or stop-watch handy to time yourself. When the six minutes are up, stop working, whether or not you're finished.

On your mark, get set, go! **ANSWERS, PAGE 120**

If the letter X appears before the comma in this sentence, cross it out. Otherwise draw a wavy line under the word SEX. Circle the odd man out: happy, glad, euphoric, gaiety, delighted. How many cubes are contained in the stack at right? __________ If a horse has five legs, draw a circle in this square, ☐ but if it doesn't, leave it blank, and answer the negative of this question incorrectly: How old are you? __________ What four coins add up to 26¢? __________ __________ __________ __________ If cats can't bark, write DOG in this space __________ but if Nebraska is larger than Texas, enter BIG here __________. Be sure to write NO here if March is the third month of the year. __________ Read each word of this sentence in reverse and answer in the space provided: tahW seod "golf" lleps drawkcab? __________ Don't write PIG in this blank __________, unless oxygen is a metal or birds can't fly. True or false: All tested students were accepted; Marty was rejected; therefore, Marty was not tested. __________ If yesterday was three days before Friday, what will tomorrow be? __________ Name five words that start and end with the letter M. __________ __________ __________ __________ __________ What relation is your brother's uncle to you? __________

Don't neglect to put a check mark in this square, ☐ even if Millard Fillmore was once President of the United States. The time shown by the clock at left is 7:12. Approximately what time would it be if the hour and minute hands were reversed? __________ Write HOT at the bottom of this page: Hold it! If the word COLD doesn't have the same number of letters as HOT, write ICE at the bottom of the page instead, unless a refrigerator is not cooler than a stove, in which case just write BRRR. Count the number of Ns in this sentence and enter your answer in this blank __________. If this quiz was too hard for you, write I QUIT at the end of this sentence. Otherwise just write I QUIT.

A TO Z #1

These directions are a little complicated, so listen up. This crossword contains 26 clues, each of which begins with a different letter of the alphabet. These initial letters have been removed and replaced by blanks. First fill in as many of the initial letters as you can be sure of. Then enter these letters in the correspondingly numbered squares in the grid.

Next, enter as many of the completed clues as you can. Each of the 26 answer words *also* begins with a different letter of the alphabet—always different from the initial letter of its clue.

Answers, naturally, can't be entered at the corresponding numbers in the grid, because their first letters will not match the initial letters you've already filled in. Instead, each answer should be filled in beginning in the space where its first letter appears.

For example, clue #1 has been completed as "Furrowed," and the letter F filled in at square 1 in the grid. Clue #19 has also been completed as "Viking harbors." Viking harbors are FJORDS. So FJORDS gets filled in starting at the F. Also, the letter V from clue #19 is entered into square 19. Now look for a clue whose answer starts with V. Work back and forth between grid and clues to complete the puzzle. **ANSWER, PAGE 120**

1. F urrowed
2. ___ unk mail receptacle
3. ___ ailroad worker
4. ___ ister
5. ___ uite
6. ___ art of a belt
7. ___ ind of jump or theory
8. ___ urger order
9. ___ aire, for example
10. ___ ift
11. ___ ine of these make a game, usually
12. ___ ith good fortune
13. ___ aft
14. ___ yclist's headgear
15. ___ ate for a goose
16. ___ eavy gas
17. ___ ake off, as soldiers
18. ___ frican fly
19. V iking harbors
20. ___ nit of weight
21. ___ mas present for a child, maybe
22. ___ 'Hare employee
23. ___ quipping with weapons
24. ___ sraeli collective
25. ___ ears and years
26. ___ ive too little light to, as film

LEFT AND RIGHT #2

There are two directions to this puzzle—left and right. Each answer is a six-letter word, which is to be entered in the grid one letter per square according to the numbers. Half the answers will read from left to right, as in the example, LIQUOR (1–2). Half will read from right to left, as in the answer to 2–3, which begins ROU-. Work both ways to complete the puzzle.

ANSWER, PAGE 120

1 L	I	Q	U	O	R 2
3					4
5					6
7					8
9					10
11					12
13					14
15					16
17					18
19					20
21					22
23					24
25					26
27					28
29					30
31					32
33					34
35					36
37					38
39					40

CLUES

1–2 Whiskey or brandy
2–3 Shook from sleep
3–4 Cactus locale
4–5 Seismograph reading
5–6 "The *3–4* Fox"
6–7 Noted 24-hour race (2 wds.)
7–8 Blunders
8–9 Experience pain
9–10 Has another tailoring session
10–11 Nursery rhyme destination (2 wds.)
11–12 Common dice rolls
12–13 Scoundrels
13–14 Brian Boitano or Katarina Witt
14–15 Eye part
15–16 Personal dislike
16–17 Bush/Gorbachev meeting
17–18 Lumberjack's cry
18–19 Prepare water for tea again
19–20 Toy train brand
20–21 Type of soup
21–22 Impersonator Rich
22–23 Matador's foe (2 wds.)
23–24 Gold-like alloy
24–25 Newspaper chief
25–26 Cheap booze
26–27 Rope puller
27–28 Observe
28–29 *American Playhouse* productions
29–30 Temple toppler of legend
30–31 Cosa ___
31–32 More pretentious
32–33 *Misery* director Rob
33–34 Louvre painting
34–35 Went wilding
35–36 Hold for questioning
36–37 Nutritional information listing
37–38 French girl's name
38–39 Forewent a family wedding
39–40 The very bottom

PICTURE PROVERB

A 16-word proverb has been scrambled into the names of 12 objects pictured below. To discover the saying, first identify each picture and enter its name on the numbered dashes beneath it. You should identify most or all of the pictures before proceeding. Next, transfer the letters that are over each number to the 16 correspondingly numbered blanks at the bottom of the page. All the letters over the number 1 will be entered on the first blank, all the 2s on the second, all the 3s on the third, etc. Finally, to find the proverb, rearrange the letters on each blank to spell a single word, and read the words thus formed in order from 1 to 16. *Voilà!* A proverb! The first picture, DISH, has been identified and its letters entered to get you started.

ANSWERS, PAGE 121

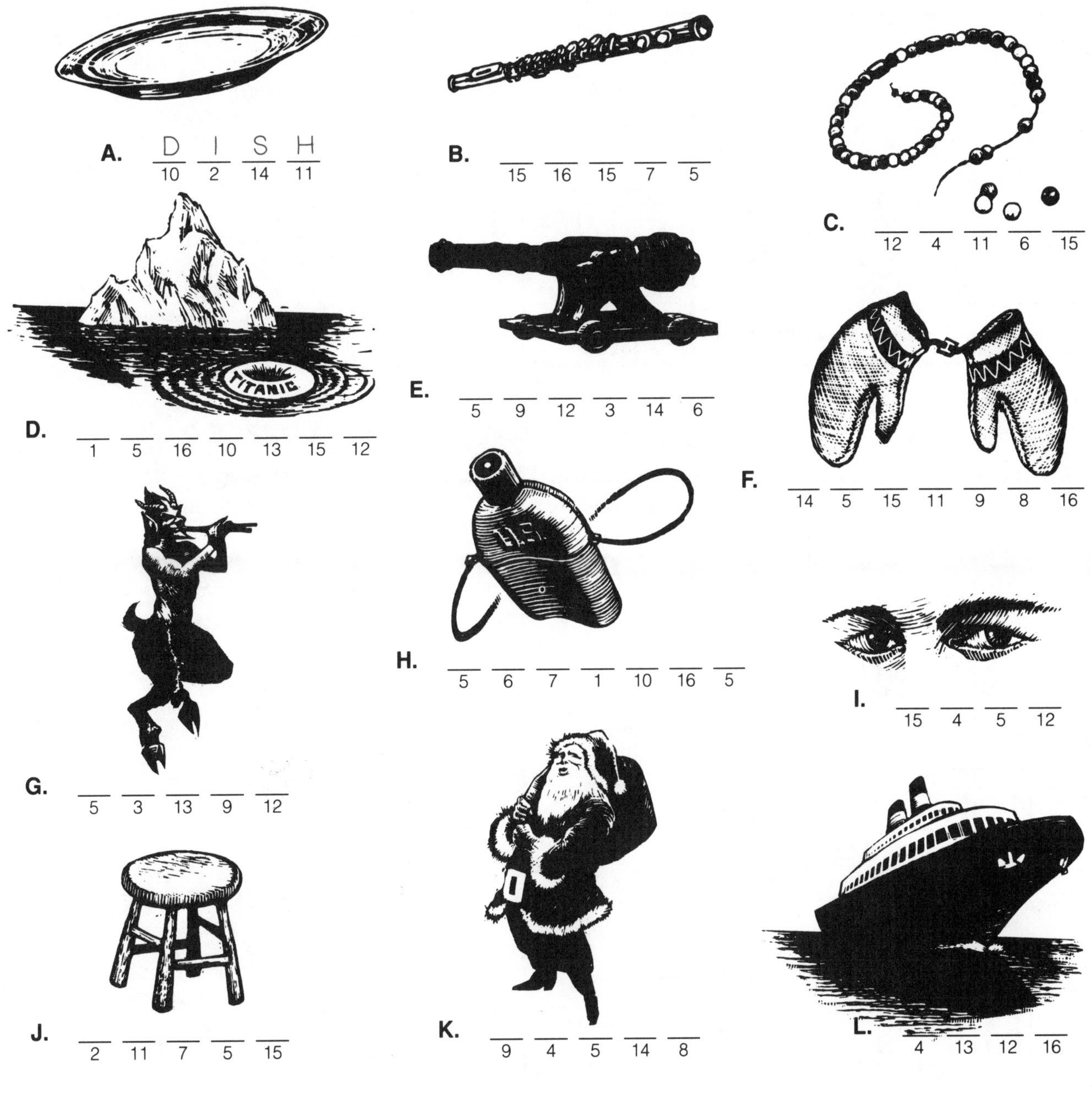

Letter Groups (to be unscrambled)

	I						
1	2	3	4	5	6	7	8

	D	H			S		
9	10	11	12	13	14	15	16

CROSS ANAGRAMS #1

Here are three puzzles for anagram fanciers. For each one, answer the clues—with the help of the letters in the grids—to discover six pairs of six-letter anagrams. Each answer in grid A has the same letters, rearranged, as the answer on the same line in grid B. (Answers read across only, not down.) For example, if the clues for the first pair in puzzle #1 were "Polished stone" and "Accuser," you could enter MARBLE and BLAMER. Only experts will find all the anagram pairs on this page.

ANSWERS, PAGE 121

PUZZLE 1

A B

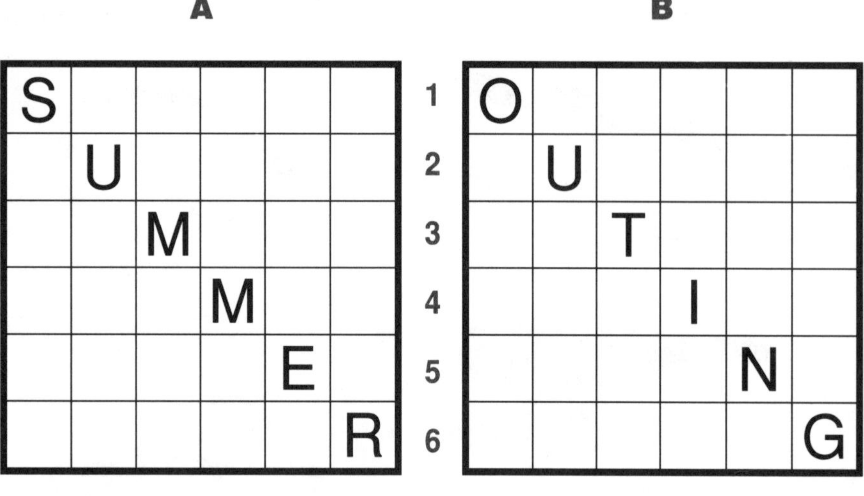

CLUES A

1. South Seas wrap-around
2. From the country
3. Hard-to-get-to
4. Inconceivably vast
5. Bumblebee's relative
6. Film director Bergman

CLUES B

1. Church instruments
2. Actor Tony
3. Shooting star
4. Sunday newspaper section
5. Bathroom "seat"
6. Preparing for war

PUZZLE 2

A

T						1
	E					2
		N				3
			N			4
				I		5
					S	6

B

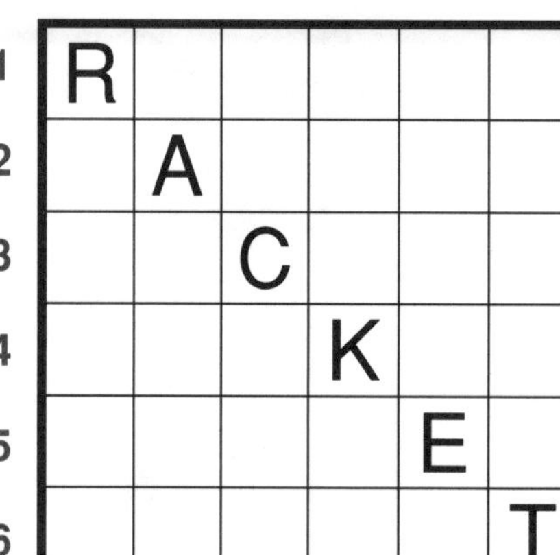

CLUES A

1. Clothes maker
2. With malice
3. Western-style home
4. Weave again
5. Stay
6. Characteristics

CLUES B

1. Theater district
2. Nonprofessionals
3. Symbol of stability
4. Fiddle (with)
5. Pilots
6. Painter

PUZZLE 3

A

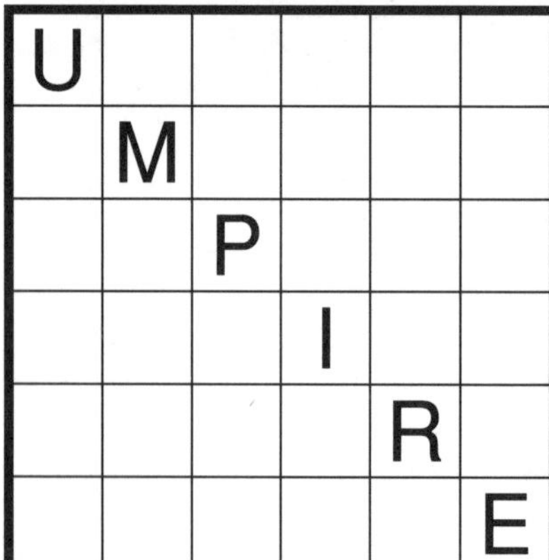

B

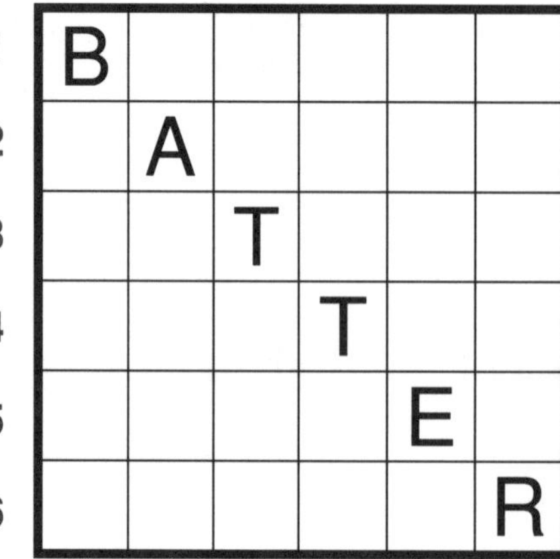

CLUES A

1. Take off a dress
2. Noted Philippine shoe lady
3. Leave
4. Thatcher's followers
5. Quickly, for example
6. Shoot by low-flying plane

CLUES B

1. Ludlum's *The ___ Identity*
2. Sent by the post office
3. Hoist by one's own ___
4. Military action
5. Withstood all danger
6. Cry of impatience

BULL'S-EYE 20 QUESTIONS #2

It's time again to take aim at the bull's-eye. The answer to each of the 20 questions in this puzzle is one of the 25 words in the bull's-eye target. Each answer scores a "hit," which you may cross off in the target since no answer word is used more than once. When all the clues have been answered, the five unused words can be rearranged to form a quotation by fashion designer Bill Blass.

ANSWERS, PAGE 121

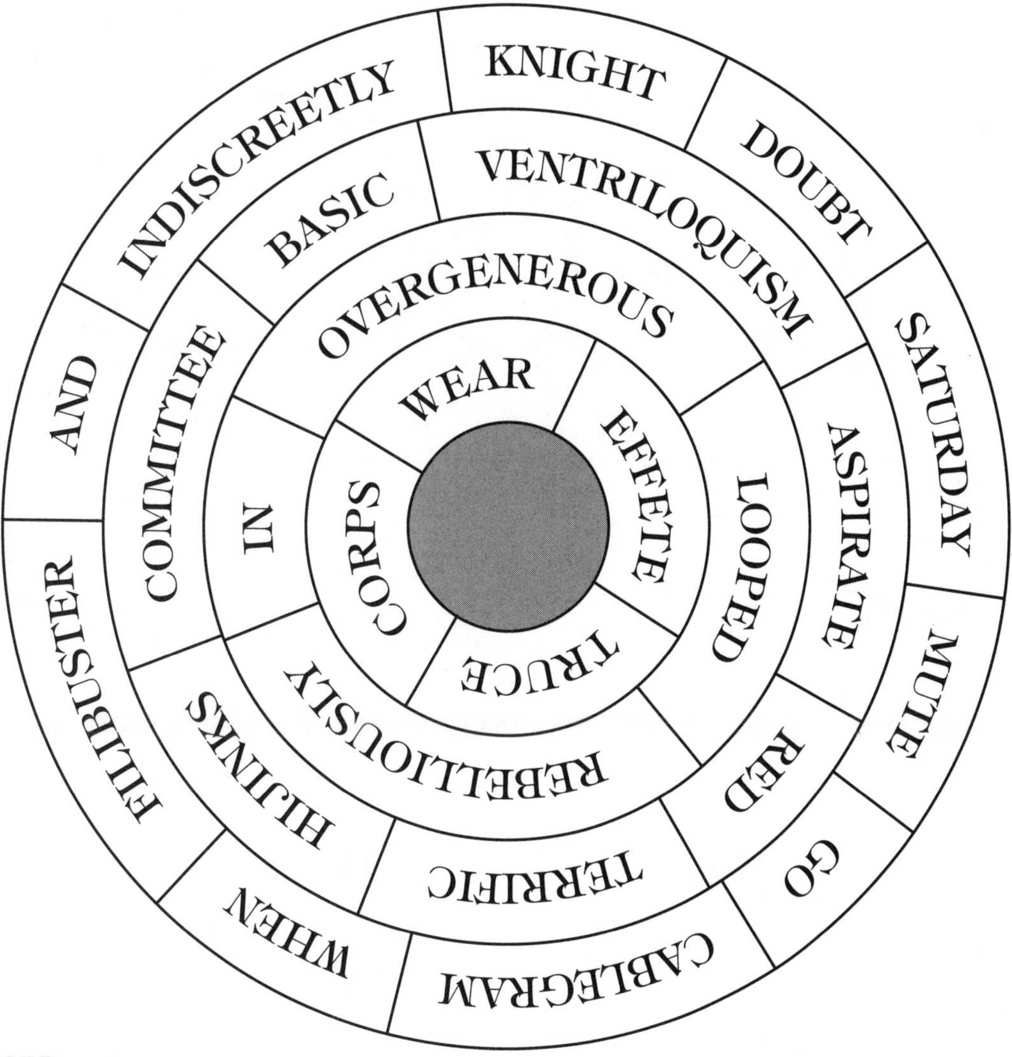

WHICH WORD ...

1. contains all the letters of the word BULL'S-EYE?
2. would become opposite in meaning if you changed the last three letters to BLE?
3. contains all the letters of the alphabet from L to V except one?
4. would have the same pattern as DOODAD in a cryptogram?
5. becomes a new word if you delete every A in it?
6. contains a word meaning "border" inside another word meaning "burdensome"?
7. would sound like a medical facility if you pronounced the first two letters last?
8. would spell a new word no matter what other vowel you made its second letter?
9. is a verb that has no letters in common with its past-tense form?
10. would have three dotted letters if written in script?
11. contains a word meaning "elegant detail" formed by every second letter?
12. would become a word meaning "deliberate" if you removed its fourth letter and read the rest backward?
13. completes this pun?: "During rush hour it's often necessary to ___ capacity."
14. can be broken into three common words of equal length?
15. is an anagram of the name of a common breed of dog?
16. has three pairs of double letters?
17. ends in two silent letters?
18. would sound like a word meaning "gospel" if pronounced with a lisp?
19. would spell a new word if you removed its first, first two, first three, first four, or first five letters?
20. has exactly one letter in common with each of the other five remaining words?

BABY BLOOMERS

If you'd like to try a smaller version of our Petal Pushers puzzles, this bud's for you. Actually, we have two buds abloom, needing to be nurtured in similar fashion. Each completed flower will contain 24 six-letter words answering the clues below its grid. Enter these words inward from the tips of the petals to the heart of the blossom, *two letters per space*. Half the words will proceed clockwise, the other half counterclockwise. Work from both sets of clues for a full bloom. **ANSWERS, PAGE 120**

PUZZLE 1

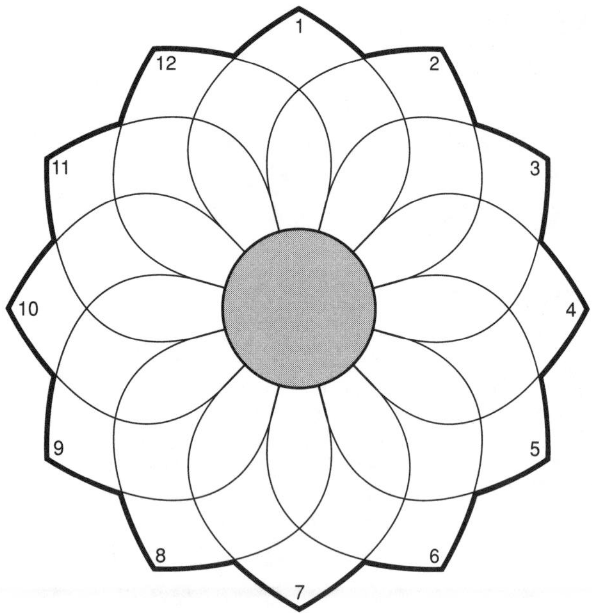

CLOCKWISE

1 Sheer strength
2 Twain's *The Innocents* ___
3 Wan
4 Member of a quartet?
5 Sources, as of knowledge
6 *Purple Rain* star
7 Kind of watch
8 Work with clay, perhaps
9 In reduced size
10 Kidnap
11 Speaker's stand
12 Clothes line?

COUNTERCLOCKWISE

1 The Smithsonian, e.g.
2 1980 political scandal
3 Conditional release
4 Love song
5 Say "no" to
6 Landscaper, at times
7 The Dionnes, e.g.
8 In short supply
9 Former Secretary of State George
10 Without warning
11 Nowheresville
12 Bring charges against

PUZZLE 2

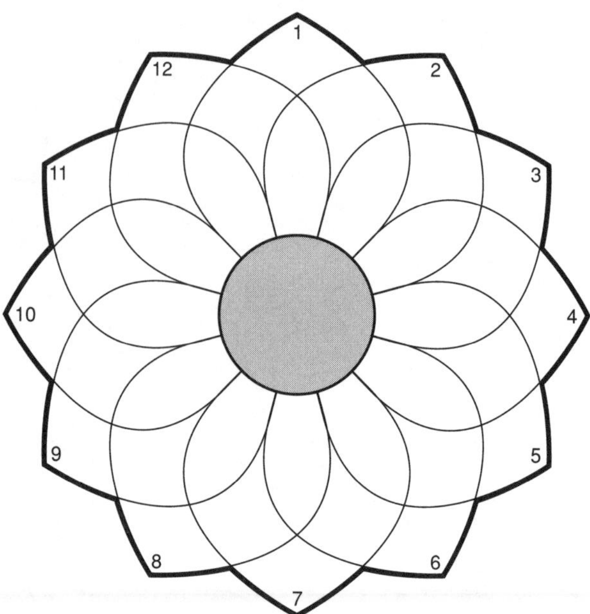

CLOCKWISE

1 High school boyfriend
2 French author Marcel
3 Lawyer's customer
4 Laud
5 Stone pit
6 Former Nicaraguan rebel
7 Cater (to)
8 Animal with a mobile home?
9 College grounds
10 Former S.F. mayor Feinstein
11 Advice
12 Fortify with vitamins

COUNTERCLOCKWISE

1 Kind of bean or bikini
2 Sermonize
3 Bad forecast for beachgoers
4 White-collar worker?
5 Cutely old-fashioned
6 Sandpaper grade
7 Kitchen closet
8 Siberian terrain
9 Ford's successor
10 Cheek mark
11 Planet beyond Saturn
12 Diesel, for one

SQUARE ROUTES #2

Each clue in this puzzle consists of three words that can each go before or after a fourth word to complete a compound word or a familiar two-word phrase. For example, the clue words LIST, BOOT, and HOLE would lead to the answer BLACK (to complete BLACKLIST, BOOTBLACK, and BLACK HOLE.)

To solve, first answer as many clues as you can. Then enter each answer in the grid, beginning in the square corresponding to the clue number and proceeding in any horizontal, vertical, or diagonal direction. The direction can be determined by logic and by the crossing letters of other answers. Work back and forth between grid and clues to complete the puzzle. When you're done, every square in the grid will be filled, and every word will have at least half its letters crossed by other answers.

WORD LIST, PAGE 128 **ANSWER, PAGE 121**

1	2	3		4	5	6		
			7					8
				9				
			10		11			12
					13	14	15	
	16							
						17		18
19			20					21
22				23	24	25	26	

CLUES

1	Paint	Index	Tip
2	Neck	Dove	Snapping
3	Rose	Variety	Party
4	Snake	Baby	Trap
5	Sun	Tone	Telephone
6	Dead	Zone	Tag
7	Fever	Log	Boy
8	Spread	Bald	Eyes
9	Gravy	Track	Mule
10	Key	Book	Bank
11	French	Party	Peck
12	Bug	Rod	White
13	Sea	Headed	Split
14	Landing	Box	Shift
15	Optic	Gas	Racking
16	Spring	Hair	Water
17	Chair	Wrestling	Strong
18	Sky	Jump	Horse
19	Drinking	Pen	Soda
20	Clover	Stalk	Loose
21	Blade	Cold	Bag
22	Beauty	Walk	Tight
23	Fashion	Home	Glass
24	Drill	Brush	Cross
25	Stool	Hole	Toed
26	Lame	Wave	Child

TRANSPLANTED CAPITALS

Are these 12 details from foreign maps? You might think so from the names of the foreign capitals highlighted. And yet, each of the map segments is actually from a road map of a U.S. state. Using your knowledge of U.S. geography, combined with clues in the pictures, how many of these 12 states with "foreign capitals" can you identify?

ANSWERS, PAGE 120

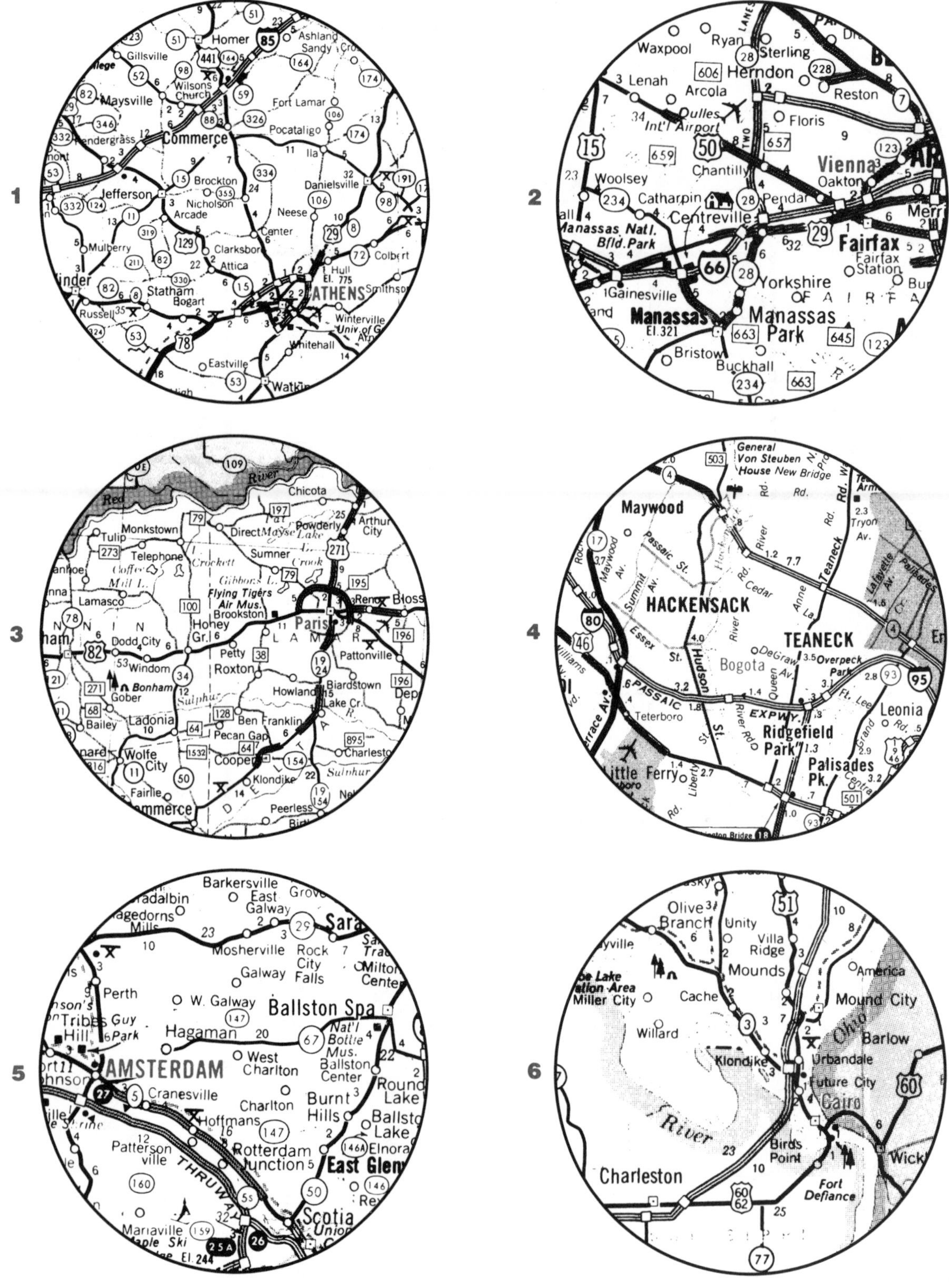

TRANSPLANTED CAPITALS

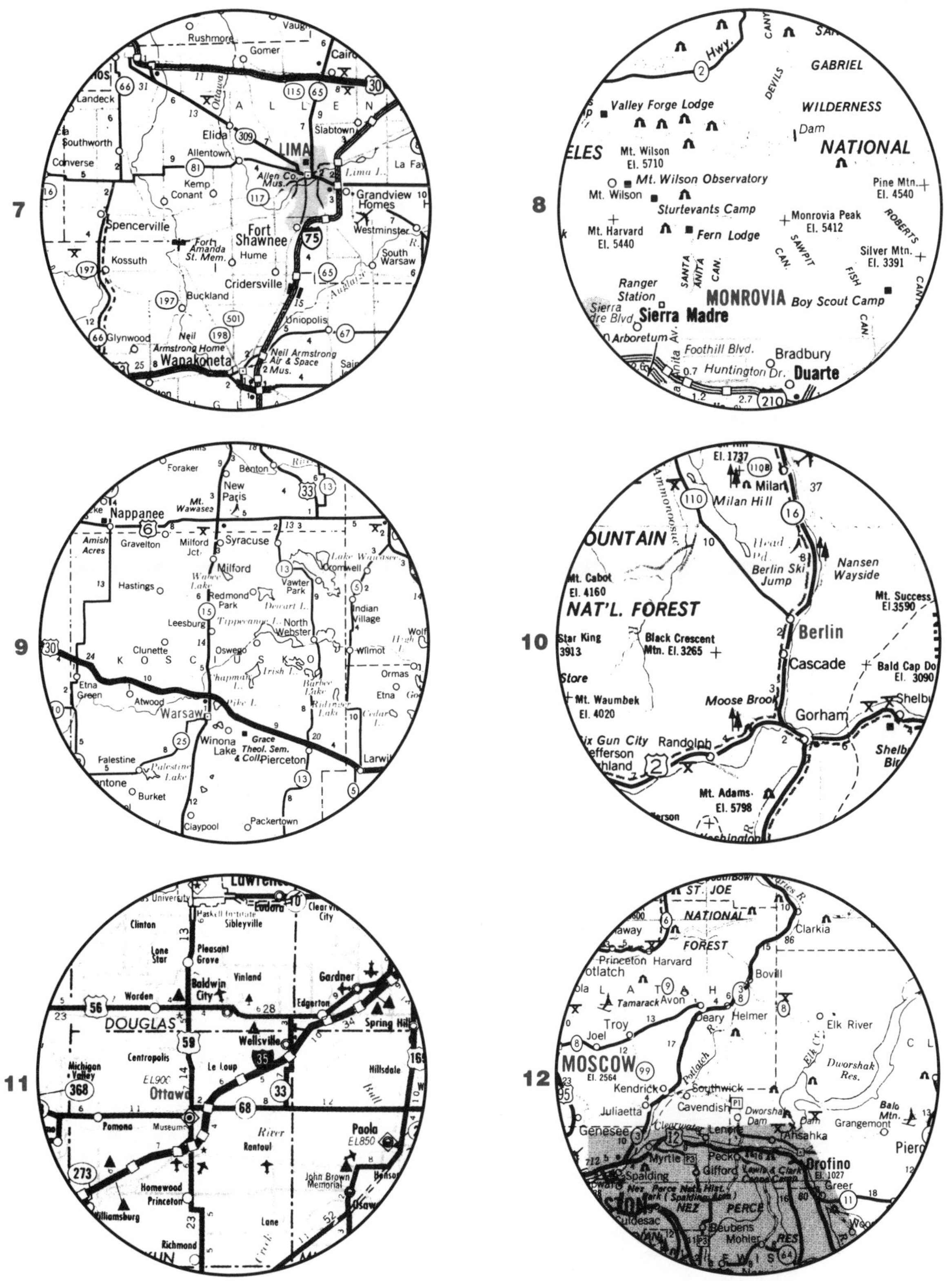

TO CATCH A THIEF

Thieves don't usually leave their calling cards at the scene of the crime. But the master crook who pulled off the great Barrington Mansion heist has gone one step further. As a brazen challenge to police, he has sent them a sheet of paper revealing: 1) his name, 2) what was stolen, and 3) the place where he can be found—as well as a fair idea of what he looks like. Can you connect all the letters below in one unbroken chain to form the thief's message and picture?

ANSWER, PAGE 121

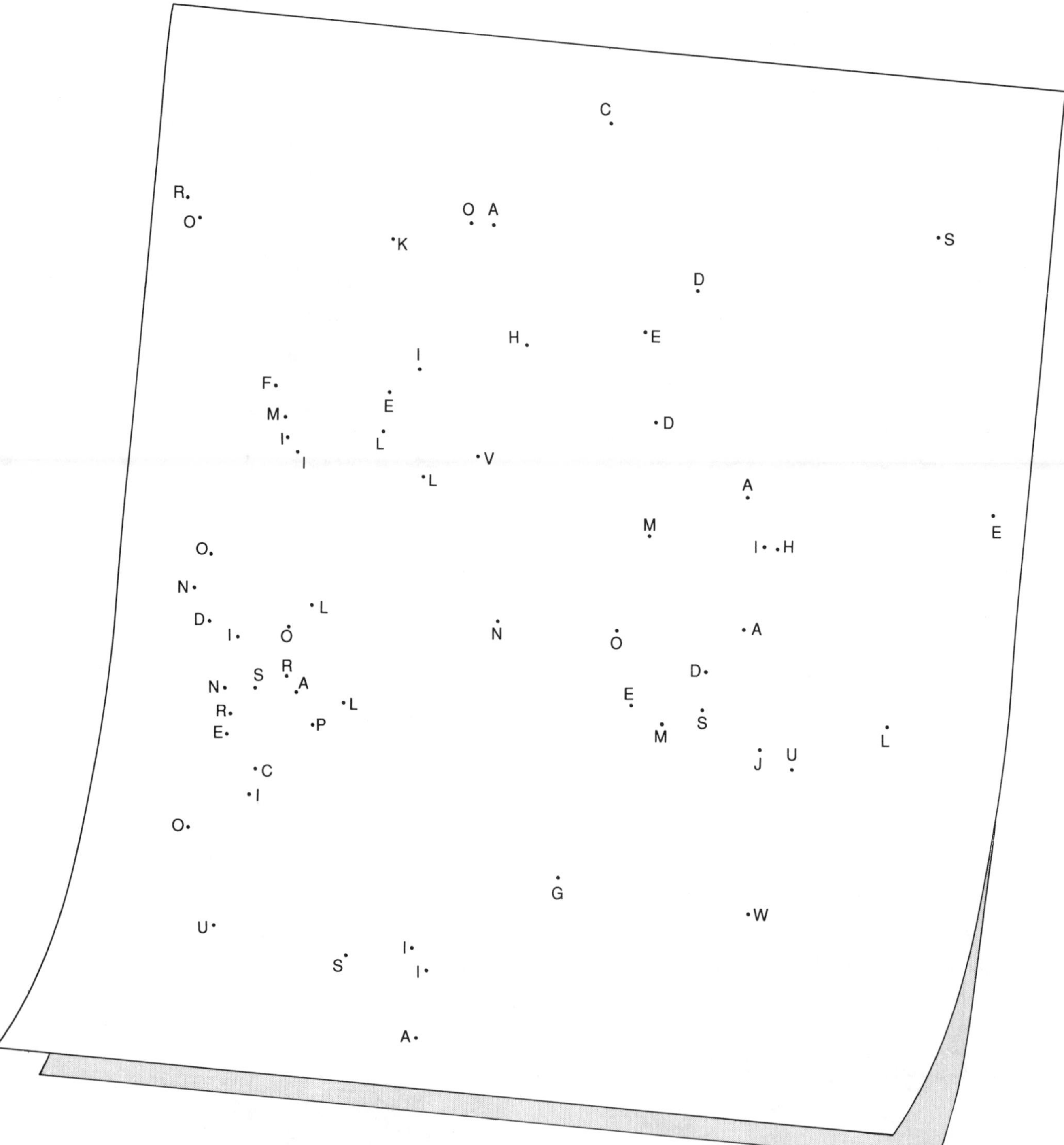

PETER FAHRNI

SYLLASTEPS #1

In each puzzle below, the two diagonal flights of stairsteps will spell related words when you are finished. To discover them, use the word fragments in the Syllabary to form eight 4-syllable words that answer the clues given. Cross off the syllables as you use them, because each is used once and only once. Enter the answer across the grid, one syllable per space—then see what the outlined spaces spell reading from upper left to lower right. ANSWERS, PAGE 121

A. WAYS TO GO

1. Steadying
2. Word book
3. Sway
4. Lawn pest
5. Award kudos to
6. Give variety to
7. Unworkable
8. Take apart

SYLLABARY

AR AS BIL BLE CAL CON DAN DE

DI DIC DIS FY GLE GLE GRAT IM

ING IZ LATE LI ON PRAC SEM SI

STA TI TION U VER WAG WIG Y

1			
2			
3			
4			
5			
6			
7			
8			

B. PRECISELY!

1. Opposite of democracy
2. Railroad official
3. Safe havens
4. Exact duplicate
5. Respectfully submissive
6. Stuffy individual?
7. Flower show exhibit
8. Guaranteed item?

SYLLABARY

AR COP DEF DER DIC EN ER FAC

GE I IES IS MAS MIST NI PHO

RA SANC SAT SHIP STA TA TAX TER

TIAL TION TION TO TOR TU UM Y

1			
2			
3			
4			
5			
6			
7			
8			

PETAL PUSHERS #2

Some people say this magic flower emanates a mystical, life-enhancing energy when you complete its pattern of 32 six-letter words. To see for yourself, answer the clues and enter the words inward from the tips of the petals to the heart of the blossom, one letter in each space. Half the words proceed clockwise from the numbers; the other half go counterclockwise. When the last letter has been entered, all the magic of the flower will be at your command. **ANSWER, PAGE 121**

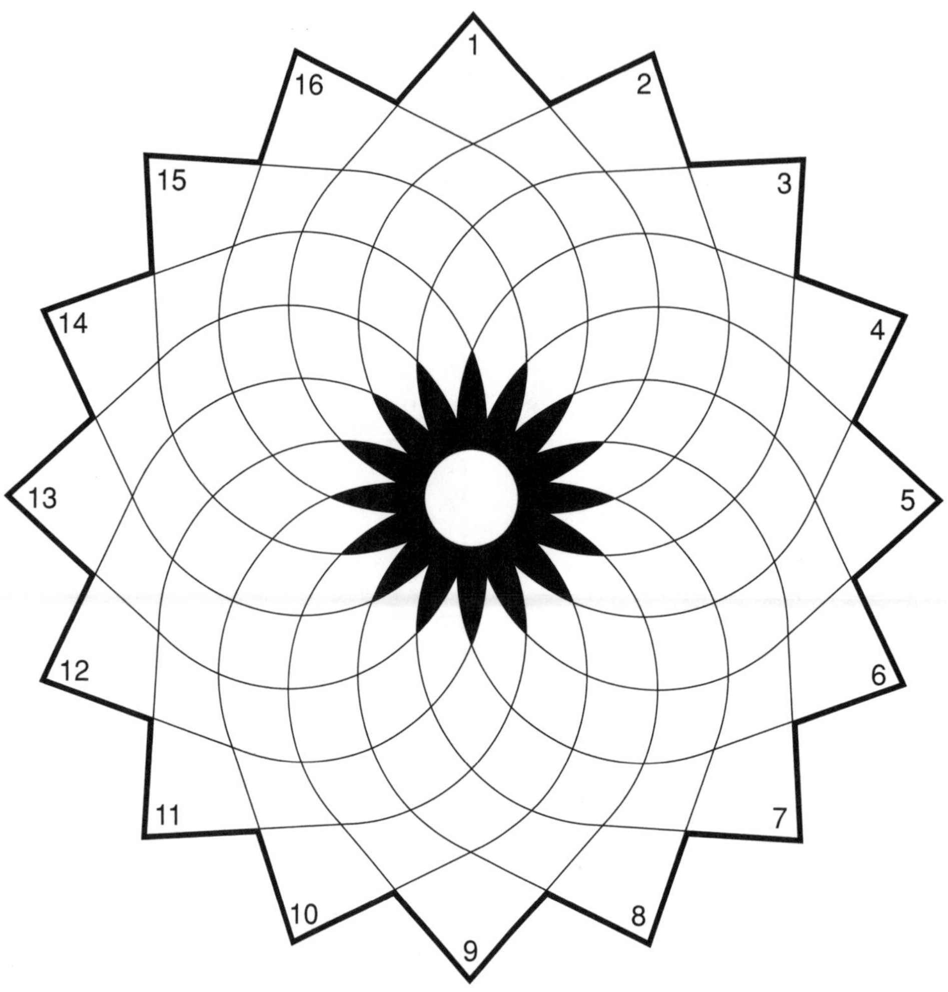

CLOCKWISE

1 Fridge
2 Jungle river
3 Pitcher's drop ball
4 Protected, as rights
5 Whodunit suspect
6 *Death of a Salesman* author
7 Like liquid lava
8 Stretching muscle
9 Kind of missile
10 *The Messiah* composer, Georg Friedrich ___
11 Wichita resident
12 Hotel or theater area
13 Health food snack
14 Turns red, as apples
15 ___ of influence
16 Available, as a doctor: 2 wds.

COUNTERCLOCKWISE

1 Have permanence
2 Difference between *ob*ject and ob*ject*
3 Libels
4 Having the capacity to survive
5 Common solvent
6 Hairy arctic beast: 2 wds.
7 Tot's hand-warmer
8 Bell ringer
9 Solidified
10 Word with head or fortune
11 WW1 German leader
12 Roosevelt's 1936 opponent
13 Over there
14 Pushed out of bed
15 Traffic light
16 Criticize

STORIES FROM THE SAFARI

How good is your memory and eye for detail? Study this scene for up to three minutes ... then turn the page to read the hunter's account of what happened. Once you turn, you will be relying solely on your memory of what you've seen.

PHIL SCHEUER

STORIES FROM THE SAFARI (PART 2)

On the previous page, you were witness to an attack on a hunter in Africa. It was a dangerous encounter, to be sure, but somehow back home the hunter's account of the attack has improved in the retelling. How many misrepresentations or other errors can you find in his story below?

ANSWERS, PAGE 121

I've had many harrowing adventures while on safari in Africa, but my closest call was wrestling with a tiger when I was armed with only a knife.

The attack occurred around noon along a deserted road in Tanzania, two miles from the small village of Bukwimba. I was all alone at the time. My throat was quite dry because I had left my canteen back at camp. A pride of lions could be seen to the left of the road ahead, and a snake was coiled on a branch of a tree above me.

Suddenly a twig snapped. I turned and saw a tiger leaping toward me. I slipped my pistol from its holster and raised my arm to shoot, but—click!—the gun wasn't loaded!

The tiger was still charging. In one more leap it would be at my throat.

In a flash I whipped out my knife and wrestled the tiger to the pavement. I repeatedly stabbed him as he bit and clawed me. Eventually I subdued him, but not without a terrible struggle. You can still see the scar where he gashed me on the arm.

Fortunately, I have another, better memento of the occasion—his head mounted on the wall behind me.

PHIL SCHEUER

SPIDER'S WEB

Each clue in this puzzle has had the letters to the answer removed in order. Thus, in #1, the letters C-R-A-W-L are missing from the phrase "Creep along slowly." Replace the letters to discover—and define—the answer. Each answer is to be written in the spider's web from the outer ring inward, beginning at the appropriate letter or letters and continuing one letter per space. The clues are given in random order and are numbered for convenience only. When the puzzle is done, the letters in two of the rings, reading clockwise, will spell a quotation from Shakespeare's *Henry VI*. **ANSWER, PAGE 122**

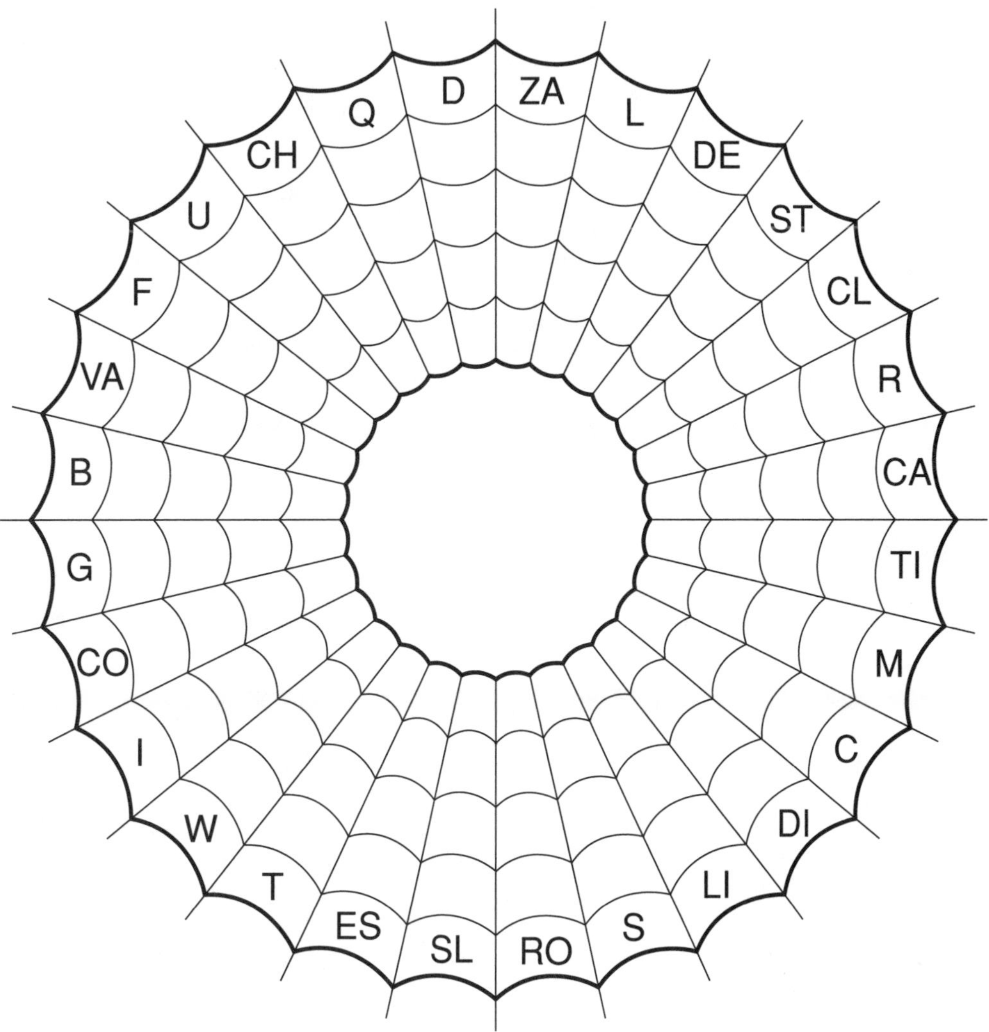

CLUES

1. _ _eep _long slo_ _y
2. _ _dira Gan_h_'s l_nd
3. _eeble _nd d_sta_ _
4. Exclama_ _on fro_ lum_ _ _jacks
5. St_a_ _ht; f_xe_
6. Produ_t _f plan_a_i_ _s
7. Pe_s_nnel regi_ _ _ _
8. _ _urchg_ing s_nge_ _
9. Ca_ _ _lly "I_y Leagu_"
10. Fa_sif_ _ _ _
11. _ _i_teen l_ss t_n
12. Peop_e w_th Octo_er bi_thd_y_?
13. _ _ _ain; pr_ _ _ure
14. U_ly _orror m_vie reg_ _ar
15. _io_ d_ _ign, perhap_
16. Ja_es B_nd p_ _tray_r
17. Tran_ _ _l; sil_n_
18. D_cea_ed's _ot_l proper_i_s
19. Tra_eler's sm_ _l_sh _uitcas_
20. _ _lgary a_d Newfoundl_n_'s loc_tion
21. Mo_t wi_ _, lik_ _ _allone?
22. Re_uced-calor_ _ ea_ _ _
23. T_inkly m_gicia_'s ro_ _
24. _ _enches; gr_ _ _ _
25. Tro_ _le f_r _llied freigh_ers
26. _ _ire/_ozam_ _que _butment
27. _ _ _uty'_ coun_erpart
28. Reme_i_s _ad comp_ter pro_ram_

HALF AND HALF #2

The unusual twist of this puzzle is that the definitions of the answers have been replaced by *hints*. Each clue consists of three words that in some way relate to the answer, but which may or may not contain a synonym of it. For example, in the first clue, "Robin," "Cape," and "Superhero" all suggest the answer BATMAN without defining it.

Each answer, like BATMAN, is a six-letter word. To put it in the diagram, divide it in the middle and enter it downward, the first half in the squares designated by the first number of the clue, the second half in the squares designated by the second number. Every word half appears in two or more answers, so every answer will help with at least one other.

Note: For an extra challenge, before you start, cover up the third column of hints and try solving the puzzle using just the first two. If you get stumped, you can always sneak a peek later.

ANSWER, PAGE 122

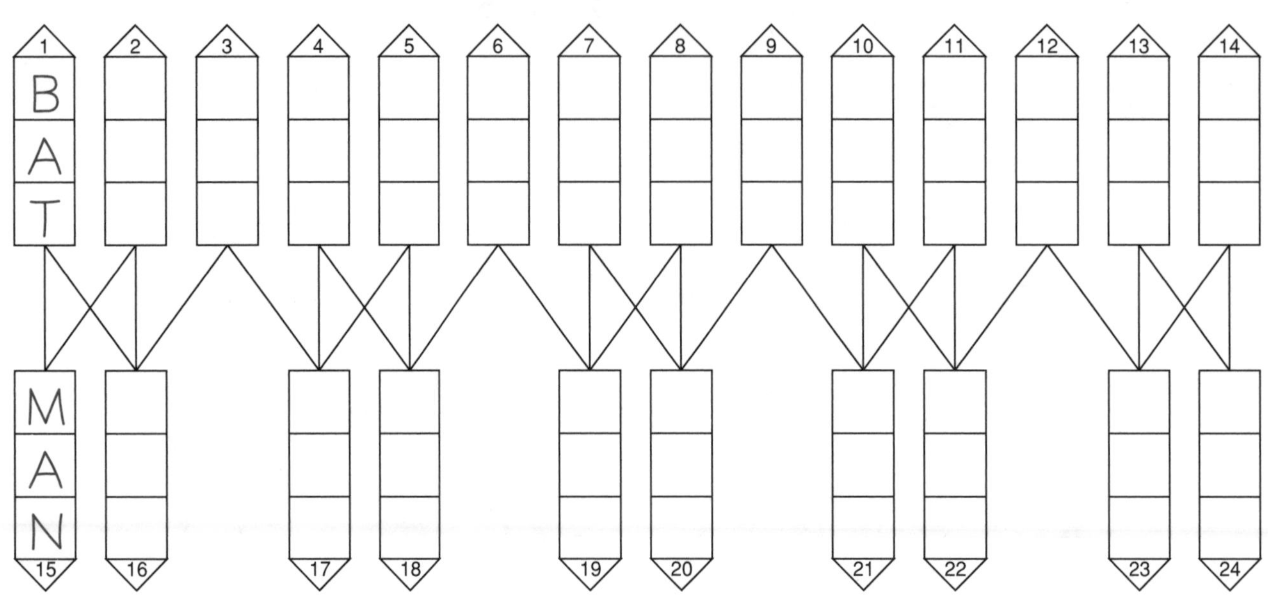

1–15	Robin	Cape	Superhero
1–16	Cake	Baseball	Pitcher
2–15	Drinks	Tavern	Server
2–16	Deal	Trade	Merchandise
3–16	Slip	Hesitate	Stumble
3–17	Hawk	Talons	Hood
4–17	Lighthouse	Warning	Bright
4–18	Canine	Hunting	Long-eared
5–17	Restaurant	French	Waiter
5–18	Mouthwash	Rinse	Throat
6–18	Rope	Hang	Participle
6–19	Roll	Breakfast	Copenhagen
7–19	Outcast	Exile	Decree
7–20	Masked	Robber	Stagecoach
8–19	Jail	Whip	Penalize
8–20	Expert	Commentator	Political
9–20	Card	Rating	Debit
9–21	Shrimp	Louisiana	Cajun
10–21	Release	Prison	Early
10–22	Discipline	Love	Father
11–21	Baltimore	Orange	Nest
11–22	Compass	China	East
12–22	Language	Easy	Flowing
12–23	Snow	Brief	Activity
13–23	Cobbler	Pit	Fruit
13–24	Squares	Balances	Money
14–23	Granite	Hunted	Excavation
14–24	Ducks	Doctors	Noises

BUILDING BLOCKS

The last three letters in every line of these puzzles are already in place. To solve, insert the "blocks" beside each grid into the remaining squares—without rearranging any letters—to complete eight nine-letter words reading across. Each of the blocks will be used exactly once, so you may cross them off as you proceed. When all the squares have been filled, two of the columns reading down in each grid will spell a pair of bonus words.

ANSWERS, PAGE 122

PUZZLE 1

AMP	DAR	EDE	ENF
GNO	HES	HOU	LIT
MAT	OCR	ORC	PRO
RIA	SEW	THE	WOM

						T	R	A
						S	I	S
						O	L	K
						U	D	E
						I	F	E
						R	C	H
						A	C	Y
						V	I	L

PUZZLE 2

ANO	ATH	BAD	DEC
ETI	FOR	IDE	KIL
MIN	NUR	NYM	SEM
SOM	TAX	TNI	UNS

						T	O	N
						R	M	Y
						A	I	D
						G	H	T
						L	O	N
						L	E	D
						M	E	S
						O	U	S

PUZZLE 3

AIN	ATA	CEL	CHD
GEM	IAL	IST	ITE
KEB	LIC	OAT	ORB
ORM	OSE	OWN	THW

T	O	U						
M	O	T						
P	O	R						
S	N	A						
E	A	R						
S	T	R						
S	O	C						
B	E	L						

READING BETWEEN THE LINES

The English teachers at Twelve O'Clock High School have distributed next semester's lists of "recommended reading" for juniors and seniors. Unfortunately, the printer misinterpreted his instructions and printed the juniors' list *on top of* the seniors'. Since no one plans to read the books anyway, it probably doesn't matter. But for the record, can you identify the 15 titles on each list?

ANSWERS, PAGE 121

1. DhetGrodhEargh
2. Myrd BfeckenFidge
3. Xanimay Farm
4. RobvesNewCWorld
5. OfcKlumberByndage
6. DonpQuixote
7. WarAmediRemembragedy
8. Bleysses
9. AheBeCaiferMAtiny
10. AesaMisSérabled
11. KatchT-22
12. Moby Dyck
13. BhedCahearbReyisited
14. SoiBby
15. GreatsExpectaIndia

BASED ON A PUZZLE BY DON RUBIN

FOUR-IN-ONE CROSSWORD

This crossword is really four crosswords in one, each part to be solved in a different way. Part 1, in the upper left corner of the diagram, is a regular crossword, to be worked in the usual manner. Part 2, in the upper right, is a fill-in. (Enter the 19 given words into the diagram across and down to complete the corner.) Part 3, in the lower left, is a diagramless. (Solve as a regular crossword, but adding the numbers and black squares in the grid as you go.) And Part 4 is a crossword with the clues in scrambled order.

Note that some of the squares in the diagram have numbers in the lower right. When all four parts of the puzzle are completed, transfer the letters in these squares to the correspondingly numbered squares in the center. The result, reading in order from 1 to 25, will spell a quotation by Goethe.

ANSWER, PAGE 122

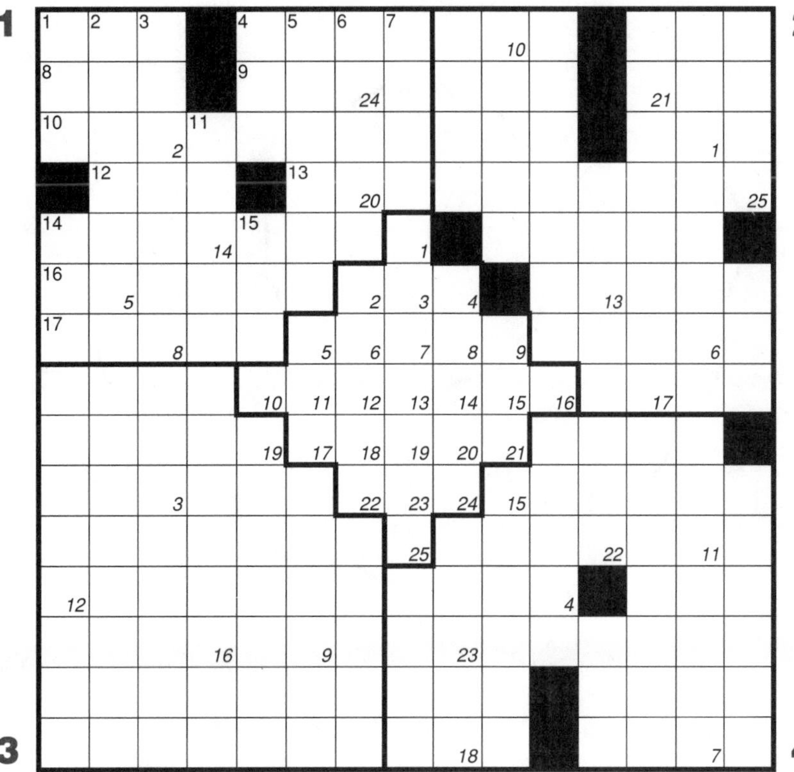

PART 1: Crossword

ACROSS

1 Witch
4 Taxis
8 Baseball stat
9 D-Day beach
10 A lot of vitamins
12 TV alien
13 Pot's top
14 Not flexible
16 Writing no-nos
17 Insurance dealer

DOWN

1 Edge of fashion
2 Floor cover: 2 wds.
3 It's enough to make you laugh: 2 wds.
4 A good chew
5 Coral islands
6 Jazz's Count
7 Backyard building
11 River of Scotland
14 This is a holdup!
15 Powerful sticks

PART 2: Fill-In

ASP
BAD
ELS
HAS
MAB
OWE
THO

ANNS
BOMB
POSY

AWARD
DRANK
KNIFE
SNAIL
VANNA

BRAVERY
DEBARKS

ATHENIAN
SHARK FIN

PART 3: Diagramless

ACROSS

1 KGB worker
4 Golfer's aids
6 Pour water on
8 Gossip
9 Gallery equipment
11 Letter after zeta
12 "Made in the ___"
13 Second coming
15 Holiday bird
16 Uncle Sam's "want"

DOWN

1 General's plan
2 Tot's game
3 Tokyo exchange
5 Cleans with a wire brush
6 Textile employee
7 Rush
10 Stadium cheer
14 Letters of debt

PART 4: Scrambled Clues

Actor DeNiro
It's never at home: 2 wds.
Commercials
Goodman, "The King of Swing"
Constrictors
Lower California
Alternative conjunctions
Scent
Farm building
Biblical king and wise man
Kernel holder
Electrical units
Turned left, as a plowhorse
Pear-shaped fruit
Clampett of *The Beverly Hillbillies*
Star Wars pilot: 2 wds.
Negative advice
Prayer's answerer
Zeal

ROUND AND ROUND

Sixteen overlapping plates have been laid in a ring below. Each answer is a word of six or more letters that spins around one of the plates, beginning in the space indicated and proceeding clockwise. The end of each answer will overlap with the front, as the H in HEALTH or the LE in LEGIBLE. The first answer, NIACIN, has been entered for you. **ANSWER, PAGE 122**

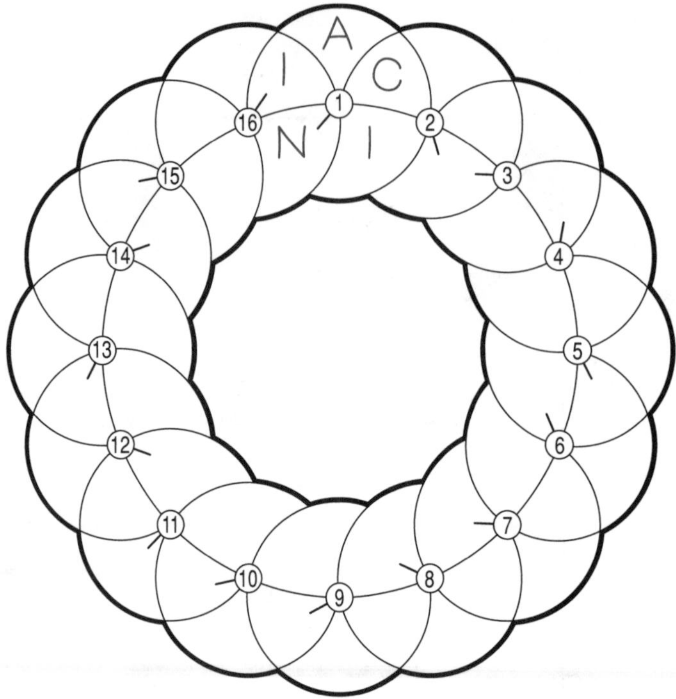

CLUES

1 B vitamin
2 The Beatles' "___ to Ride"
3 Wood-eating insect
4 Follower of Mohammed
5 "Half" or "full" wrestling hold
6 Perk up
7 Make clear
8 College or parish head
9 Home of the Blue Jays
10 Loyal team fan
11 Roman dawn goddess
12 Ship's turning mechanism
13 Refused, as permission
14 Geniuses
15 Marksman's aim
16 Fix firmly, as habits

OY, A QUIZ!

Every answer in this quiz is a word or name that ends in the *sound* of "oi." For example, with the clue "combination of metals," the answer would be ALLOY. How many of the others can you get? **ANSWERS, PAGE 122**

1. Shipmate's cry ______
2. Russian ballet ______
3. Sturdy fabric ______
4. WW1 infantryman ______
5. He "was here" ______
6. Largest of the Virgin Islands ______
7. Parade of truckers ______
8. Popular magazine ______
9. Man with a *Complaint*? ______
10. False duck ______
11. Abe Lincoln's home ______
12. Author of *Anna Karenina* ______
13. Inner tube, e.g. ______
14. American Indian confederacy ______
15. Colonial governor of India ______
16. Famed London theater ______
17. Rodeo rider ______
18. Wet blanket ______
19. Diplomatic representative ______
20. Common people ______

CONNECT-A-WORD

When the grid below is correctly completed, each pair of adjacent boxes will contain a compound word or a familiar phrase. Clues are identified by the numbers in the boxes, and the answers are to be entered left to right and top to bottom. The answer to 1–2 Across, SHORTHAND ("Secretary's scribble"). has been filled in as an example. Now you know that the first part of 1–6 Down is SHORT and that the first part of both 2–3 Across and 2–7 Down is HAND. Every box is part of two or more answers, so if the clue in one direction stumps you, try another connection.

ANSWER, PAGE 123

1 SHORT	2 HAND	3	4	5
6	7	8	9	10
11	12	■	13	■
14	15	16	17	18
19	20	21	22	23
■	24	■	25	26
27	28	29	30	31
32	33	34	35	36

ACROSS

1–2 Secretary's scribble
2–3 Acrobatic flip
3–4 Young person, jocularly
4–5 Insignificant amount of money
6–7 Topple
7–8 Pay-and-a-half
8–9 Athlete's rest period
9–10 Surpass in pugilistic skill
11–12 Montana Indian
14–15 Stage illuminator
15–16 Unit of distance
16–17 For all seasons
17–18 Locomotive repair shop
19–20 Mug or delay
20–21 Overturn
21–22 Furniture item
22–23 Dining surface
25–26 Beginning, as a journey
27–28 Refer to prior records
28–29 One's personal history
29–30 Land-based gun attack
30–31 Kind of chat
32–33 Library chute
33–34 Visit unexpectedly
34–35 Situated
35–36 Field goal try

DOWN

1–6 Deficiency, as of money
2–7 Relinquish control
3–8 When flowers bloom
4–9 Become scared
5–10 Grain receptacle for animals
6–11 Fail unceremoniously
7–12 General business expenses
9–13 Opposite of income
11–14 Policeman
12–15 Auto's "eye"
13–17 Bout
14–19 Secure position
15–20 Start a cigarette
16–21 Late December
17–22 Group discussion
18–23 Roof
20–24 Raise spiritually or emotionally
22–25 Plate, silverware, napkin, etc.
23–26 Refill, as a drink
24–28 Car model with a rear hatch
25–30 Igniting
26–31 Football call
27–32 Item that needs monthly balancing
28–33 Rear stage scene
29–34 Deeply embedded, as dirt
30–35 Site of an andiron
31–36 Tonto, to the Lone Ranger

THROUGH-THE-HOUSE TREASURE HUNT

Some time ago the GAMES staff had a party that featured a through-the-house treasure hunt. Each team of four was given a starting puzzle, the solution to which identified some place in the house, where another puzzle was hidden. The solution to the second puzzle identified a spot in the house where a third puzzle awaited, and so on. In all, nine puzzles of varying types had to be solved to reach the treasure—a cache of giant chocolate bars concealed ... well, you discover where ...

To play at home, begin with the Starting Puzzle below. Its solution will name a location shown in one of the eight illustrations on these two pages. Jump to that picture and solve the puzzle attached to it to discover the hiding place of the next clue. Continue from one part of the "house" to the next, solving each puzzle as you go. The last puzzle in the chain will reveal the location of the treasure (candy bars not provided).

Note that most of the puzzles have no solving directions, so the first challenge of a clue may be figuring out what to do with it. If you get stuck on any part of the treasure hunt, you'll find your "teammates" on page 128 to provide hints.

Final words to party hosts: If you stage your own treasure hunt, warn teams to take only the clues designated for them, leaving other teams' clues hidden. If possible, vary the order of the clues so that not all teams are working on the same puzzle at once. And since every nook and cranny of your house is fair territory to the players, you may want to chase away cobwebs before the party begins.

HINTS, PAGE 128 **ANSWERS, PAGE 122**

Starting Puzzle
Alphabetize this list of words; then read columns 4 and 6.

CHERUB
DRAWER
KILOWATT
ABANDON
TURNIP
CLOTHED
EPITOME
TERROR
VIBRATE
ECHELON
HAYCOCK
DASHED
BEHOOF
UTTERED
EPISCOPAL

KSEAJMPNFMPBSEC! GSN DMRU CSFRUQ PDU FMCP WNLLFU. PDU PJUMCNJU BC ZUDBEQ PDU UEKGKFSWUQBMC.

THROUGH-THE-HOUSE TREASURE HUNT

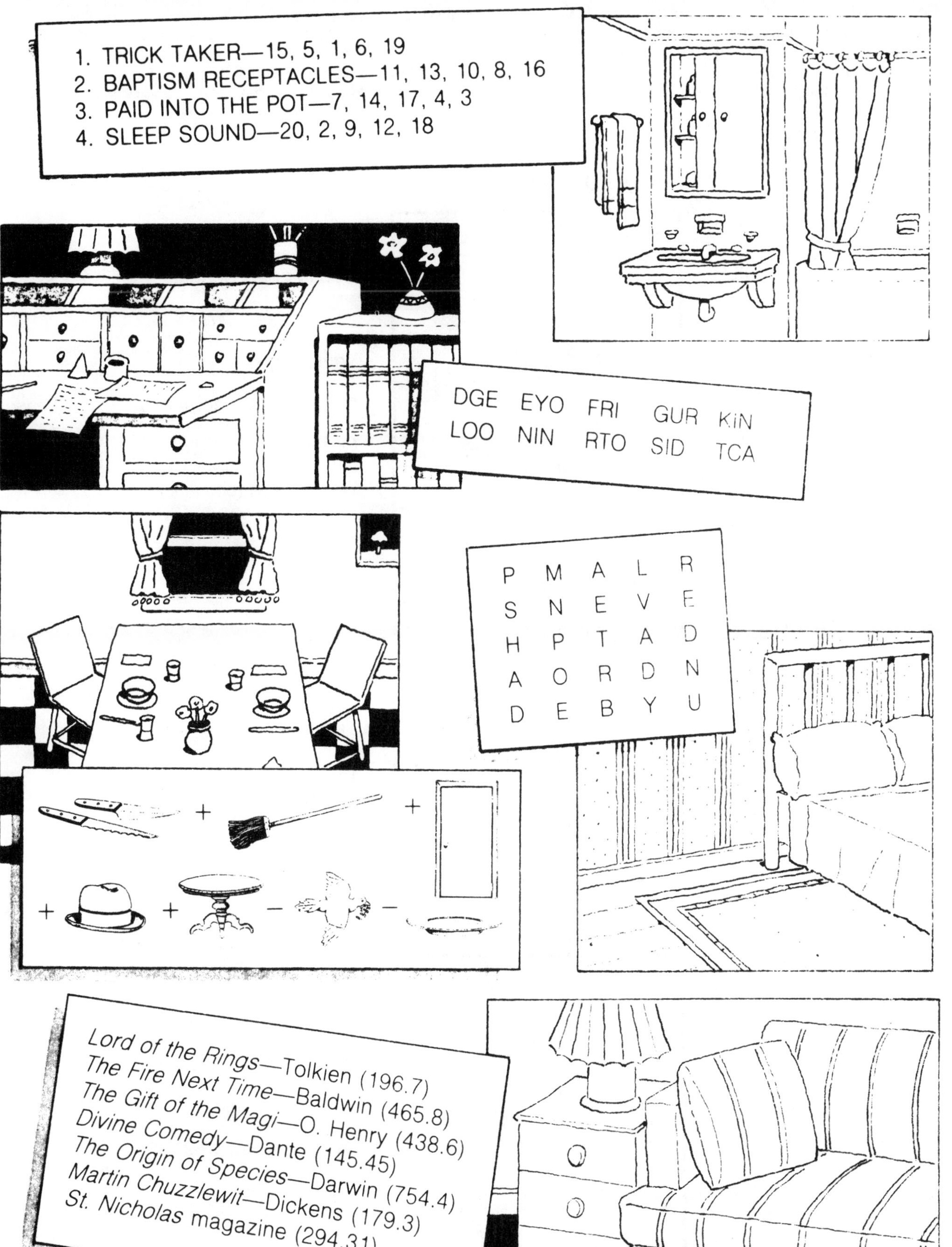

1. TRICK TAKER—15, 5, 1, 6, 19
2. BAPTISM RECEPTACLES—11, 13, 10, 8, 16
3. PAID INTO THE POT—7, 14, 17, 4, 3
4. SLEEP SOUND—20, 2, 9, 12, 18
DGE EYO FRI GUR KiN
LOO NIN RTO SID TCA
P M A L R
S N E V E
H P T A D
A O R D N
D E B Y U
+ + + + − −
Lord of the Rings—Tolkien (196.7)
The Fire Next Time—Baldwin (465.8)
The Gift of the Magi—O. Henry (438.6)
Divine Comedy—Dante (145.45)
The Origin of Species—Darwin (754.4)
Martin Chuzzlewit—Dickens (179.3)
St. Nicholas magazine (294.31)
KURT VARGO

WRY SANDWICHES #2

Rearrange the letters of each word on the left below, and add two or three letters in the middle, to form a seven-letter word answering the clue on the right. The words on the left are the outside letters, or "bread," of the seven-letter "sandwich." The letters you add are the "filler" and will appear consecutively in the shaded squares inside. For example, given the word ASTER and the clue "Weird," you would answer STRA<u>NG</u>E, with the letters NG appearing in the shaded squares. When a puzzle is completed, read the shaded letters in order, line by line, to spell a daffynition of the puzzle's title. **ANSWERS, PAGE 114**

1. BASEBALL UMPIRE

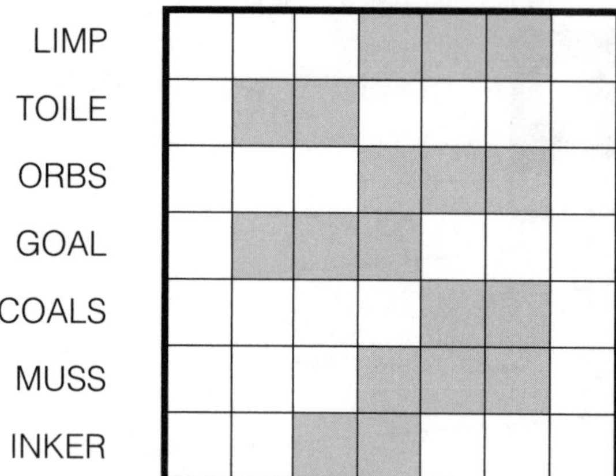

Word	Clue
LIMP	Select a jury
TOILE	Use to one's benefit
ORBS	___ *Rules of Order*
GOAL	Venice "taxi"
COALS	Not caring for company
MUSS	Order in the court?
INKER	Washington footballer

2. CASINO CHIPS

Word	Clue
ORALS	College-goer
REST	Suitable for "Ripley's"
CAPER	Introductory remarks
HENS	Abbreviate
NAGS	The whole ___
CLUE	Moolah
VICED	Come off without a hitch?

3. EGOTISTICAL

Word	Clue
HEADY	Country bumpkin
RULES	Off-work time
MOATS	Situated in the middle of
METER	One who breaks up homes?
SLOTS	Aria singer, for example
KNELT	What stars do
ELATE	Jock

TRIMMING THE TREE

Each answer is a four-letter word that is to be entered in the Christmas tree beginning in the appropriately numbered space and proceeding clockwise around the three adjacent triangles. The exact order of placement is for you to determine. The first word, OBOE, has been entered as an example. When the puzzle is completed, the letters in the 39 numbered spaces, read in order, will form 1½ lines of a popular Christmas carol.

ANSWER, PAGE 123

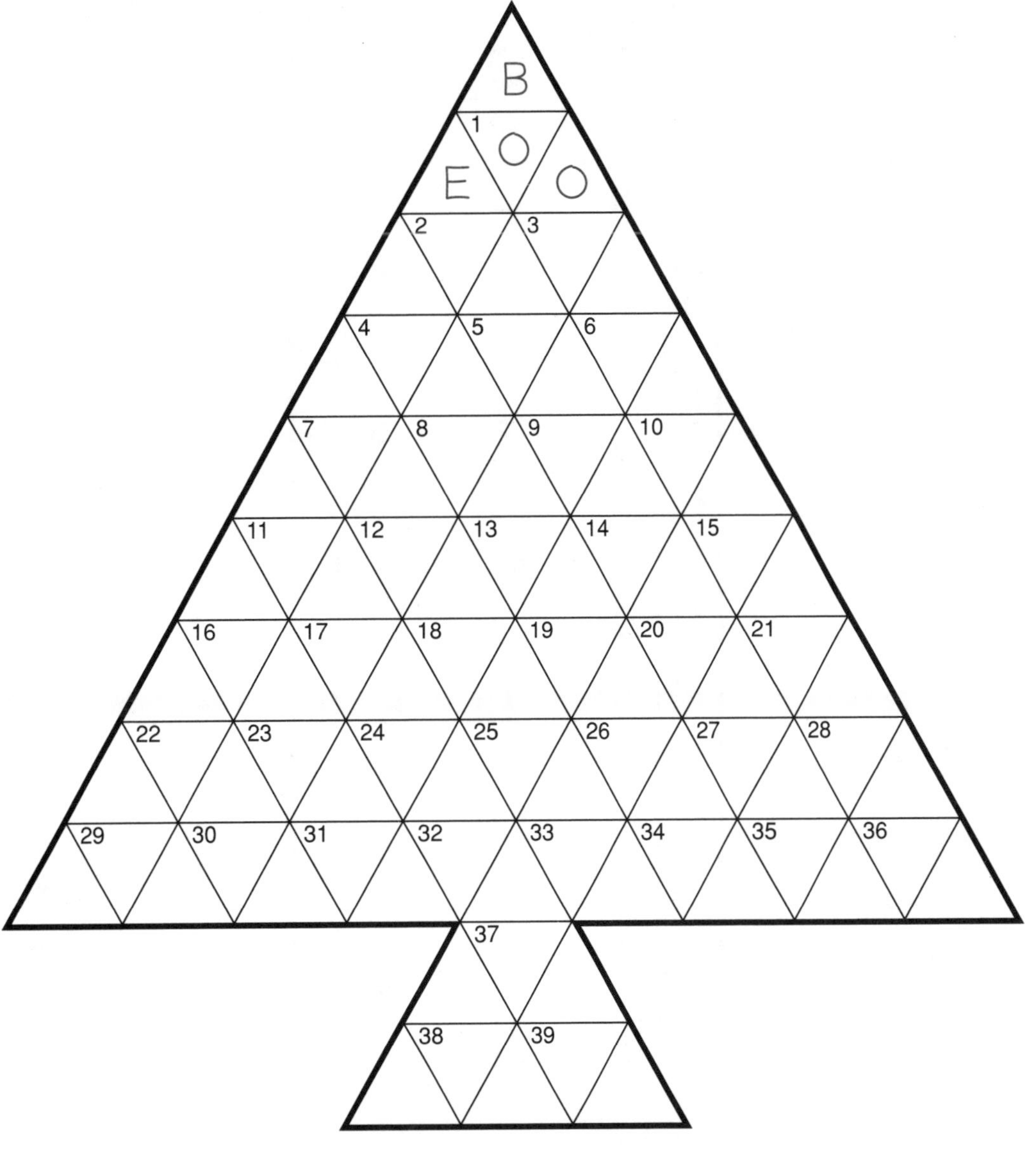

CLUES

1 Instrument in *The Nutcracker Suite*
2 "I'll Be ___ for Christmas" (1943 song)
3 Host Perry of holiday specials
4 Camel feature
5 Play friskily
6 Ayatollah's title
7 Catch a wave
8 Heavy cover
9 1974 part for Lucille Ball
10 Carpet layer's calculation
11 Divan
12 Something to do along the dotted line
13 Steak order
14 Raison d'___
15 In former times
16 Instrument in Handel's *Messiah*
17 By word of mouth
18 Trick, especially in love
19 The Emerald Isle
20 Presidential "no"
21 Bruised items, sometimes
22 Pealed, as Christmas bells
23 Yuletide drink
24 Word with bank or jelly
25 Yalies
26 Alternatively
27 Christmas carol
28 Safecracker
29 Poet Khayyám
30 Advocate
31 Part of an actor?
32 ___ weevil
33 Optimistic
34 Treaty signer
35 Actress Patricia
36 Zoo enclosure
37 Angel's headgear
38 And others: 2 wds., abbr.
39 Christmas tree decoration

ALPHABOXES

Arrange the 26 letters of the alphabet in the first empty column in the grid, and again in the second empty column, to complete the 26 seven-letter words reading across. Some of the individual words may be completed in more than one way, but the whole puzzle has only one solution. The first word has been finished as an example. **ANSWER, PAGE 123**

First Column

A B C D E F ~~G~~ H I J K L M N O P Q R S T U V W X Y Z

R	E	G	I	M	E	N
S	C		O		A	R
N	I		P		C	K
P	I		U		N	T
A	N		L		S	T
I	N		E		E	D
P	O		O		E	R
S	U		Z		R	O
D	I		O		C	E
G	L		M		S	E
B	A		O		U	E
P	R		T		E	L
L	O		K		A	W
L	A		N		R	Y
H	A		S		E	R
S	I		A		L	E
B	E		E		E	L
R	E		U		E	E
B	O		L		U	L
A	S		A		C	E
A	M		E		I	A
S	N		R		E	L
V	U		T		R	E
G	A		O		O	L
A	N		B		D	Y
T	A		I		A	B

Second Column

A B C D E F G H I J K L ~~M~~ N O P Q R S T U V W X Y Z

SUPER SEVEN SEARCH

Hidden in the word search grid below are 49 words that can be grouped into seven categories of seven words each. Six of the categories are listed beside the grid; the seventh is a mystery category for you to discover. Each answer is a single word that reads in a straight line forward, backward, or diagonally. Shade the letter spaces as you use them in the grid—but do so lightly, because some will be used more than once. When you've found all 49 answers, exactly seven letters will remain unshaded in the grid, and these will also relate—in an enigmatic way—to the number seven. Can you see how?

WORD LIST, PAGE 128 **ANSWER, PAGE 124**

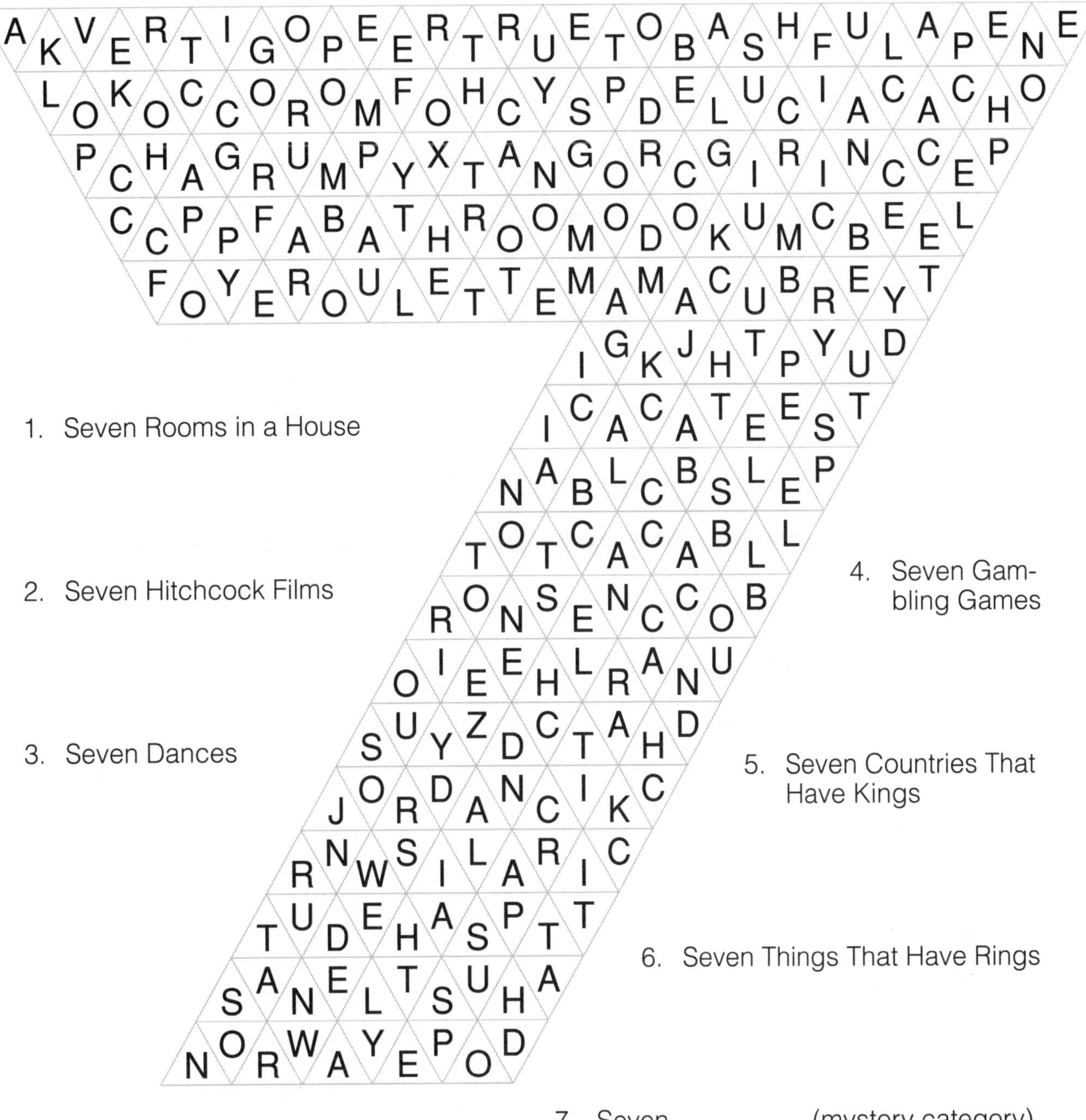

1. Seven Rooms in a House
2. Seven Hitchcock Films
3. Seven Dances
4. Seven Gambling Games
5. Seven Countries That Have Kings
6. Seven Things That Have Rings
7. Seven __________ (mystery category)

THE SPIRAL #3

This puzzle turns in two directions. The spiral's Inward clues yield a sequence of words to be entered counterclockwise in the spaces from 1 to 100. The Outward clues yield a different set of words to be entered clockwise from 100 back to 1. Fill in the answers, one letter per space, according to the numbers beside the clues. Be sure to follow directions, both ours and yours, or you'll be heading for—or getting back into—trouble.

ANSWER, PAGE 123

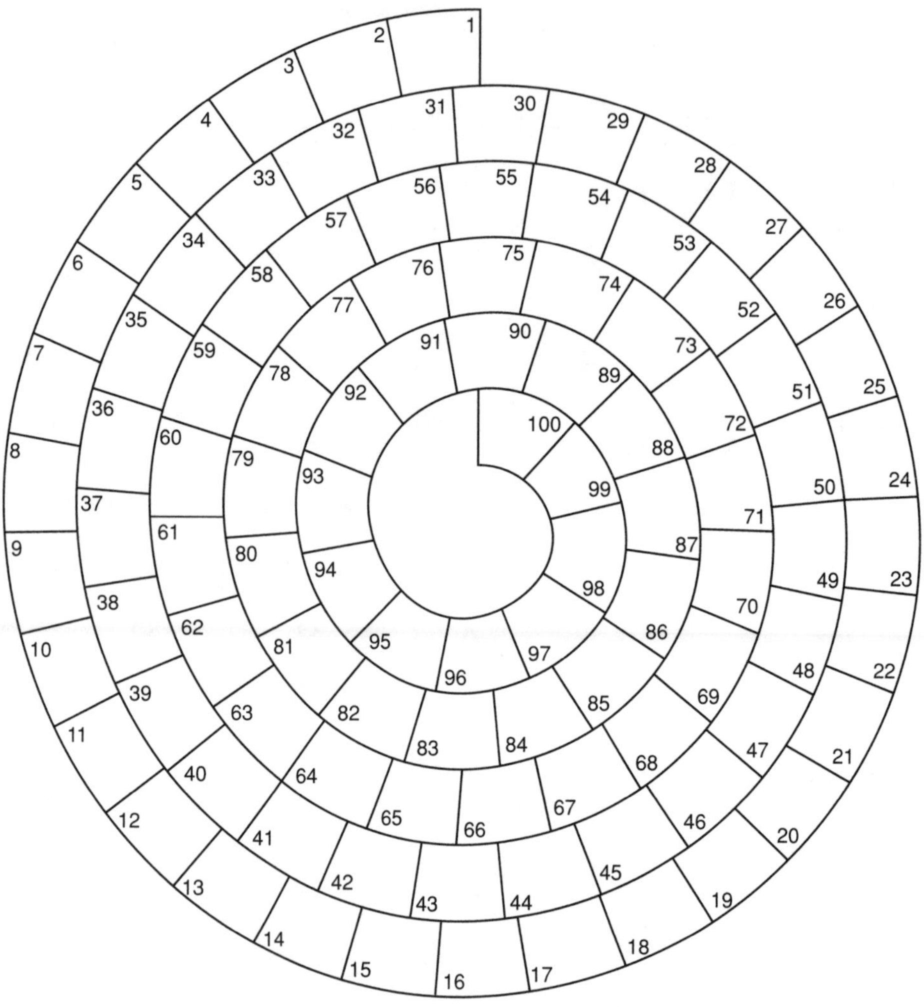

INWARD

1–4 Streetcar
5–9 Razor sharpener
10–15 Repeat, as the party line
16–23 Fancy breakfast dish
24–39 Candidate for the "*Forbes* 400"
40–45 Actress Jacqueline of *The Deep*
46–56 Exact to a fault
57–64 Fatherly
65–75 The guilty one
76–82 Resident of Switzerland's largest city
83–91 Baseball Hall-of-Famer Harmon
92–100 Small percussion instrument (2 wds.)

OUTWARD

100–95 Start of many a mystery
94–89 The "A" in Q&A
88–84 Attorney Melvin
83–79 Jack of cards
78–74 United ___ College Fund
73–69 French pastry
68–62 Do advance strategy
61–55 Makes another recording
54–51 Bakery employee
50–43 Fills out an absentee ballot
42–35 ___ Husky
34–32 Lube
31–27 "The sky's the ___"
26–22 Film director Sidney
21–13 Engine run by remote control
12–6 Harmonious relationship
5–1 Brainy

TELESCOPES

This challenge "lens" itself to focused thinking. In each of the two puzzles below, all the letters in the names of the objects pictured can be "telescoped" into a line of just 21 consecutive letters. To solve, first identify the objects and enter their names on the adjoining lines. The start and/or end of each word will overlap with at least one other word in the chain. For example, if one answer were TRAP, another might be APRON, another might be PRONG, etc. The objects are pictured in random order, so part of the puzzle is to determine where each name belongs in the chain. When you've identified all the objects correctly, eliminate the overlapping letters (and the spaces between them) to form one string of 21 letters, and enter it in the telescope.

ANSWERS, PAGE 122

Puzzle #1

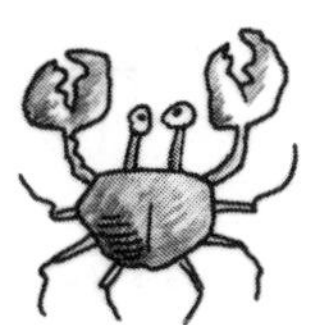
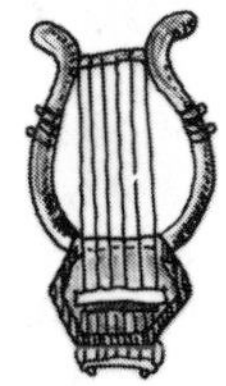

1. ______ 2. ______ 3. ______ 4. ______

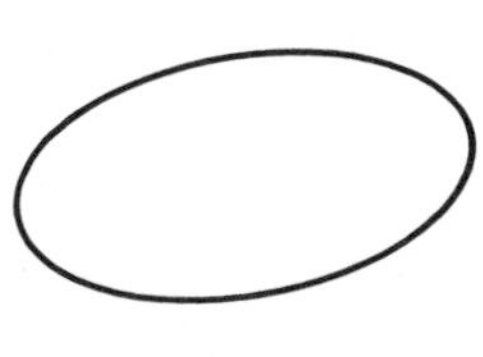

5. ______ 6. ______ 7. ______ 8. ______ 9. ______

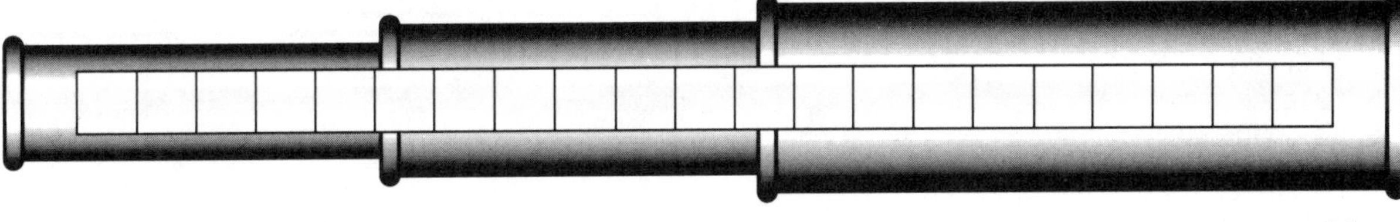

Puzzle #2

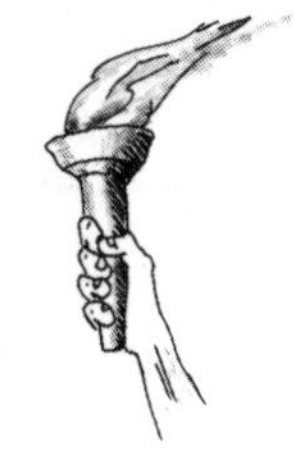

1. ______ 2. ______ 3. ______ 4. ______

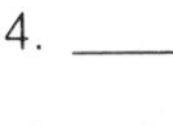

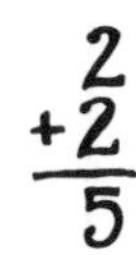

5. ______ 6. ______ 7. ______ 8. ______

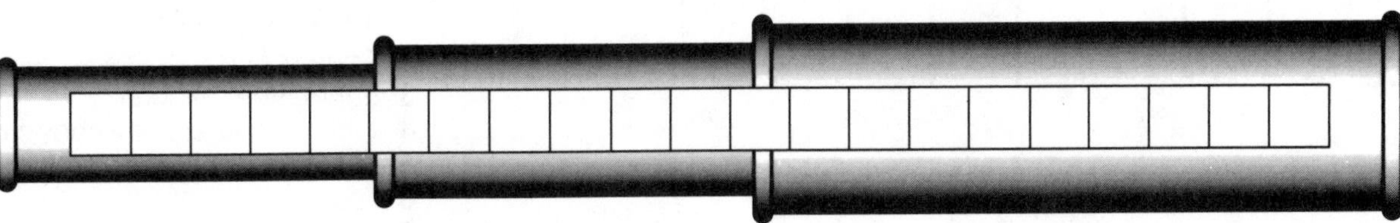

ROBERT LEIGHTON

LINK ACROSTICS #2

To solve these puzzles, answer the clues for three five-letter words reading across each line. The last two letters of the words in box A are the first two letters of those in box B, and the last two letters of the words in box B are the first two letters of those in box C. For, example, if the clues in the first line were "Miss Garbo," "Piece of furniture," and "Exit," you would fill in GRE(TA)B(LE)AVE. When each puzzle is done, three additional related words will read down the shaded columns.

ANSWERS, PAGE 123

1. CAN YOU TOP THIS?

A. **1** ___ being
2 Octopus's cousin
3 *Joie de vivre*
4 Aluminum, e.g.
5 Bird at a construction site?
6 Polo in the Far East?
7 Olympics award

B. **1** "Well-turned" body part
2 Perfect
3 Site of funny faces?
4 Big name in aluminum
5 '60s jacket style
6 Davenport
7 Aristotle's initial

C. **1** Patient of Father Damien
2 From the same mold
3 Game show host
4 "The Old ___ Bucket"
5 12" stick
6 It's "in the mail"
7 Overly fast

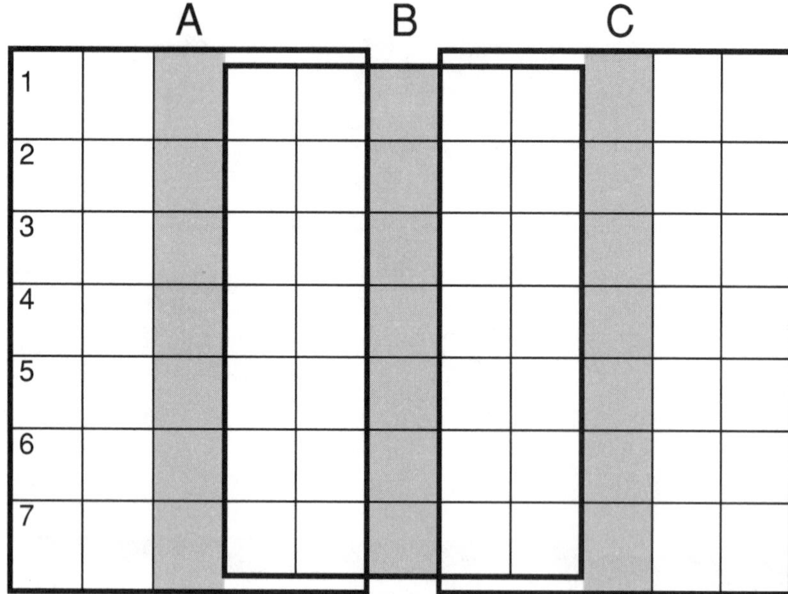

2. WELL, WHAT DO YOU KNOW?

A. **1** Poker pot
2 The silent Marx
3 Ecuador's capital
4 Santa's helpers
5 Friend, south of the border
6 Suntanning locale
7 Pancho ___

B. **1** Printing goofs
2 Tobacco receptacle
3 Trunk of the body
4 County north of the Thames
5 Dig out, painfully
6 Beijing's country
7 Caesar's language

C. **1** Academy Award
2 Church singers
3 Submarine detector
4 When repeated, newsboy's cry
5 Fowl in a gaggle
6 Foul
7 Preface, for short

SPLIT ENDS #1

Each clue in this crossword has been cut into two parts, and the parts have been given numbers from 1 to 76. To solve the puzzle, find and rejoin each matching pair of clue parts to produce the original clue. Enter the answer to each clue at the grid space indicated by the sum of the numbers of the clue's two parts. For example, #23 and #6 below combine to form the clue "Nut/Enjoyed by squirrels." The answer, ACORN, is filled in at #29 (23 + 6). Either part of the clue may appear first in the numbered list. Every part will be used exactly once in the completed puzzle.

ANSWER, PAGE 123

CLUES

1 Mongolia
2 Shaped like a boot
3 Checkers
4 Four-sided
5 Country
6 Enjoyed by squirrels
7 Direction in which
8 Decoration
9 Geometrical figure
10 Propelled by oars
11 Pearl's
12 Von Bismarck
13 Christmas tree
14 To throw coins
15 Less
16 A cigarette
17 Take into
18 The Earth's
19 What's inside
20 *The Canterbury Tales*
21 On the second
22 That snap shut
23 Nut
24 Shake
25 From the heart
26 Chancellor
27 Or spy
28 Voice heard
29 A clock
30 Contaminated
31 Residents of
32 Air
33 Adjust, as
34 Insurance man
35 An old photograph
36 Line
37 Dinner
38 Kings and
39 Kind of
40 In the pot
41 Informal
42 Feeling of
43 Exclusive
44 Place
45 Mecca
46 ___ (consider)
47 Essential
48 Pony or cock
49 Vessel
50 It comes straight
51 Plant with leaves
52 Person who
53 In a canyon
54 Color of
55 That has been mended
56 Reporter's
57 For horses
58 Placed money
59 Part of something
60 With fear
61 Being closed in
62 King
63 Tire
64 Desert of
65 Word after
66 On a weather map
67 Opposite of
68 Author of
69 Lends a hand
70 Of the jungle
71 Floor of a house
72 Queens, collectively
73 The sun comes up
74 Source
75 Photograph
76 Awake

SPINOFFS

Each clue (1-8) consists of a sentence with two missing words. Think of a five-letter word to go in the first blank, which, if you remove its initial letter, will make a four-letter word that will go in the second blank and complete the sentence. For example, "Mom threw a COVER OVER the new sofa." Each five-letter answer is to be entered clockwise around the appropriate number in the grid, beginning in the circle that appears in the overlapping disk. When you've finished all eight discs, rearrange the highlighted letters to make an eight-letter word that can be similarly "beheaded" to complete the Bonus Clue.

ANSWER, PAGE 124

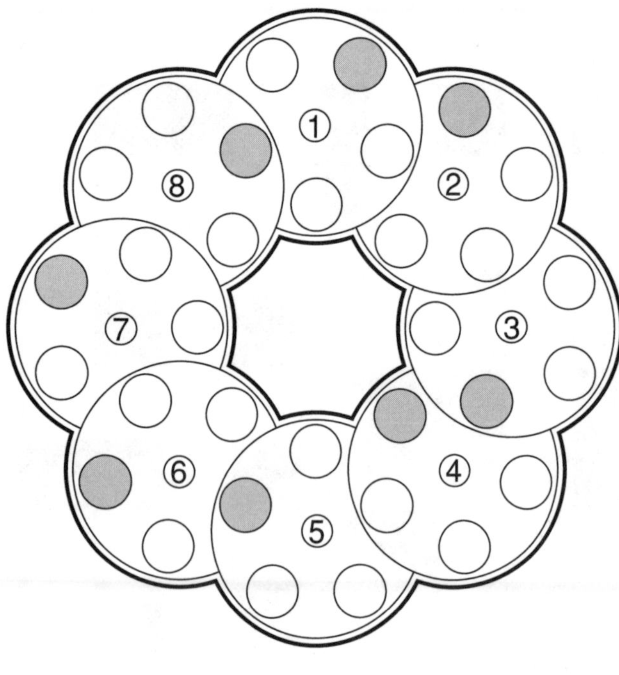

CLUES

1. To get the closest possible ________, ________ a fresh blade in your razor.
2. Nothing ________ ________ more than the quirks of their divorced partners.
3. The farm agent who was checking to see if the soil would ________ ________ in a tractor all around the field.
4. If that's where the tribesmen want to ________, ________, they can stay there as long as they want.
5. A handy lesson of life is, as you'll one day ________, ________ as much money as you can while you're young.
6. If a usually even-tempered exterminator ________, ________ are probably crawling up his leg!
7. The striptease artist wears a black garter around her ________, ________ above her knee.
8. At the end of this year's Halloween party, everyone agreed to make the ________ ________ the next one.

BONUS CLUE

In last night's broadcast, viewers heard the Pacific ________ ________ a rival across the sea.

EX TERMINATIONS

This quiz will give you a chance to express yourself. The answer to each clue is a word, name, or title ending with the letters EX. For example, the clue "Mark or accent over a foreign vowel" would be answered CIRCUMFLEX, while "Alpine mountain goat" would be answered IBEX. Twelve correct answers is exemplary, 14 is exceptional, and a score of 16 or more is simply extraordinary.

ANSWERS, PAGE 124

1. Knee-tapping reaction ________________
2. Highest point ________________
3. Heat-resistant glassware ________________
4. Kind of hair salon ________________
5. Cast an evil spell ________________
6. Mystify ________________
7. Two-family house ________________
8. Point of a triangle ________________
9. Back-of-book listing ________________
10. Paint ingredient ________________
11. Curved outward ________________
12. "Is it live, or is it ..." ________________
13. Building wing ________________
14. Popular glass cleaner ________________
15. Elaborate and intricate ________________
16. Watch that "keeps on ticking" ________________
17. Cablegram's alternative ________________
18. Part of the brain ________________

WORD DERBY

Ladies and gentlemen, the horses are at the starting gate. Pick your favorites (A, E, I, O, or U—this is purely a matter of luck) and you're ready to begin. Answer the clues below the racetrack and enter the answers in the blanks at their right. Vowels go in the blanks with numbers; consonants go in blanks without. Next, advance each horse counterclockwise on the track the number of spaces indicated below the corresponding vowels in the answers. For example, if the vowel A appeared above the number 4, you would cross out four spaces of A's lane on the track. The position of the horses at the end of the puzzle determines the order of placement. Solving hint: All the answer words have something in common.

ANSWERS, PAGE 124

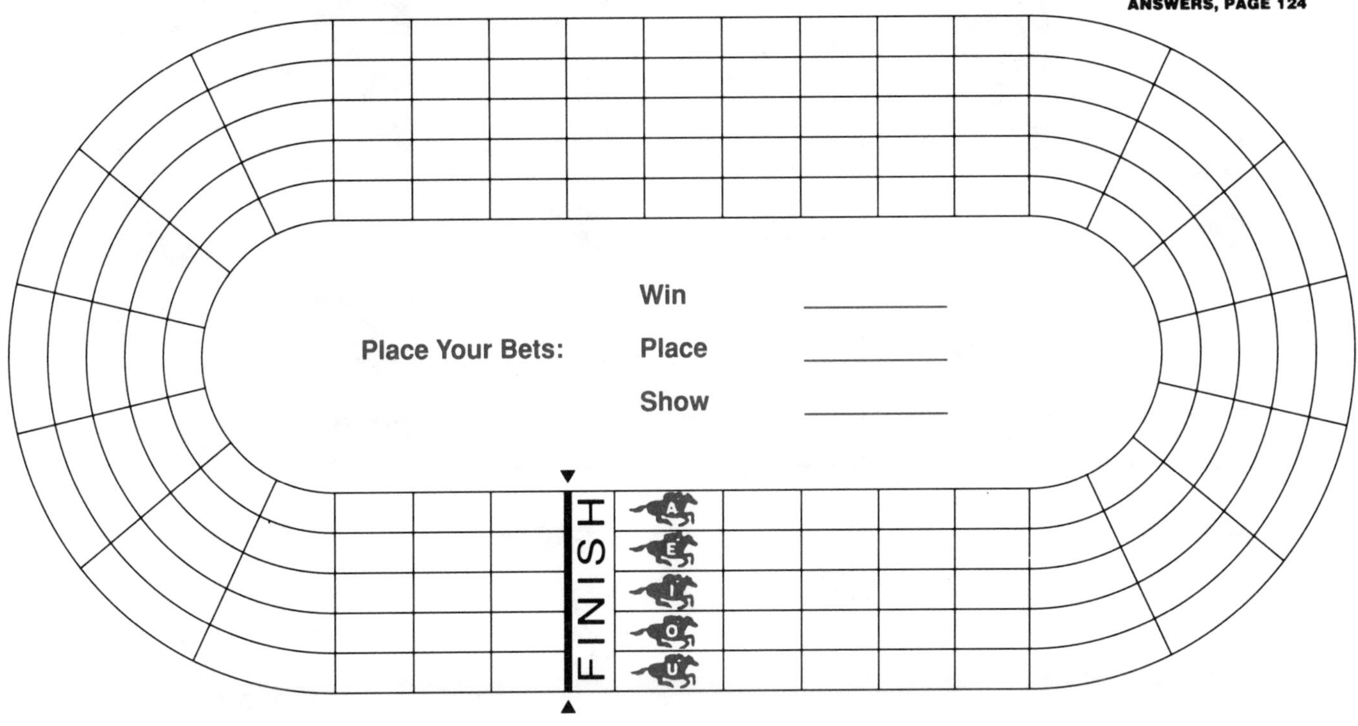

1. Riddle — C _2_ ___ _4_ N ___ ___ _5_ M
2. Breach, as of the law — V _4_ _3_ ___ _3_ T _6_ _2_ N
3. Envoy — _2_ ___ B _3_ ___ ___ _3_ D _4_ ___
4. Mouseketeer Annette — F _6_ ___ _5_ ___ _4_ ___ L _2_
5. "Nonsense!" — F _5_ ___ ___ ___ _4_ S ___ _6_ ___ K ___
6. Alp famed for mountain climbers — ___ _5_ ___ T _6_ R ___ _3_ ___ N
7. Kings of the road — ___ _2_ B _1_ _6_ ___
8. Financier J.P. — ___ _3_ ___ G _5_ ___
9. Without qualification whatsoever — _4_ B ___ _2_ L _6_ T _5_
10. Whaler's missile — ___ _4_ R ___ _3_ _3_ N

BASED ON A PUZZLE BY EUGENE R. NECKAR

DOUBLE PARKING

Solve these two puzzles as you would regular crosswords, except instead of filling in squares, put one letter in each triangular space.

ANSWERS, PAGE 124

Puzzle 1

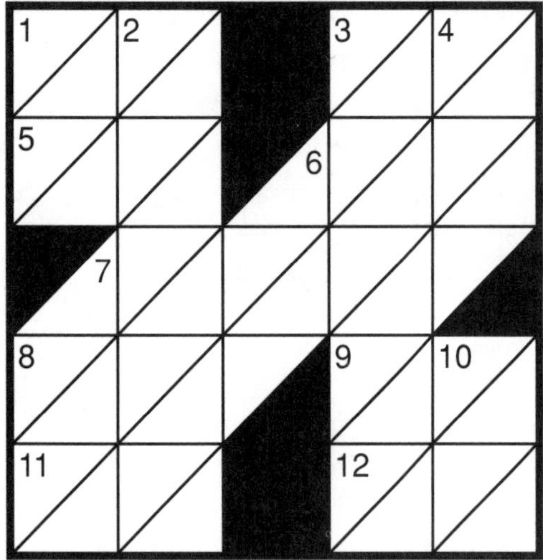

Puzzle 2

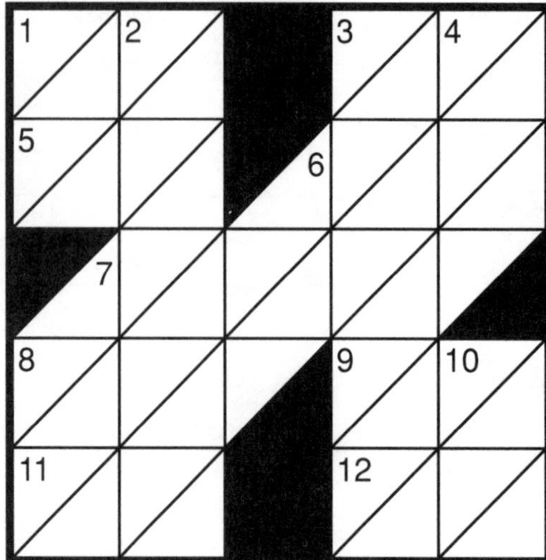

Puzzle 1

ACROSS

1 Halloween cover-up
3 Stallion or bull, e.g.
5 Lock openers
6 Snowbank
7 Harsh feeling
8 Beats, as wings
9 Draw permanently
11 One in debt
12 Eye-dropper?

DOWN

1 Brand of car
2 Chicago's Sears Tower, e.g.
3 It has strings pulled
4 Southpaw
6 Turns down (the lights)
7 Moving, like lava
10 Scorch

Puzzle 2

ACROSS

1 Big party
3 Fictional detective
5 Nimble
6 Buffalo's home?
7 Give rise to
8 South American capital
9 Story teller
11 Some Islamic names
12 Thus

DOWN

1 Sound of astonishment
2 Why one might be at a loss for words?
3 Ballroom fixture
4 Rile
6 Gambling haven
7 A twin
10 Jason's ship

CONFUSABLES

Was it Charlotte or Emily Brontë who wrote *Wuthering Heights*? If you have to guess, good—this quiz on common confusables may be your sort of challenge. These are all facts all of us have read and heard many times, but many of us still have trouble remembering.

A score of eight or more is good.

ANSWERS, PAGE 124

1. Was Romeo a member of the Capulet family and Juliet a member of the Montague family, or was it the other way around?
2. In a cave you notice rock formations hanging from the ceiling. Are those stalagmites or stalactites?
3. On a loom, is the series of lengthwise yarns known as the warp or the woof?
4. Copper and tin are melded to form a common alloy. Is that alloy brass or is it bronze?
5. Between apogee and perigee, which is the high point of an orbit and which the low?
6. You need to be treated for an eye infection. Should you see an optometrist, an ophthalmologist, or an optician?
7. Is the boiling point of water higher or lower at higher elevations?
8. At graduation ceremonies, do you shift the tassel from the right side of the mortarboard to the left, or from the left to the right?
9. Was Plato a student of Socrates or Socrates a student of Plato?
10. Of the Civil War ships the *Monitor* and the *Merrimac*, which was the Union ship and which the Confederate?
11. Was Alaska or Hawaii admitted to the Union first?
12. At sea, your captain calls all passengers to the ship's starboard. If you're facing the bow, do you head left or right?

“B” HIVE #2

When this puzzle is completed, 30 six-letter words will swarm in circular fashion around the numbers in the beehive. To solve, answer the clues (which all just happen to start with the letter B) and enter each answer word around the corresponding number in the grid. Answers begin in the spaces indicated by the arrows and proceed clockwise or counterclockwise—the direction is for you to determine. As a solving hint, we'll tell you that all 26 letters of the alphabet are used at least once in the completed grid.

ANSWER, PAGE 124

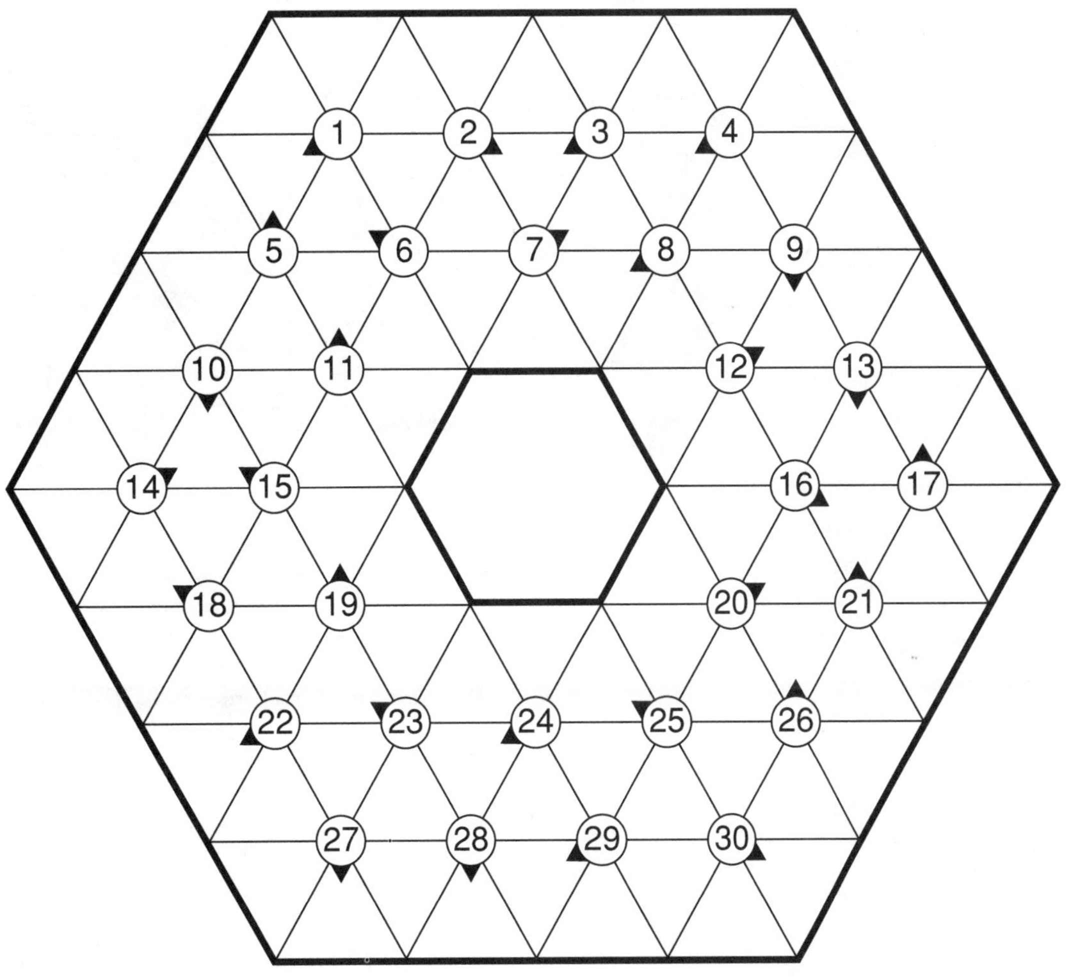

1 Begonia or bluebell
2 Barring two-directional traffic (hyph.)
3 Busy (oneself with)
4 Block volume
5 Bordeaux's country
6 Big ditch
7 Betting establishment
8 Be acquiescent
9 Bridges/Close film ___ *Edge*
10 Blanketlike cloak
11 Burial place of King Arthur
12 Bewitched in a bad way
13 Bring a plane to Havana?
14 Big, weightwise
15 Blue Cross/Blue Shield contract
16 Brightly-colored cloth
17 Bad art
18 Broadway theater of note
19 Bygone refrigerator
20 Blindly enthusiastic one
21 Bohemians, today
22 Between Newfoundland and Ontario
23 Breast-feeding alternative
24 Boardinghouse resident
25 Belushi's ___ *House*
26 Bothersome skin inflammation
27 Be choosy?
28 Bombarded
29 Blue jeans
30 Batter-maker Aunt ___

CARTOON REBUSES

It's said that a picture is worth a thousand words. We're not asking for *that* many words, but we are looking for some specific ones to solve the 14 Cartoon Rebuses pictured on these two pages. The answer to each puzzle is a name that's found by combining any or all of the following elements from the cartoon:

- Words or synonyms of words spoken by the characters or found elsewhere in the picture;
- Names of prominent objects in the picture;
- Isolated letters in the picture;
- Words implied by the cartoon's action or scene.

These elements are combined *phonetically* to form the name fitting the category and the number of letters given as clues above the cartoon.

For example, the answer to the cartoon shown at upper left is *Vanity Fair.* It's found by combining VAN, pictured in the background; the word IT spoken by the cabbie; the letter E on the van; and the word FARE, suggested by the scene. Put them together phonetically and you get VAN-IT-E-FARE.

How many of the others can you solve? **ANSWERS, PAGE 124**

Ex. Magazine: 6,4

1. Cartoon Character: 5,10

5. Supreme Court Justice: 8,8

6. Novel: 7,2,5

10. Indian Tribe: 8

11. World Capital: 8

CARTOON REBUSES

2. Singer/Actress: 6,7

3. Old Automobile: 10

4. Religious Leader: 5,6

7. 1600s Invention: 5,4

8. Drink: 9

9. Former Baseball Player: 4,7

12. Fictional Character: 10

13. Game: 9

14. Old Song: 3,5,2,3,5

KIMBLE MEAD

FLOWER CROSS

To solve this hybrid puzzle, first answer the clues for words to be entered in the grid. Answers proceed outward from the numbered spaces to the tips of the petals. Half the words will read clockwise, the other half counterclockwise. When you're done, take the letters in the 17 shaded spaces and arrange them in the empty spaces in the middle of the grid to form a word square, with five five-letter words reading across and five different five-letter words going down. **ANSWER, PAGE 124**

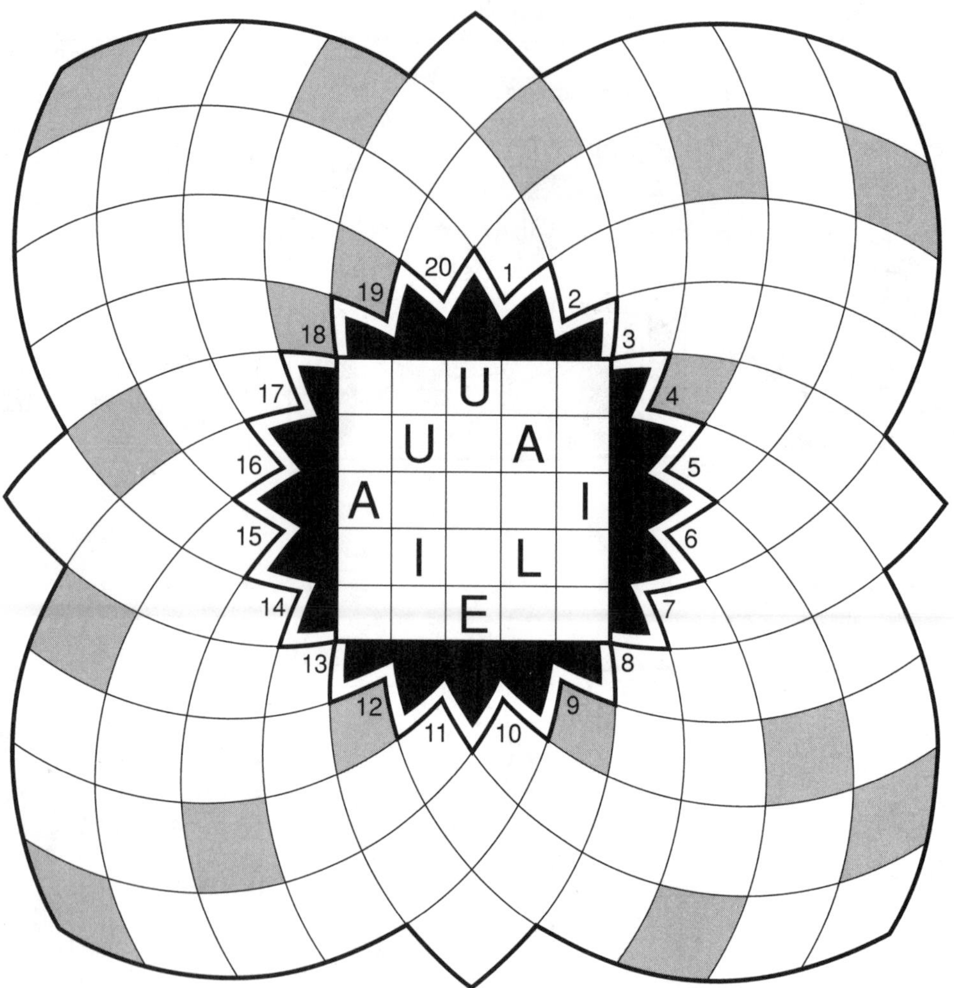

CLOCKWISE

1 Old fuddy-duds
2 Fountain of Rome
3 Target ship at Pearl Harbor
4 Religious group
5 Quick investigation (hyph.)
6 Kids' put-together game
7 Grieve
8 Doughnuts, mathematically
9 Reading aid
10 "Sit!" or "Heel!"
11 Kramden's best pal
12 Five, in compounds
13 The Tower of London, formerly
14 New York City stadium
15 Laundry worker
16 Tristram's beloved, in legend
17 Arabian leader?
18 Fancy alternative
19 Loverboy
20 Cabinet department

COUNTERCLOCKWISE

1 Tickler
2 Literally, "bean ferment"
3 Nudge
4 Alice B. Toklas's "autobiographer"
5 Foliage
6 Noted Apache chief
7 Not worth arguing about
8 Conned
9 Oafs
10 Stephen King novel
11 Conventional favorite?
12 Pageantry
13 It can make you sick!
14 Elf supervisor
15 Futuristic torpedo type
16 Cork's location
17 Far from land
18 ___ Yellow Rose (TV diner)
19 Bad pitches
20 The '80s, e.g.

SYLLASTEPS #2

To solve each puzzle, enter the syllables of the Syllabary into the grid, one syllable per space, to form eight four-syllable words answering the given clues. All answers read across. Cross off the syllables as you use them, because each will be used once. When you're done, the shaded diagonals in the grid will spell bonus words relating to the puzzle's title.

ANSWERS, PAGE 125

A. STAR MAN

1. Utter surprise
2. Annoyingly condescending
3. Some pudding
4. The flicker, familiarly
5. European capital
6. Summer reading?
7. Gold Rush participant (hyph.)
8. Tonsillitis cause

SYLLABARY

A AS CA CO COC CUS FOR GEN
HA HAM I ING ISH IZ LOW MENT
MER NER NI O PA PEN PER STREP
TAP TEM TO TON TRON TURE TY YEL

1			
2			
3			
4			
5			
6			
7			
8			

B. THE WRITE STUFF

1. Battle site of 1876 (2 wds.)
2. Butterfly's alter ego
3. Society governed by women
4. Accepted thinking
5. Official bulletin
6. He has his ups and downs
7. Fan
8. Picture

SYLLABARY

AR AST BIG CAT CHY COM DOX EN
ER HORN IL IST LAR LIN LIT LUS
MA MU NI OR PIL PO QUE SI
THO THU TION TLE TRA TRAM TRI Y

1			
2			
3			
4			
5			
6			
7			
8			

EQUATION ANALYSIS TEST #2

This test does not measure your I.Q., verbal ability, or talent for math. It will, however, give you some indication of your mental agility, creativity, and awareness of the world around you. It may also drive you bonkers!

To solve, figure out what words the initials represent in each equation. For example, *36 = I. in a Y.* would be *36 = Inches in a Yard.* Some answers, you'll find, will come to mind immediately with a quick, intuitive leap. Others, though, may remain frustratingly stuck on the tip of your tongue or in the back of your brain. If the words don't occur to you right off, move on to something else and come back later. Creativity sometimes strikes when least expected; so don't be surprised if while you're doing the dishes or reading the paper, an equation you weren't even thinking about suddenly makes absolute sense.

ANSWERS, PAGE 125

a. 36 = I. in a Y. Inches in a Yard

b. 6 = W. of H. the E. ________

c. 212 = D. at which W.B. ________

d. 3 = P. for a F.G. in F. ________

e. 20 = Y. that R.V.W.S. ________

f. 101 = D. ________

g. 60 = S. in a M. ________

h. 7 = H. of R. ________

i. 56 = S. of the D. of I. ________

j. 5 = F. on the H. ________

k. 40 = T. (with A.B.) ________

l. 30 = D.H.S.A.J. and N. ________

m. 1 = D. at a T. ________

n. 10 = A. in the B. of R. ________

o. 435 = M. of the H. of R. ________

p. 16 = O. in a P. ________

q. 31 = I.C.F. at B.-R. ________

r. 50 = C. in a H.D. ________

s. 2 = T.D. (and a P. in a P.T.) ________

t. 4 = H. of the A. ________

u. 13 = C. in a S. ________

v. 8 = P. of S. in the E.L. ________

w. 20,000 = L.U. the S. ________

x. 9 = I. in a B.G. ________

CROSS-O #2

Hidden in each box on this page are five words—four related objects or names, plus a fifth that identifies what the other four have in common. Each word is divided into five parts and concealed sequentially from left to right in consecutive columns.

For example, one of the names in box #1 is ORANGE, with the letters OR in the first column, A in the second, N in the third, G in the fourth, and E in the fifth. The category, FRUIT, is similarly concealed in left-to-right fashion. Now see if you can find the three remaining fruits. Then try the other boxes on your own. You may cross out squares as you solve, because each will be used only once.

ANSWERS, PAGE 124

CH	R	N	N	E
B	U	U	R	T
OR	E	A	QU	A
F	AN	M	G	Y
K	A	R	I	AT

1. FRUIT

ORANGE

D	O	AM	Y	LD
J	ET	E	RA	Z
E	I	W	ON	ST
T	E	H	A	L
AM	M	P	E	D

2.

BE	A	OD	E	O
P	G	R	I	Y
PA	O	RC	L	L
M	AI	H	BO	VE
H	E	E	D	E

3.

CO	L	T	L	R
M	T	A	K	UM
Y	E	V	A	EL
SI	I	TR	E	T
N	B	C	I	L

4.

WH	O	EN	N	Y
E	R	T	O	E
MA	V	IS	S	OR
IN	I	R	NE	N
M	D	CO	T	I

5.

F	IT	E	O	E
A	E	I	N	S
R	T	EA	C	M
CH	L	C	OO	NE
S	OS	R	R	P

6.

R	OL	U	M	Y
D	R	CH	A	D
CU	O	B	NC	E
DR	U	RE	L	R
P	A	L	N	A

7.

E	S	D	B	R
DE	E	S	I	O
S	C	R	IN	RT
P	HE	L	E	G
J	UD	LA	L	ET

8.

A LITTLE OFF THE TOP

Three words complete each verse below. Remove the first letter of the first word to get the second word, and remove the first letter of the second word to get the third. For example, if SCREAM completed the first line, the next two lines would end in CREAM and REAM.

ANSWERS, PAGE 125

1. That traveling minister surely could ______________ ,
For far from the pulpit his sermons would ______________ .
(They say his revivals grossed many grand ______________ .)

2. My Halloween costume makes everyone ______________ .
I dress as a warty, repulsive old ______________ .
The hot rubber mask, though, sure makes my face ______________ .

3. The fans in the bleachers made hollers and ______________ .
Their team had scored seven straight basketball ______________ .
The coach for the visiting cagers said, " ______________ !"

4. One thing I can live without, thanks, is the ______________
Of rushing to dress and get off to a ______________ ...
And finding it's late on account of the ______________ .

5. Remarkably bright and exceedingly ______________
Is he who conceived the mechanical ______________
(For prying up rocks the most useful thing ______________ !).

6. The Suicide Stoppers have taken a ______________
To calm any "jumper" who's out on a ______________ .
They give him support so he's not so "on ______________ ."

7. Some friendly advice when you visit your ______________ :
Provide a small push when he's going up ______________ ;
And if there's a stereo, turn up the ______________ .

WORD MAZE

How many of the names of fish and other sea creatures can you find in the grid below? Each name is concealed in a series of consecutively connected squares. For example, CARP can be spelled beginning with the C in the second column, then moving up to the A, diagonally down to the R, and diagonally down to the P. In spelling a word, do not stand on a letter (as the D in HADDOCK) before going on. You may, however, reuse a letter in a word. Getting 6 answers is good; finding 9 is expert. Our answer list contains 12 common fish and sea creatures.

ANSWERS, PAGE 124

M	H	N	U	R
D	A	S	O	T
O	C	R	I	L
R	P	K	E	P

1. ______________
2. ______________
3. ______________
4. ______________
5. ______________
6. ______________
7. ______________
8. ______________
9. ______________
10. ______________
11. ______________
12. ______________

BULL'S-EYE 20 QUESTIONS #3

Ready to set your sights on another bull's-eye? The answer to each of the 20 questions in this puzzle is one of the 24 words in the bull's-eye target. Each answer scores a "hit," which you may cross off in the target since no answer word is used more than once. When all the clues have been answered, the four unused words can be rearranged to form a quotation by chess grandmaster Savielly Tartakower.

ANSWERS, PAGE 125

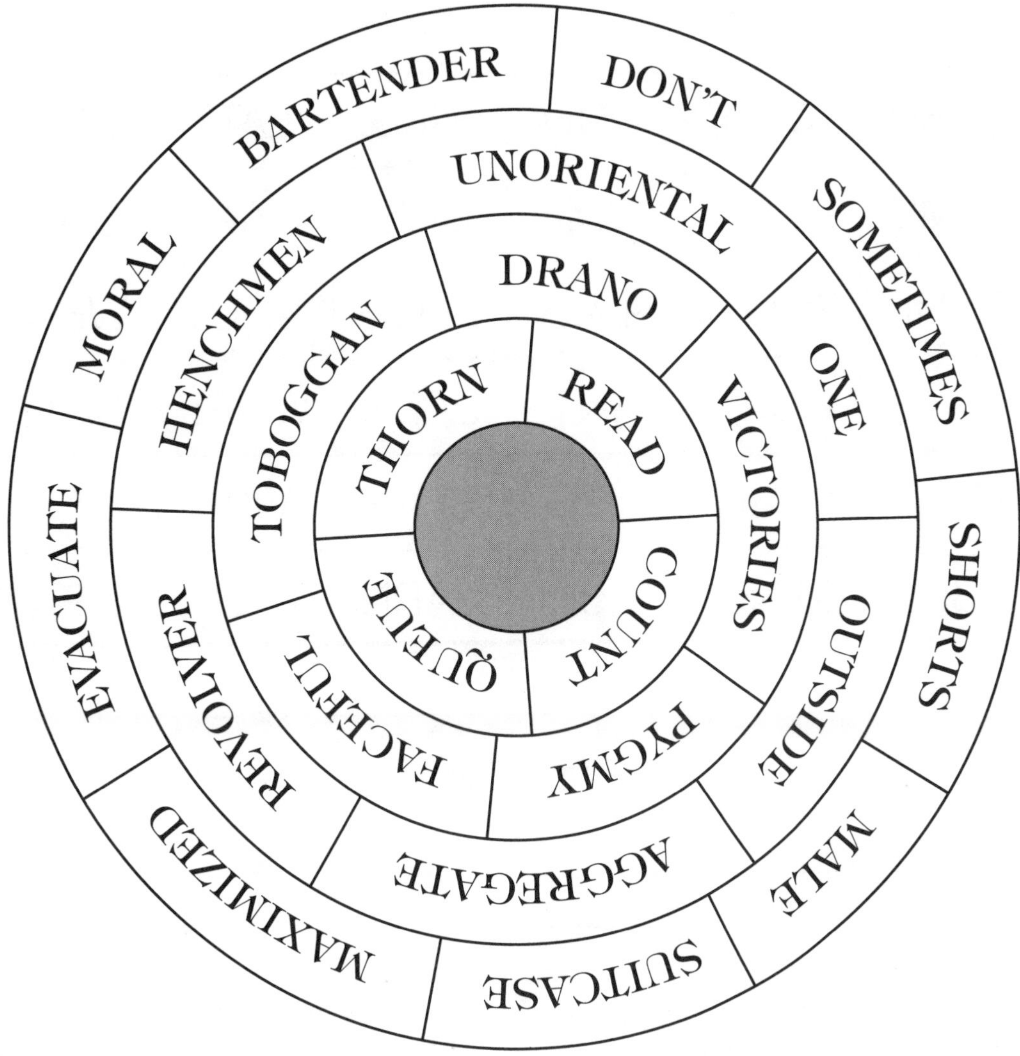

WHICH WORD ...

1. contains only the letters in the word TARGET?
2. spells the name of a brand of beer in reverse?
3. would spell a synonym of itself if you dropped its first and fifth letters?
4. sounds like two consecutive arithmetical operations?
5. would have the same pattern as ADELAIDE in a cryptogram?
6. would spell the name of a movie if you dropped its middle letter?
7. has, when written in lower-case script, strokes below the line in all but one of its letters?
8. is an anagram of a compass direction?
9. would sound like a word meaning "trustworthy" if spoken with a lisp?
10. would be pronounced the same if you dropped its last four letters?
11. contains all five vowels in reverse order?
12. is a verb whose present and past tense forms are spelled the same?
13. would become a word meaning "trade" if you removed its end?
14. consists of two consecutive words meaning "a legal matter"?
15. would become an antonym of itself if the letters FE were placed in front of it?
16. contains Roman numerals totaling 2,512?
17. means, to a punster, "The purpose of attending a Boston flea market"?
18. can be prefixed by any of 10 different letters to form a common new word?
19. would spell itself backward if you reversed its middle two letters?
20. begins with a letter that appears in each of the other remaining four words?

WORLD TOUR

This puzzle features a round-the-world tour of 18 major cities outside the United States. Three cities—each made up of six letters—are hidden among the six words in each row of the grid. The cities are spelled out left to right, one letter per word. For example, WARSAW is found in the first row by taking the W in the first word, the A in the second, the R in the third, etc. (Two more cities are also concealed in the first row.) You may cross off letters as you proceed, because no letter will be used more than once. One letter in each word will remain when you're done. Can you identify all 18 cities? **ANSWERS, PAGE 125**

SWAM	AWAY	RIND	PINS	LATE	YAWN
LAMB	AUTO	HYMN	BIDE	CANT	SHAY
BUMP	ROOM	SLAG	CLOG	LOUT	WEAR
LONG	COAT	PINT	LADY	WORE	SNAP
TOLD	LAUD	BITE	SLAP	VISE	LAIN
ABLE	MINE	DISK	BARN	TOUR	NEAT

1. WARSAW
   ______
   ______
2. ______
   ______
   ______
3. ______
   ______
   ______
4. ______
   ______
   ______
5. ______
   ______
   ______
6. ______
   ______
   ______

THE THREE R'S

In early school days the three R's were reading, 'riting, and 'rithmetic. In the 1884 presidential election they were Rum, Romanism, and Rebellion. To modern puzzlers, though, they're simply words that contain three R's. How many of the following can you complete, filling in one letter per blank?

ANSWERS, PAGE 125

Ex. Mistake E R R O R

1. Newspaper worker R _ _ _ R _ _ R
2. Wire-haired dog _ _ R R _ _ R
3. Storyteller _ _ R R _ _ _ R
4. Club officer _ R _ _ _ _ _ R _ R
5. Image-maker? _ _ R R _ R
6. Toward the back R _ _ R _ _ R _
7. Roadblock _ _ R R _ _ R
8. Ask for more stock R _ _ R _ _ R
9. Hallway _ _ R R _ _ _ R
10. Fruit flavor R _ _ _ _ _ R R _
11. Backside, politely _ _ R R _ _ R _
12. Wizard _ _ R _ _ R _ R
13. "Golden" dog R _ _ R _ _ _ _ _ R
14. Not uniform _ R R _ _ _ _ _ _ _ R
15. Constant fretter _ _ R R _ _ _ R _

A TO Z #2

This crossword contains 26 clues, each of which begins with a different letter of the alphabet. These initial letters have been removed and replaced by blanks. First fill in as many of the initial letters as you can be sure of. Then enter these letters in the correspondingly numbered squares in the grid.

Next, enter answers to as many of the completed clues as you can. Each of the 26 answer words *also* begins with a different letter of the alphabet—always different from the initial letter of its clue.

Answers, naturally, can't be entered at the corresponding numbers in the grid, because their first letters will not match the initial letters you've already filled in. Instead, each answer should be filled in beginning in the space where its first letter appears. The initial letter for #1, S, has been entered in both the clues and the grid to help get you started.

ANSWER, PAGE 125

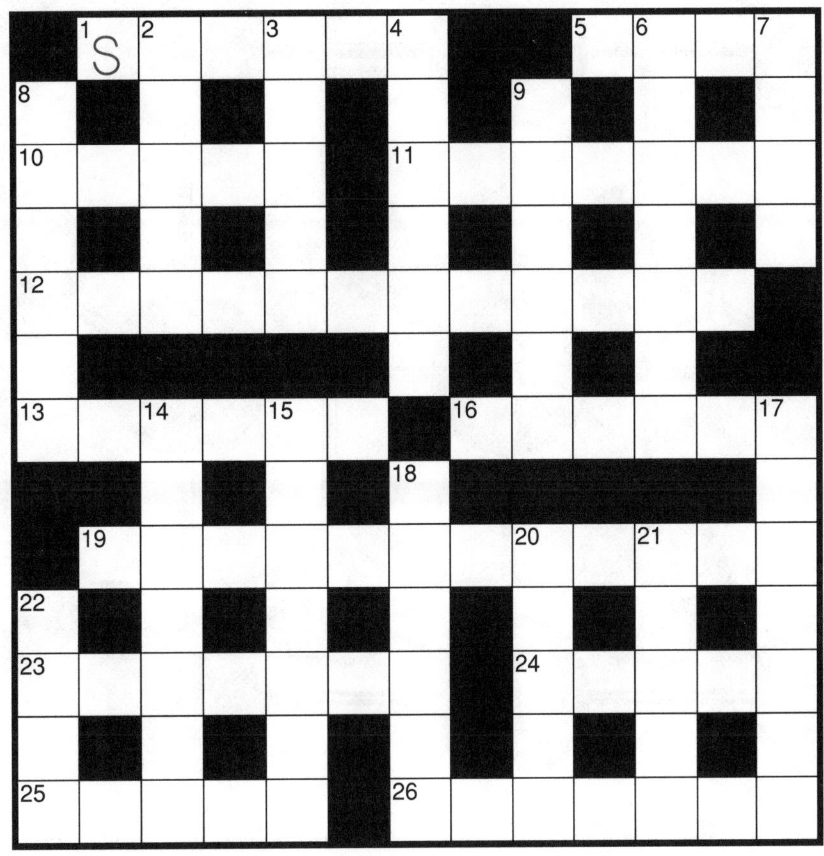

1. S ea
2. ___ uiet hideaway
3. ___ xtinguish, as a rebellion
4. ___ ashmir is there
5. ___ oin a cabal
6. ___ bject hopelessness
7. ___ apped at the dentist's (hyph.)
8. ___ eed oil
9. ___ omely
10. ___ slo's country
11. ___ *rave New World* author
12. ___ here bats hang out
13. ___ awning feeling
14. ___ ive advice over cards
15. ___ adio type (hyph.)
16. ___ ake a tough decision (with "over")
17. ___ orm of "me"
18. ___ -rated lady's room
19. ___ tah basketball team
20. ___ ipher
21. ___ mprecisely
22. ___ art of a breakfast menu
23. ___ ord of Sith, in *Star Wars*
24. ___ enice "taxi"
25. ___ hird Reich title
26. ___ annon, for one

3-D WORD HUNT #2

In the three-dimensional block of letters below, how many five-letter words can you find? A word may start at any letter, but must proceed along balls that are consecutively connected by straight lines. For example, the word STOVE starts at the S in the lower right corner of the front of the block, moves left to the T, backward to the O, up to the V, and forward to the E. In forming a word you may return to a letter and use it twice (like the S in LASTS), but you may not stand on a letter and use it twice before proceeding (like the B in RABBI). Proper names are not counted, but plurals are fine. A score of 20 or more words is good; 28 is excellent. We found 44 relatively common five-letter words in the block. And you?

ANSWERS, PAGE 125

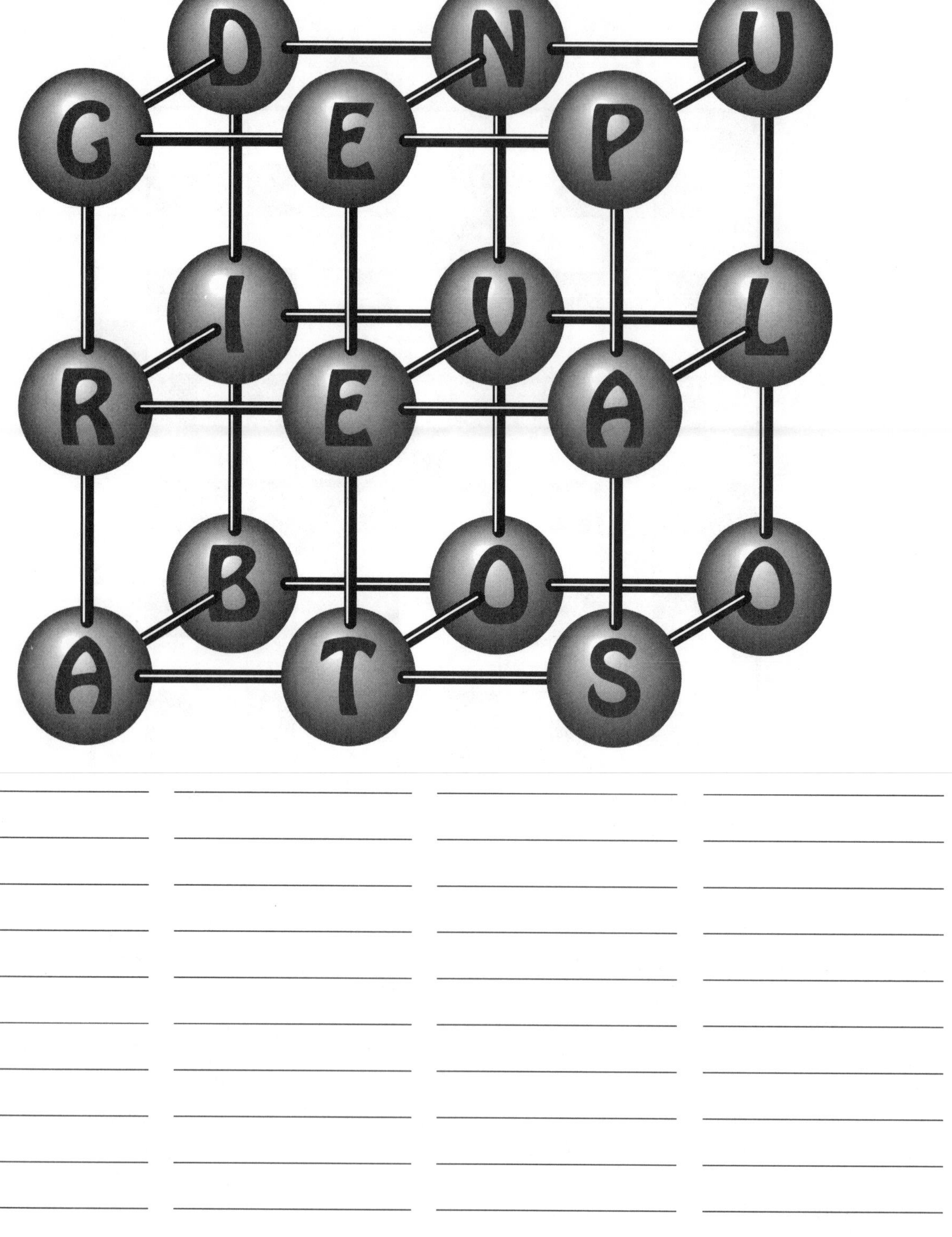

SKELETON

At the bare bones, this skeleton is two puzzles in one—a combination word game and crisscross puzzle. In the word game, which you solve first, pairs of words are given: one of them (you determine which) has a synonym that rhymes with the other. The answers are grouped according to their length in letters. In the example, the three-letter answer to the pair "Strike" and "Mitt" is HIT. When you have solved all the clues, you are ready to begin the crisscross. Fit the answer words in their proper spaces in the skeleton grid to complete an interlocking pattern of words reading across and down.

WORD LIST, PAGE 128 **ANSWER, PAGE 125**

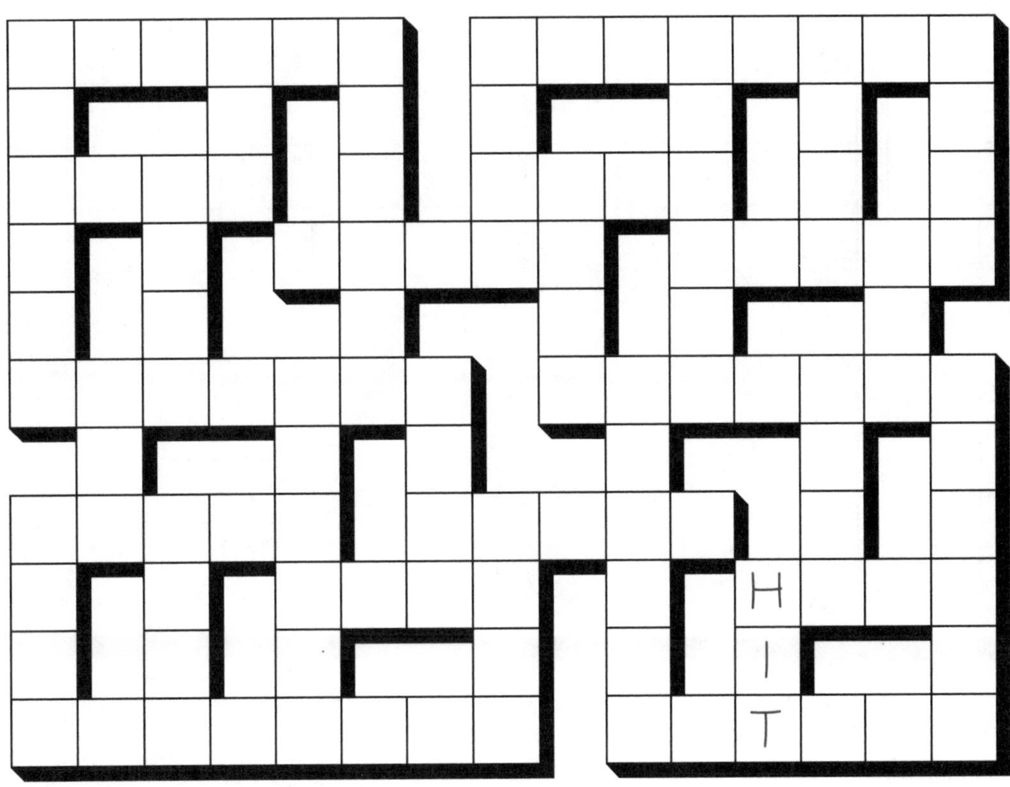

3-LETTER WORDS

Strike, Mitt ____HIT____
Peon, Age ________
Couple, You ________
Point, Blot ________

4-LETTER WORDS

Happy, Sad ________
Waive, Hoard ________
Chicken, Prowl ________
Expert, His ________
Best, Leisure ________
Summit, Seek ________
Orient, Leased ________
Yearn, Whirl ________
Boat, Carry ________
Crave, Bead ________
Stockings, Goes ________
Virgo, Therefore ________
Kelp, Aid ________
Stop, Go ________

5-LETTER WORDS

Tang, Vice ________
While, Grin ________
Districted, Moaned ________
Dresses, Towns ________

6-LETTER WORDS

Estimate, Beckon ________
Girl, Laden ________
Crystal, Gun ________
Quarrels, Ethics ________
Bar, Cavern ________
Station, Land ________
Usual, Formal ________
Puzzle, Drink ________

7-LETTER WORDS

People, Spire ________
Here, Pheasant ________

8-LETTER WORDS

Whiten, Scare ________
Stalemate, Wedlock ________

HALF AND HALF #3

The novelty of this puzzle is that the definitions of the answers have been replaced by words that *suggest* them. Each clue consists of three words that in some way relate to the answer, but which may or may not contain a synonym of it. For example, in the first clue, "Poll, " "Observe," and "Geological" all suggest the answer SURVEY without necessarily defining it.

Each answer, like SURVEY, is a six-letter word. To put it in the diagram, divide it in the middle and enter it downward, the first half in the squares designated by the first number of the clue, the second half in the squares designated by the second number. Every word half appears in two or more answers, so every answer will help with at least one other.

If you're up for more of a challenge, before you begin, cover up the third column of hints and try solving the puzzle using just the first two. If you get stuck, you can always peek later.

ANSWER, PAGE 126

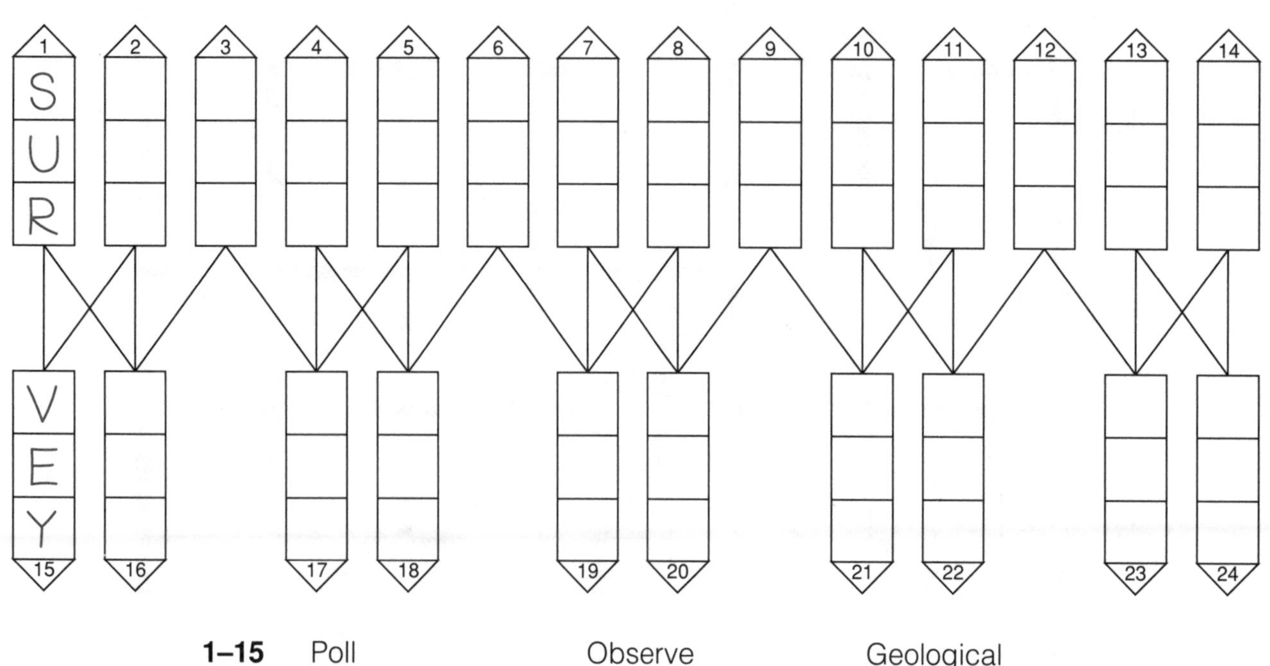

1–15	Poll	Observe	Geological
1–16	Board	Ocean	Daredevil
2–15	Transport	Deliver	Idea
2–16	Meet	Discuss	Bestow
3–16	Iron	Player	Green
3–17	Rule	Fleece	Opportunity
4–17	Flower	Vegetable	Variety
4–18	Mix	Confuse	Voice
5–17	Prison	Game	Official
5–18	Sing	Bird	Quaver
6–18	Horse	Barn	Steady
6–19	Russia	Dictator	Yalta
7–19	Elf	Mischievous	Halloween
7–20	Wine	Glass	Stem
8–19	String	Bow	Concerto
8–20	Lavender	Shrinking	Bloom
9–20	Village	Tragedy	Shakespeare
9–21	Carpenter	Detective	Head
10–21	Reader	Elementary	Paint
10–22	Father	Church	Catholic
11–21	Past	Earlier	Once
11–22	Sherwood	Black	Primeval
12–22	Capture	Police	Book
12–23	Reach	Come	Guests
13–23	Salad	Leaf	Chicory
13–24	Last	Abide	Suffer
14–23	Indian	Son	Intelligence
14–24	Mother	Second	Wilderness

LETTER "S" PICTURE TEST

In this picture, it's not hard to find objects whose names begin with the letter S. But how many of these objects, when the initial S is dropped, are "transformed" into *other* objects also pictured here? For example, the STRAP hanging from the horse's bridle becomes the TRAP seen under the table. We know of 18 other such pairs, but we doubt that anyone will be able to find all of them.

ANSWERS, PAGE 125

ANDERS WENNGREN

PUZZLE POTPOURRI

We don't mean to get emotional, but this potpourri of posers should be a moving experience. That is, you'll need to move letters, matchsticks, math symbols—and gray matter—in order to solve them. Together these six separate brainteasers offer a diverse mental workout.

ANSWERS, PAGE 126

1. NEW MATH

This equation in Roman numerals (9 – 12 = 3) is obviously incorrect. Move one match to produce a correct equation. The solution does not involve creating an inequality sign.

2. TARGET WORD

The bull's-eye target below has 16 different letters in the outer ring. Place 8 letters in the second ring that are all different from one another, 4 letters in the third ring that are all different from one another, and 1 letter in the bull's eye in order to complete 16 four-letter words reading from the outer ring to the middle. Can you do it?

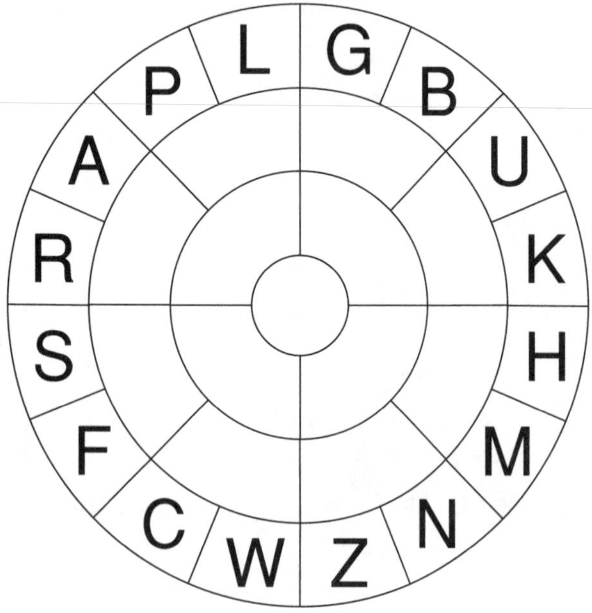

3. CHANGE OF CLOTHES

Change one letter in each word below to a new letter to get an item of apparel.

Ex. COST ______ COAT ______

1. PRESS ______
2. SCARE ______
3. CLOCK ______
4. GROVE ______
5. SHALL ______
6. SONNET ______
7. BIKING ______
8. RACKET ______
9. STRONG ______
10. SWELTER ______
11. GROUSERS ______
12. SHOCKING ______

PUZZLE POTPOURRI

4. SIX-PACKS

Insert the arithmetic symbols (+, −, ×, ÷) between the 6s in each line to make the eight different equations true. In each case the arithmetic operations should be performed in order from left to right.

a. 6 6 6 6 = 5
b. 6 6 6 6 = 8
c. 6 6 6 6 = 13
d. 6 6 6 6 = 42
e. 6 6 6 6 = 48
f. 6 6 6 6 = 66
g. 6 6 6 6 = 108
h. 6 6 6 6 = 180

5. MISCHMASCH

Lewis Carroll, author of the Alice books, also found a wonderland in creating puzzles and games. Mischmasch is a game he invented and published in 1882. To solve these new examples, think of a familiar English word that contains each of the following uninterrupted groups of letters. For example, the letter combination GP could be answered by MAGPIE, PIGPEN, or BAGPIPES. Proper nouns and hyphenated words are not allowed. Most of our test solvers found our Mischmasch to be surprisingly tricky—and nobody was able to get number 12. See how *you* do.

1. INDM ______
2. BMA ______
3. PRECH ______
4. ROH ______
5. CHNO ______
6. GERN ______
7. THT ______
8. DK ______
9. TENUS ______
10. XOPH ______
11. YDRE ______
12. HPU ______

6. SOLITAIRE JOTTO

The three solitaire puzzles here are based on the popular commercial game Jotto. The object, as in the regular two-player version, is to identify the five-letter secret words. In each case, you are given seven "guess" words and seven numbers. The number reveals the number of letters in that guess that also appear in the answer word. For example, a zero means that no letters in the guess appear in the answer; a one means that one of the letters will appear in it (although it doesn't identify which one, or which position that letter occupies in the answer); etc. First discover the five letters of each answer by deduction and process of elimination. Then rearrange the letters to form the secret word.

1. □□□□□

USAGE — 1
GUILT — 4
CRAMP — 0
QUALM — 1
THEIR — 3
STERN — 1
CLINK — 2

2. □□□□□

QUAKE — 2
THEIR — 1
ASKEW — 2
FINAL — 0
OPIUM — 3
WOMAN — 2
TWERP — 1

3. □□□□□

DRAWL — 2
IMAGE — 3
BLIND — 1
ANGEL — 1
SHADY — 2
RHYME — 1
GLEAM — 2

LEFT AND RIGHT #3

There are two directions to this puzzle—left and right. Each answer is a six-letter word, which is to be entered in the grid one letter per square according to the numbers. Half the answers will read from left to right, as in the example, COBWEB (1–2). Half will read from right to left, as in the answer to 2–3, which begins BEW-. Work both ways to complete the puzzle.

ANSWER, PAGE 126

1 C	O	B	W	E	B 2
3					4
5					6
7					8
9					10
11					12
13					14
15					16
17					18
19					20
21					22
23					24
25					26
27					28
29					30
31					32
33					34
35					36
37					38
39					40

CLUES

1–2 Spider's snare
2–3 "___ the Ides of March!"
3–4 It gets the lead out
4–5 Vacation spot
5–6 Gardening tool
6–7 More raunchy
7–8 Charge the quarterback (hyph.)
8–9 "Bare"back rider
9–10 Certain car rental agencies
10–11 Last six lines of a sonnet
11–12 Group of four
12–13 Monkey Trial defense lawyer
13–14 Crawled stealthily
14–15 Shy
15–16 Blows one's top
16–17 New York cathedral, for short (2 wds.)
17–18 1953 movie ___ *17*
18–19 Horse race, informally
19–20 Allergy sufferer's bane
20–21 "Full" or "half" grip
21–22 0, on a cash register (2 wds.)
22–23 Slip by
23–24 Glimpsed
24–25 Winter windshield clearer
25–26 Guinness datum
26–27 Surprise guest (hyph.)
27–28 Bit gently
28–29 Train stations
29–30 High, in a way
30–31 Robert of *Raging Bull*
31–32 Baltimore player
32–33 Weds sans consent
33–34 Kind of tank
34–35 One source of Vitamin C
35–36 "___ Girl" (Beach Boys hit)
36–37 Put in a different folder
37–38 Bring out
38–39 Tiny breath mint (2 wds.)
39–40 Hamburger topper

QUIZ-ACROSTIC

This puzzle works like a double-crostic, a cryptogram, and a trivia quiz all rolled into one. To solve, first circle the correct answer for as many of the multiple-choice questions as you can. Next, transfer the first letter of each answer to all the squares in the grid that match the question number; that is, if the answer to question 1 were BICYCLING, you would enter the letter B in all squares numbered 1. When the puzzle is completed, an interesting fact will be spelled out line by line in the grid. To answer questions you don't know, use letter frequencies and letter positions to work backward from the grid to the quiz. A word of caution: Not all 26 letters of the alphabet will appear in the completed grid, and some letters may be represented by more than one number.

ANSWER, PAGE 126

8	3	5	12	10	1	6	5	4	7	20	4	10	7	19	3	16	17	10	14
6	20	17	14	19	8	4	18	1	8	13	1	11	14	17	7	19	20	14	1
3	11	7	10	5	18	13	5	15	2	5	11	4	12	5	16	4	18	19	5
1	6	8	3	1	14	8	8	4	18	4	7	9	14	17	15	5	16	4	18

1. The first motion picture copyrighted in the United States showed a man...

BICYCLING JUGGLING PLOWING READING SNEEZING

2. Flag Day is celebrated on the 14th of what month?

AUGUST FEBRUARY JUNE MAY NOVEMBER

3. Who was the only 20th-century President not to attend college?

COOLIDGE EISENHOWER HARDING NIXON TRUMAN

4. Which of the following does not complete the title of a Hope-Crosby-Lamour "road" film, *Road to* ___?

MOROCCO NORWAY RIO UTOPIA ZANZIBAR

5. What automobile was once advertised with the slogan "Have one built for you"?

BUICK CHEVROLET FORD OLDSMOBILE PONTIAC

6. Leslie Hornby is better known as...

BATMAN DALI HOUDINI TWIGGY ZORRO

7. What is the familiar name of the annual writing award given by the Mystery Writers of America?

AGATHA DASHIELL EDGAR MICKEY RAYMOND

8. Which of the following is not a woodwind?

ACCORDION BASSOON CLARINET FLUTE OBOE

9. Which of these planets has no moons?

JUPITER MARS PLUTO URANUS VENUS

10. Which of the following solids weighs the least per cubic inch?

BUTTER GELATIN IVORY PORCELAIN SUGAR

11. Which of these states elects more than one delegate to the House of Representatives?

ALASKA DELAWARE HAWAII VERMONT WYOMING

12. What musical group sang "Last Train to Clarksville"?

CARPENTERS KINKS MONKEES RASCALS SUPREMES

13. The first color comics in American newspapers were printed in...

BLUE GREEN ORANGE PINK YELLOW

14. Which of the following names belonged to the most English kings?

CHARLES EDWARD GEORGE RICHARD WILLIAM

15. What unit of measurement equals six feet?

ANGSTROM CHAIN FATHOM HAND ROD

16. Which of these magazines is not published by Time, Inc.?

FORTUNE LIFE MONEY PEOPLE US

17. Who wrote *All Quiet on the Western Front*?

FAULKNER HEMINGWAY KIPLING REMARQUE WELLS

18. The United States bought the Virgin Islands from...

DENMARK ENGLAND FRANCE GERMANY SPAIN

19. Which of these words is not on the front of a $1 bill?

BANK LIBERTY PRIVATE RESERVE WASHINGTON

20. Which of the following is not a weapon in the Parker Brothers game Clue?

CANDLESTICK IRON KNIFE ROPE WRENCH

ILLUSTRATED HONEYCOMB

This puzzle is like earlier Honeycombs (page 26) except that written clues have been replaced by illustrations. First figure out what each picture is; then enter its name around the appropriate number in the honeycomb, beginning at the triangle indicated by the short line and proceeding one letter per space. All answer words have six letters and read clockwise or counterclockwise—the direction in each case is for you to determine. **ANSWER, PAGE 126**

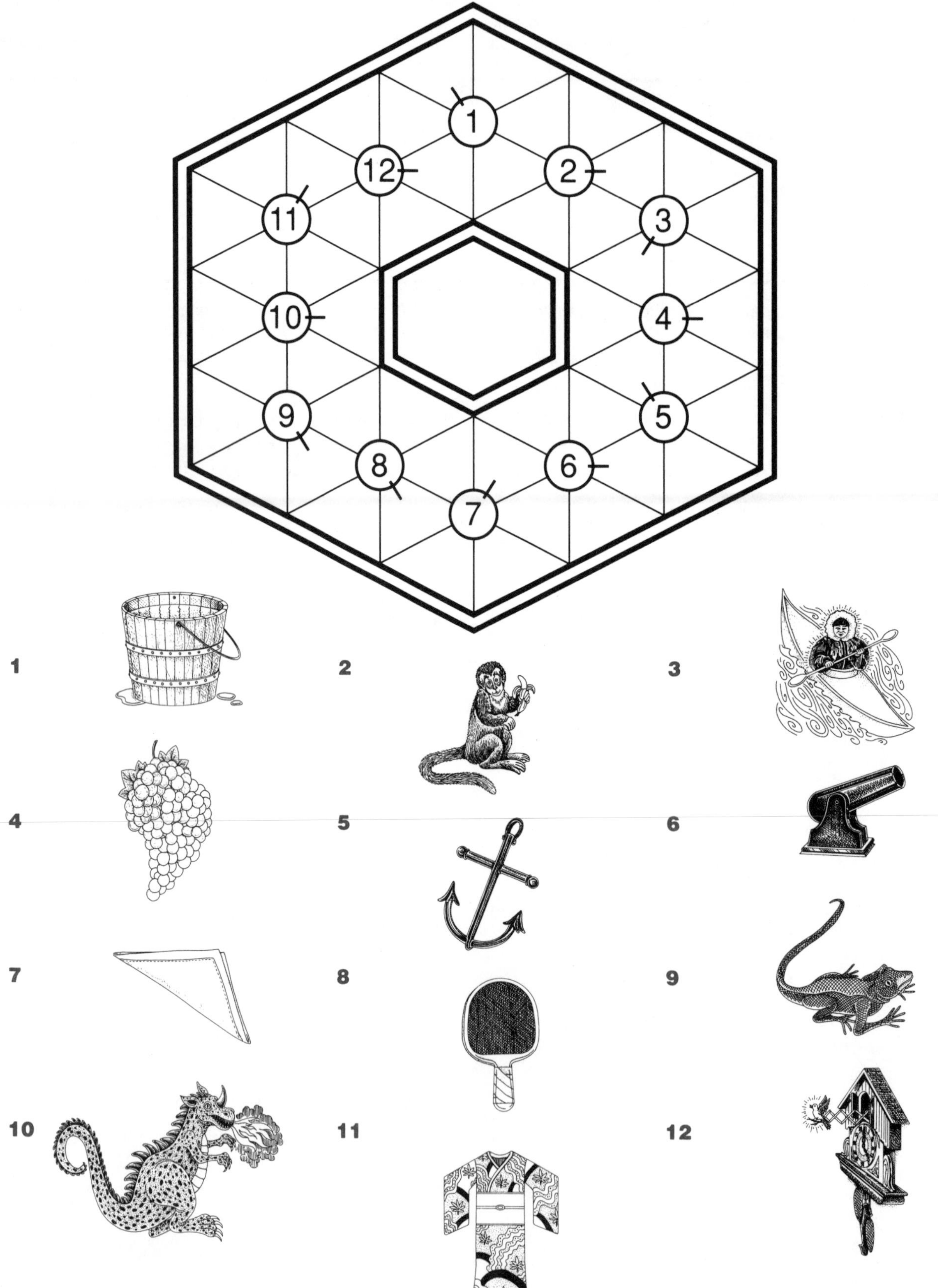

CLAUDIA KARABAIC SARGENT

SQUARE ROUTES #3

This version of Square Routes, differing from earlier ones, is a word game within a puzzle. Each clue consists of two words, one of which is a synonym of an anagram of the other. For example, the clue words RECALL and BASEMENT would lead to the answer CELLAR (an anagram of "recall" and a synonym of "basement.") Either the synonym or the anagram may come first—determining which word is which is part of the puzzle.

To solve, first answer as many clues as you can. Then enter each answer in the grid, beginning in the square corresponding to the clue number and proceeding in any horizontal, vertical, or diagonal direction. (The direction can be determined by logic and by the crossing letters of other answers.) Work back and forth between grid and clues to finish. When you're done, every square in the grid will be filled.

CLUE ANSWERS, PAGE 128 **PUZZLE ANSWER, PAGE 126**

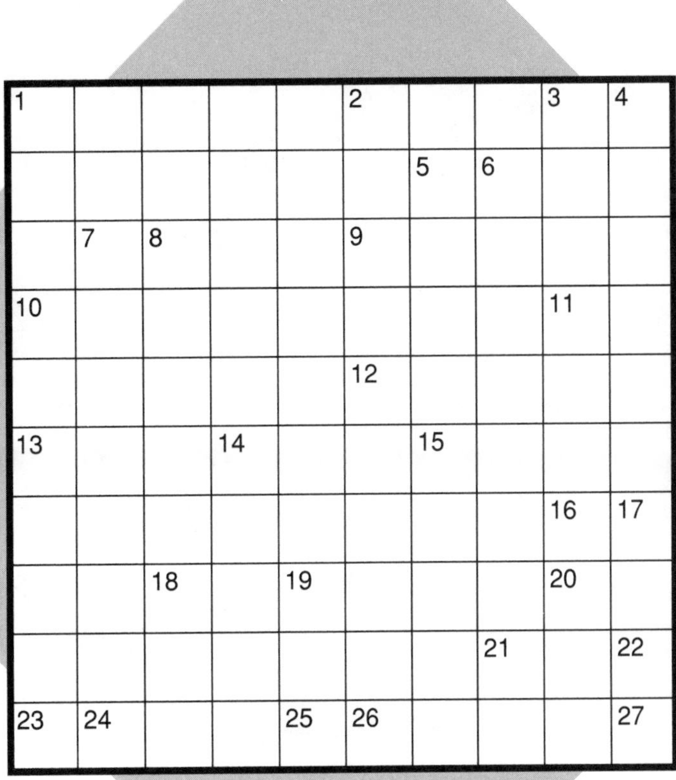

1					2			3	4
						5	6		
	7	8			9				
10								11	
					12				
13			14			15			
								16	17
		18		19				20	
							21		22
23	24			25	26				27

CLUES

1	BROADEN	RASPED
2	ASSUME	DIVERTS
3	TURTLES	TRANSPIRE
4	COURSE	MASTER
5	NEST	MAILED
6	COLLAPSE	BAKE
7	ANOINT	REPUBLIC
8	DIRE	MARGINAL
9	ANGLE	REAP
10	RELAY	PREMATURE
11	POUND	SHAM
12	CENTER	EARTH
13	SCATTER	PRESIDES
14	LOPE	SPAR
15	SCANTY	SPEARS
16	ATTIRE	MINARET
17	SKEPTIC	STAKES
18	SIRE	ASCEND
19	STATE	SAVOR
20	EVENING	THING
21	ADMIRES	PISTOL
22	CLEAN	DELUSION
23	STAR	AUTOCRAT
24	LOAFER	RILED
25	VISION	GENIES
26	ASTUTENESS	PRIEST
27	PLUG	SWALLOW

THE SPIRAL #4

This puzzle turns in two directions. The spiral's Inward clues yield a sequence of words to be entered counterclockwise in the spaces from 1 to 100. The Outward clues yield a different set of words to be entered clockwise from 100 back to 1. Fill in the answers, one letter per space, according to the numbers beside the clues. Always know when you're going clockwise or counterclockwise—unless you've got a lot of time on your hands.

ANSWER, PAGE 126

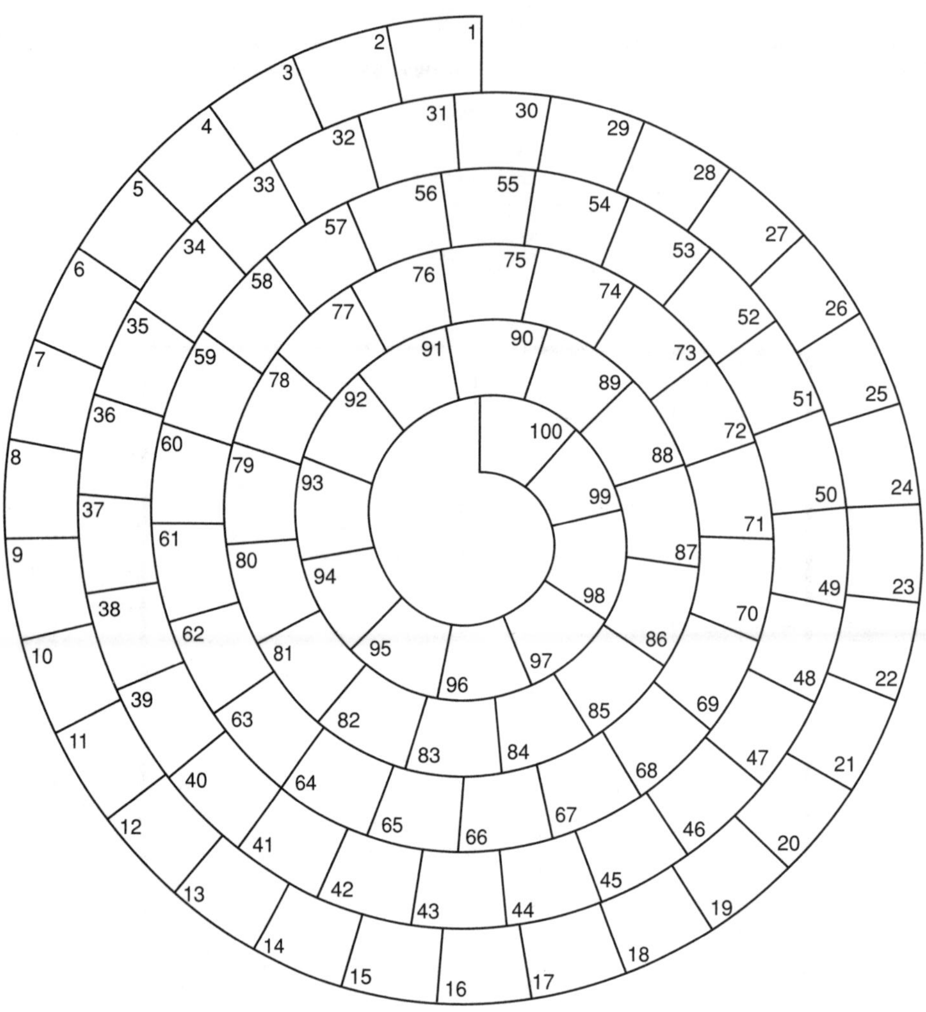

INWARD

1–5 Send, as payment
6–13 Large, fragrant white flower
14–20 He can't keep his hands to himself
21–27 Graceful antelope
28–36 Site of Fort McHenry
37–40 Actress Capshaw
41–47 Ship's capacity
48–57 Opposite of pulchritude
58–62 Belt holders
63–69 Hush-hush matters
70–76 Kind of fishing or diving (hyph.)
77–83 Scotland's largest city
84–86 Queasy, only more so
87–95 Limitless (hyph.)
96–100 More biting, as the wind

OUTWARD

100–93 Gave a gold star to
92–89 Hawaii's state bird
88–80 Future frogs
79–75 Lake gunk
74–66 One who puts the pedal to the metal
65–57 Stinky pits
56–51 A bit dotty
50–44 One-time Connecticut tribesman
43–35 Classroom scribe
34–31 Leave off
30–24 Singer Patti
23–18 Industrial city of Yugoslavia
17–9 Dickered
8–1 Scott Joplin, notably

AT THE SCENE OF THE ACCIDENT

How good an eyewitness are you? Study this picture for up to three minutes ... then turn the page for questioning. Once you turn, you will be relying on your memory of what you have seen.

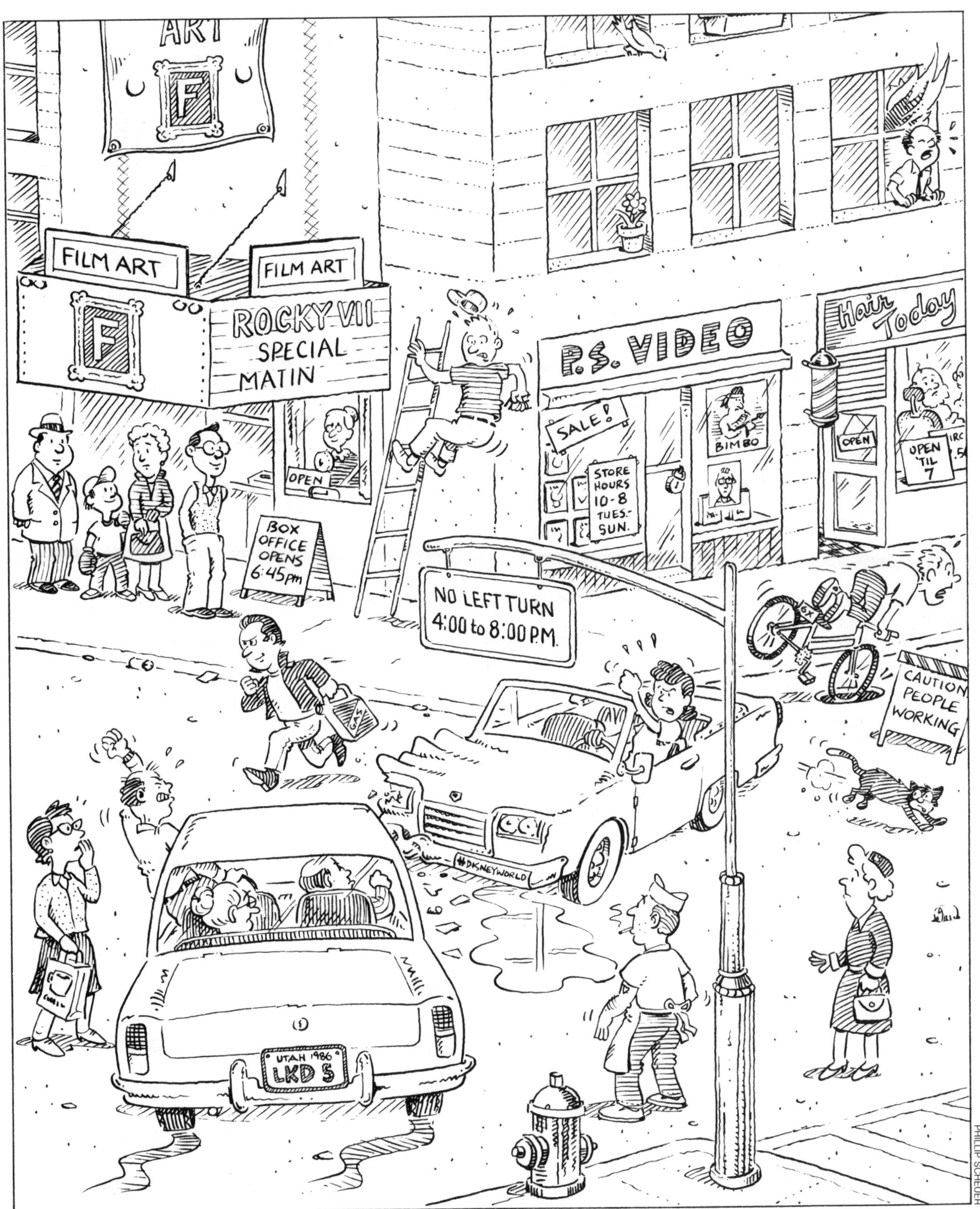

PHIL SCHEUER

SCENE OF THE ACCIDENT (PART 2)

In the street street scene on the previous page, you were witness to an auto collision, a bicycle accident, an impending injury, and a probable case of arson. The police would like your firsthand account of what happened. Please answer the following questions to the best of your memory.

ANSWERS AND RATINGS, PAGE 127

1. Approximately what time was it? ____________
2. What day of the week was it? ______________
3. How many onlookers were standing in the intersection after the collision? ______________
4. Was a policeman present? ______________
5. What was the license number of the car in the foreground? ____________________________
6. What state was it from? ________________
7. What was the expiration date of the license? ____________________________
8. How many people were in the car? __________
9. What traffic law had the driver broken? ________ ____________________________
10. Did the convertible's driver wear glasses? _____
11. What did her bumper sticker say? ___________
12. What immediate hazard was her car causing? ____________________________
13. What movie was playing at the theater? ____________________________
14. What mishap was the marquee worker about to suffer? ________________________
15. What letter was he holding in his hand? _______
16. Above what store was the fire? _____________
17. On what floor of the building did it start? ______
18. Who, among the people at the scene, looked the most likely to have started it? ______________
19. What sign was posted at the open manhole? ____________________________
20. What was the license number of the bicycle that ran into it? ______________________
21. Why was it probably not the rider's own bike? ____________________________

Bonus Questions:

22-24. The police would also like to question other eyewitnesses to the accident. Which three of the following persons were present?

25. How has one of them changed his or her appearance since the accident? ________________

MEASURE FOR MEASURE

There is a box in the corner of our office that has the mysterious notation "Cu. 0.9" printed in a corner of each side. After giving the problem more consideration than it probably deserves, we decided that the "Cu. 0.9" must stand for the measurement nine-tenths of a cubic foot, which is about the right size of the box. In the quiz below are 18 more numerical measurements, all frequently encountered in modern life. Match the measures on the left to the products and things (a–r) on the right to which they relate.

ANSWERS, PAGE 126

1. ____ 19" diag.	10. ____ 150W	a. air conditioner	j. radio wavelength
2. ____ 64K	11. ____ 200X	b. telescope	k. typing
3. ____ 9½D	12. ____ 17⅜ + ¼	c. shoes	l. medicine
4. ____ 200 hp	13. ____ 102.7 MHz	d. film	m. pants
5. ____ 14 kt	14. ____ 95 dB	e. light bulb	n. television
6. ____ 10cc	15. ____ 16 fl. oz.	f. gold	o. photograph
7. ____ 35mm	16. ____ No. 2	g. computer	p. engine
8. ____ 32W 35L	17. ____ 250 BTU	h. pencil	q. soft drink
9. ____ 8" x 10"	18. ____ 95 wpm	i. noise	r. stock price

RHYME AND REASON #2

Each clue below consists of a regular definition in which, as an extra hint, one of the words rhymes with the answer. For example, the first clue, "Kept the floor clean," is answered by SWEPT, which rhymes with "kept." If you drop one of the letters in the answer word and rearrange those that remain, you'll spell one of the words in the diagram. For example, by dropping the W in SWEPT and anagramming the rest, you get PEST, found in the third row of the grid. (The clue numbers have nothing to do with the locations of the answers.) Cross off that word and write the extra letter beneath it. When all 28 clues have been solved in this manner, the letters written in the grid will spell, in order, a quotation by Oscar Wilde.

ANSWER, PAGE 127

RANCH	HIRE	GISHES	TAYLOR	RACE	ASKING	ROCS
SEGUED	DIRT	PORTS	SAFE	SAPID	STAB	THEIST
ANTS	CADRE	RANG	~~PEST~~	CHITS	LUTES	BARK
			W			
RIPE	HAMS	PETE	WINKER	FLORA	PARCH	HIKER

1. Kept the floor clean
2. Pie maker
3. Patterns for Scottish lads
4. Play waiter (to)
5. European wine region
6. That which in time saves nine
7. Yell, "Eek!"
8. Made a wild stab on a test
9. Quaking
10. Lightest in color
11. Arthur Ashe hit
12. These bother dogs
13. Vehicles for snowy days
14. Had a rank odor
15. Where an Indian goes when he's sleepy
16. Moan
17. Item on a tanker or scow
18. Church master
19. Teach in church
20. Word before base, degree or dimension
21. Stablemate of Prancer
22. Something to savor
23. First in time or rank
24. Make the most of oneself?
25. To whom the British show loyalty
26. One more than nineteen
27. Crinkle
28. One seeking the truth to a mystery

PETAL PUSHERS #3

This seven-letter rose puzzle is a little thornier than the six-letter variety we presented earlier in the book—but you don't need to be a budding genius to solve it. As usual, the flower is to be filled in with 32 words answering the clues below the grid. Enter these words inward from the tips of the petals to the heart of the blossom, one letter in each space. Half the words proceed clockwise from the numbers; the other half go counterclockwise. Work from both sets of clues for a full bloom.

ANSWER, PAGE 126

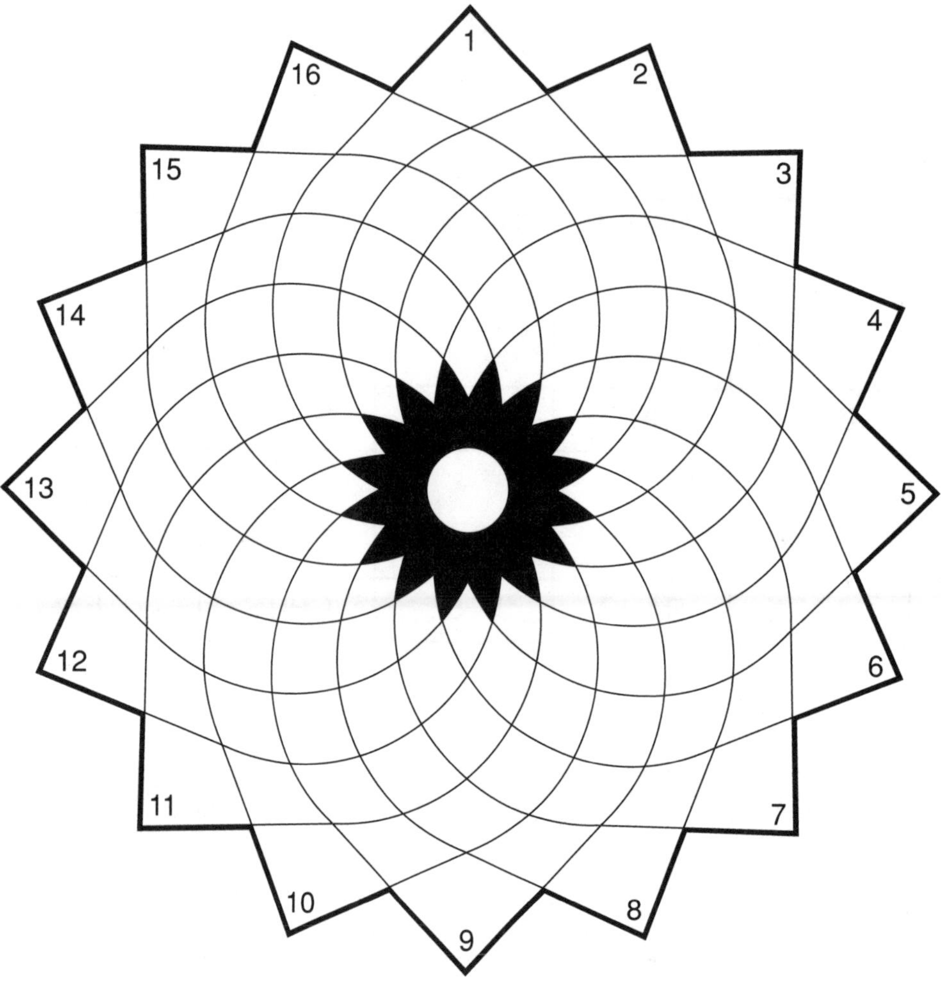

CLOCKWISE

1 French automaker
2 Medical breakthrough
3 Noted 18th-century biographer
4 Longer limbed
5 Computer language
6 Pocketbook
7 Transmitting
8 Combining against, with "up"
9 Preparation made from barley grain
10 Feeling
11 Inhumanly mean
12 Talkative
13 Athlete's weak spots
14 Tropical American trees
15 Uncontrollable mirth, with "the"
16 Acquired through underhandedness

COUNTERCLOCKWISE

1 1964 Four Seasons hit (2 wds.)
2 Popular auto motor (hyph.)
3 Ornamental bracelets
4 Areas
5 Meadow grasses
6 Extravagantly enthusiastic (hyph.)
7 John Singer ___ , American portrait painter
8 Non-Jewish
9 Machine shaft
10 Harbor peril
11 From Brussels
12 Letting off steam
13 Preparing a salad
14 Walloping
15 The real McCoy
16 Pretentious talker

INSIDE AND OUT

Each sentence below has a hidden word that is defined somewhere in the line. For example, sentence #1 conceals the word AFFINITY, which is defined as "liking." (The number of letters in the answer is shown in parentheses.) Enter each answer in the grid beginning in the appropriately numbered square and proceeding along the outlined path. When all the answers have been entered in this way, the shaded squares on the grid's border—starting in the upper left corner and reading clockwise—will spell a quote by Christopher Morley.

ANSWER, PAGE 127

CLUES

1. By covering the sheet with paraffin, it yielded a luster to the worker's liking. (8)
2. If the girls look promising, let one try out for the team. (9)
3. The sound of the bird in Handel's oratorio left me bewildered. (6)
4. Seven visitors remained in part of New England. (5)
5. The darkness had everyone scared. (5)
6. Ray, the clean-up man, described the circus to Diana. (9)
7. The hungry fox encircled the sleeping farm animals. (4)
8. We discussed a political theory of freedom in our philosophy class. (6)
9. Our next entry in the talent competition shows room for improvement. (6)
10. It's hard to overcome a downwind in a field of expert bicyclists. (6)
11. The metal pin enabled me to fix the Swiss watch. (6)
12. Several taxpayers don't think the rate adjustment is fair. (4)
13. The Indian language is behind in the development of new words. (5)
14. Father ran downtown on a quick trip to the store. (6)
15. We need to repair a diode in the receiver. (5)
16. Martha taught the yogi some tricky kind of exercises. (9)
17. Color showed in the violent anger in each man's face. (9)

SCRAPBOOK MIXUP

For over a decade, Harold has meticulously kept a scrapbook of newspaper clippings that have been sent to him by his pen pals around the world. However, one day Harold's plans for a well-ordered scrapbook were almost blown away. Before he could paste up the 10 clippings shown on these two pages, the wind from an open window scattered them all around the room. The clippings weren't marked with their sources, but Harold knew that each had come from one of the newspapers listed at bottom right, and that all had been published during January. Fortunately, Harold was as smart as he was orderly. From the clues in the clippings, can you, like Harold, match each to its original paper?

ANSWERS, PAGE 127

1.

LAST WEEK in review

SATURDAY:

IS COCONUT WATER TO FEEL TAX AXE?: The Ministry of Finance has presented Customs and Excise with a problem with the imposition of a new ten per cent purchase tax on locally produced foodstuff and juices. Customs officials are in a frenzy to determine whether drinking water and coconut water fall within the tax list which includes spa waters and aerated waters as taxable items. More troublesome areas for the Customs Department will be food preparation which is wide ranging. It can include roti, barra, doubles, black pudding, souse, pelau and other local foods. The question is how will Customs monitor the operation.

2.

MOVIE DIRECTORY

AMOR — "TENG TENG DE SARAPEN"
AVENUE — "HOT PROPERTY"
BARON CINEMA — "GUNFIGHTER"
CAPRI — "KARNAL"
DILSON — "TENG TENG DE SARAPEN"
EASTERN — "KARNAL"
EVER — "BAGO KUMALAT ANG KAMANDAG"
GALAXY — "GUNFIGHTER"
GOTESCO — "BAD BANANAS SA PUTING TABING"
GOTESCO A — "HOT PROPERTY"
GOTESCO B — "OVER MY DEAD BODY"
HARRISON 1 — "OVER MY DEAD BODY"
HOLLYWOOD — "GUNFIGHTER"
JENNET — "TENG TENG DE SARAPEN"
LIFE — "THE GODSON"
LORDS — "KARNAL"
LUNETA — "BAD BANANAS SA PUTING TABING"
MAIN — "BAD BANANAS SA PUTING TABING"
…AIR — "THE GODSON"
…A — "GUNFIGHTER"
…MAR — "TENG TENG DE …APEN"
…LOVE 1 — "TENG TENG DE …APEN"
…LOVE 2 — "OVER MY DEAD …DY"
…ON — "THE GODSON"
…MON — "BAGO KUMALAT … KAMANDAG"
…EN — "OVER MY DEAD BODY"
…BINSON 1 — "HOT PROPERTY"
…BINSON 2 — "THE GODSON"
…BINSON 3 — "GUNFIGHTE…"
…XAN — "BAGO KUMA… …AMANDAG"
…TATE — "BA…"

3.

WARWICK SCHOOL LUNCH MENU

Week of Jan. 9-13
Elementary Schools

Monday

Weiner wink or hot dog, homemade baked beans, potato chips, carrot sticks, cookies.

Tuesday

Baked lasagna, or mac. and cheese, tossed salad w/french dressing, roll, buttered green beans, popsicle.

Wednesday

Hot turkey sandwich, mashed potatoes w/gravy, buttered broccoli or corn, fruit compote.

Thursday

Cheeseburger, french fries, tomato and lettuce salad, fresh fruit.

Friday

Pizza boat, celery and peanut butter, potato chips, applesauce.

Secondary Schools & Faculty

Monday

1. Weiner wink, homemade baked beans, potato chips, carrot sticks, cookies.

2. Veg beef soup, meat ball sandwich, carrot sticks, fruit or cookies.

Tuesday

1. Baked lasagna or mac. and cheese, tossed salad w/french dressing, roll, buttered green beans, popsicle.

2. Salad bar at high school and middle school. Cold platter for faculty and elementary schools- carrot and raisin salad w/cheese wedge.

Wednesday

Hot turkey sandwich, mashed potatoes w/gravy, buttered broccoli or corn, fruit compote.

Thursday

1. Cheeseburger, frenc… fries, tomato and lettuce sala… fresh fruit.

2. Salad bar at high sch… and middle school. Cold pla… for faculty in elemen… schools- cottage che… w/apricots.

Friday

1. Pizza boat, celery … peanut butter, potato … applesauce.

2. Garden salad, veal … fruit

4.

SNOW REPORT

LAURENTIANS: It may be cold for skiing, but for snowmaking it's ideal. Surfaces are generally hard packed with well groomed runs offering machine-groomed powder over a solid base. All centres are in full operation. There is free skiing today at **Mt. Alta**, just south of Ste. Agathe.

EASTERN TOWNSHIPS: All centres are in full operation with the exception of **Mt. Orford** where they are changing a lift tower which should be ready by tomorrow. Surfaces are generally hard packed with machine groomed runs offering powder over a good base.

QUEBEC CITY: All centres are in full operation with the exception of **Mont Ste-Anne** where one lift on the west side is out of commission, but should be operating today or tomorrow. Surfaces are of packed powder over an excellent base with complete cover on all runs.

NEW ENGLAND: All centres are in full operation with surfaces of packed and machine-groomed powder over a frozen granular base. Cover is complete on all runs.

5.

Mr DIGWELL...All about early tomatoes

NOW'S THE TIME TO SOW TOMATOES FOR EARLY GREENHOUSE CROPS
SPACE SEED OUT IN TRAYS OF SEED COMPOST
WHEN LEAVES HAVE FORMED, POT UP SINGLY
MOVE TO LARGER POTS AS PLANTS GROW
AND PLANT IN THE GREEN-HOUSE BORDER WHEN FLOWERS START TO OPEN
SOW SUPER ROMA FOR MAKING SOUP OR KETCHUP— IT'S A MUST!
AND AM… YOUR PL… BE SURE… MARIG…
28-1-84
SOW IN MID-MARCH FOR OUTDOOR OR UNHEATED GREENHOUSE PLANTS
DUNKLEY
IT'S REP… W…

SCRAPBOOK MIXUP

7.

Take off on a Spring SuperSaver Weekend!

LONDON FROM £66

EUROPE FROM £119

U.S. FROM £239

Shearer pre[...] his radio show in the KCRW studio.

8.

BROADWAY

TONIGHT 8, TOM'W 2 & 8
THE LONGEST RUNNING SHOW
IN BROADWAY HISTORY:
BEST MUSICAL
1976 TONY & PULITZER PRIZE WINNER
New York Shakespeare Festival
presents
A CHORUS LINE
TELE-CHARGE: (212) 239-6200
8 AM-Midnight • 7 Days a Week
Mon.-Sat. 8 PM, Mats. Wed. & Sat. 2 PM
Groups: (212) 398-8383/598-7107
Ticketron: (212) 977-9020
SHUBERT Thea. 225 W. 44th St. 239-6200

On television

)NIA HUMPHREY, the appable and gracious host ie ABC's arts series, Sum- Spectrum offers another rtaining documentary at m on Channel Two. Song arewell focuses on one of nost successful collabora- in musical history – that eing Yorkshiremen, Eric y, and Frederick Delius. vision programmers ensured the competition ce in this time slot, for her prime choices of the ıg also screen at 8.30pm.

The Kremlin Letters on Channel 10 stars Richard Boon, Max Von Sydow, Orson Wells and Barbara Parkins.

It has a tangled plot about an freelance American spy team comprising specialists in various fields. They are assigned to retrieve a bogus treaty supposedly signed by the United States and Russia and proposing the annihilation of Red China.

Also at 8.30pm on Channel

Seve[...] brated pop [...] actor, stars in Nic[...] film, The Man Who F[...] Earth.

Roeg who is known for his striking films and bad timing created a science fiction, fantasy drama with this tale of a space creature who looks remarkably like a human. After landing on earth he proceeds to build a financial empire of such proportions it is capable of devouring huge corporations.

10.

Currencies

Currency	Sell	Buy
US	0,7830	0,7930
UK	180,5875	176,6705
Can	0,9705	0,9940
Belg C	44,7000	45,7500
Belg F	44,9500	45,9500
Swiss	1,7500	1,7845
French	6,7265	6,8555
Italian	1337,0000	1363,0000
Dutch	2,4730	2,5200
Deutsche	2,1970	2,2395
Swede	6,3690	6,4915
Norw	6,1500	6,2690
Danish	7,9730	8,1245
Austrian	15,4500	15,7500
Port	105,4000	107,6000
Japanese	182,4000	186,1000
Span	123,7500	126,2500
Aus	0,8545	0,8730
NZ	1,2015	1,2295
Zamb	1,2570	1,2670
Mal	0,9940	1,0785
Zimb	0,8877	0,9042
Hong Kong	6,0855	6,1985
Indian	8,3725	8,6025

The Newspapers

___ Australia: *The Australian*

___ Canada: *The* (Montreal) *Gazette*

___ England: (London) *Daily Mirror*

___ Ireland: *Irish Independent*

___ Philippines: *Metro Manila Times*

___ South Africa: *The* (Johannesburg) *Star*

___ Trinidad and Tobago: *The Sunday Guardian*

___ USA: *The Lititz* (Pa.) *Record-Express* (weekly)

___ USA: *Los Angeles Herald Examiner*

___ USA: *The New York Times*

SIT FOR A SPELL

How many words of five or more letters can you find in the grid below, provided that each word uses at least one set of doubled letters? Words may be spelled by moving from letter to letter along the lines connecting the circles. For example, you can form the word MOOSE below by starting at the M at the lower right, moving up to the O, repeating the O, continuing up to the S, and then down to the E. You may return to a letter and use it twice in the same word (as the O in COMMON), but this does not count as doubling. Not allowed are plurals or verbs formed by adding -s or -es, past tenses ending -ed, hyphenated words, and proper names.

Each answer scores 1 point, except words with two pairs of doubled letters, which score 2. A score of 15 or more points is good; 25 is excellent; 35 exceptional. Our list of relatively common words, including the two examples, totals 51 points.

ANSWERS, PAGE 126

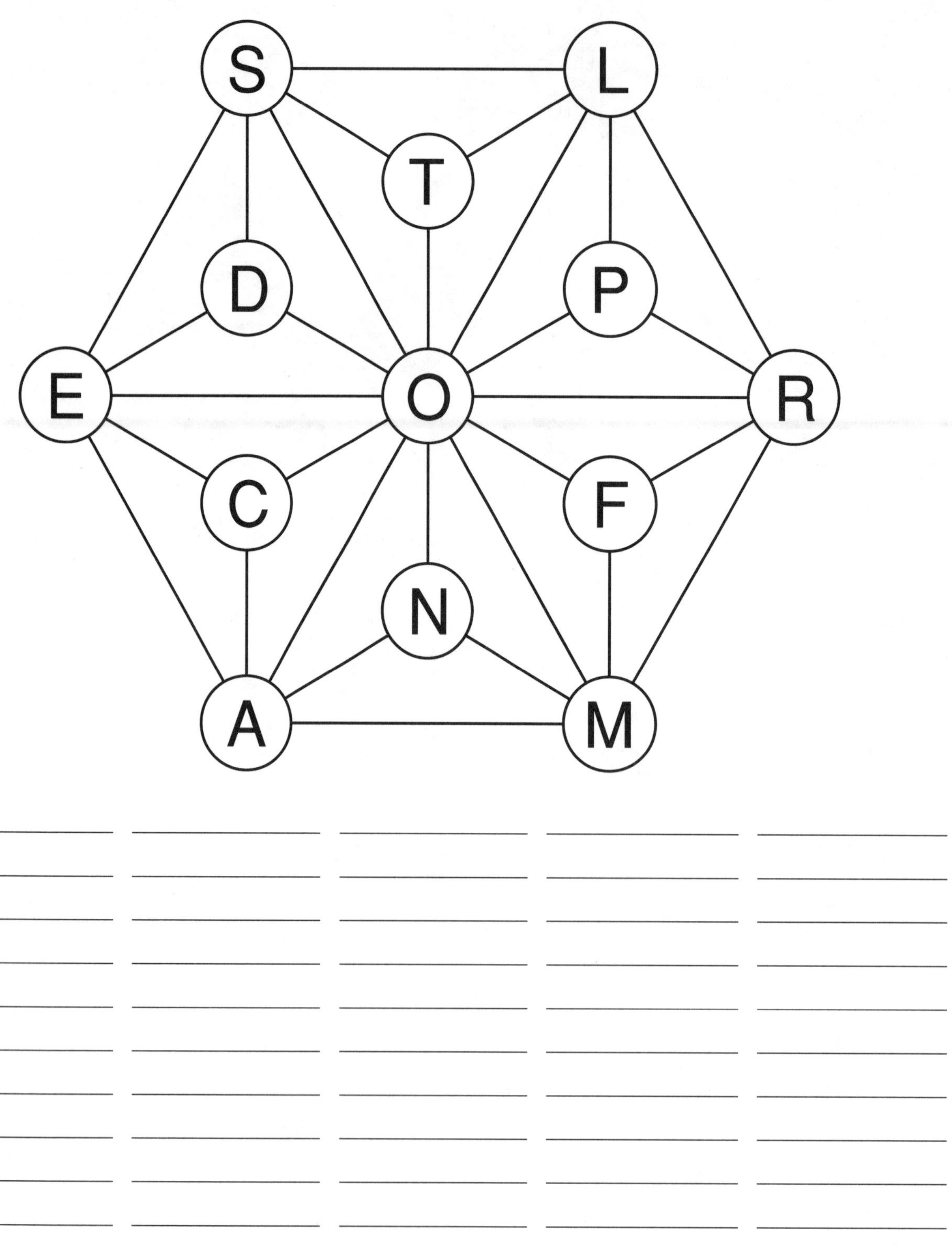

SPLIT ENDS #2

Each clue in this crossword has been cut into two parts, and the parts have been given numbers from 1 to 78. To solve the puzzle, find and rejoin each matching pair of clue parts to produce the original clue. Enter the answer to each clue at the grid space indicated by the sum of the numbers of the clue's two parts. For example, #70 and #29 below combine to form the clue "Popular television/Canine." The answer, LASSIE, is filled in at #99 (70 + 29). Either part of the clue may appear first in the numbered list. Every part will be used exactly once in the completed puzzle.

ANSWER, PAGE 127

CLUES

1 Ocean
2 People who have no
3 Swings on
4 B&O Railroad
5 Drink popular
6 What a door
7 Prohibition's
8 Two
9 Opposite of
10 Around Christmas
11 Dirty dishes
12 Money
13 Miss
14 "Filthy"
15 Basketball team
16 Person of
17 Injury
18 Speed or fire
19 Tennis star
20 Boys
21 Club
22 Any whole
23 Person who reads
24 Or seawater
25 Not
26 Amendment
27 For breeding
28 Noted Harlem
29 Canine
30 Low IQ
31 Northernmost
32 Red ink
33 From Stockholm
34 According to
35 Invention
36 Item shown in
37 Turkey is eaten
38 Bumps on the head
39 Golf
40 Alexander Graham Bell
41 The Soviet government
42 Clothes on
43 Under, in
44 Center of
45 Hearst
46 Census
47 Amount of
48 Of perfection
49 Quite
50 William
51 Overnight
52 Word after
53 Stock ___
54 Standard
55 New York
56 Stallion kept
57 What follows
58 Data
59 Bird that has
60 Like pretzels
61 Or Bryan, e.g.
62 Ankle or wrist
63 Holiday on which
64 Law
65 Playwright
66 Poetry
67 The "O" in
68 Clay
69 Place to stay
70 Popular television
71 Precipitation
72 Nap
73 A comb
74 Number
75 Performance
76 A Mexican
77 Place for
78 Met

CROSS ANAGRAMS #2

Here are three puzzles for anagram fanciers. For each one, answer the clues—with the help of the letters in the grids—to discover six pairs of six-letter anagrams. Each answer in grid A has the same letters, rearranged, as the answer on the same line in grid B. (Answers read across only, not down.) For example, if the clues for the first pair in puzzle #1 were "Polished stone" and "Accuser," you could enter MARBLE and BLAMER. Only experts will find all the anagram pairs on this page.

ANSWERS, PAGE 127

PUZZLE 1

CLUES A
1. Attacked riotously
2. Frankness
3. Quit office
4. Connected
5. Theater passages
6. Mean (to)

CLUES B
1. Failed in a big way
2. Synthetic fabric
3. Vocalist
4. Start, as a fire
5. TV dog
6. Set in from the margin

A

M						1
	A					2
		S				3
			K			4
				E		5
					D	6

B

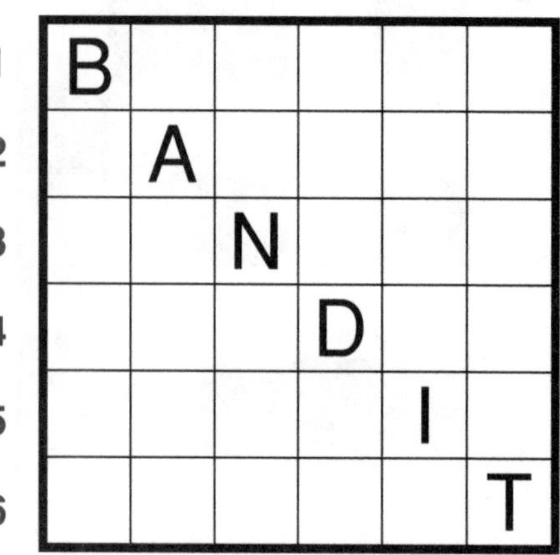

PUZZLE 2

CLUES A
1. Church officer
2. Kind of shepherd
3. Save
4. Take into custody
5. Happens
6. Pre-talkie movie

CLUES B
1. Paddled
2. Feeding trough
3. Safe
4. French existentialist
5. Early spring bloom
6. Coves

A

D						1
	E					2
		S				3
			E			4
				R		5
					T	6

B

C					
	A				
		C			
			T		
				U	
					S

PUZZLE 3

CLUES A
1. Texas city (2 wds.)
2. ___ de corps
3. Thrown skyward
4. Mideast ally
5. Angel
6. Steal cattle

CLUES B
1. Slanting
2. Minister
3. Topping for fries
4. Story in installments
5. Express in words
6. Outcome

A **B**

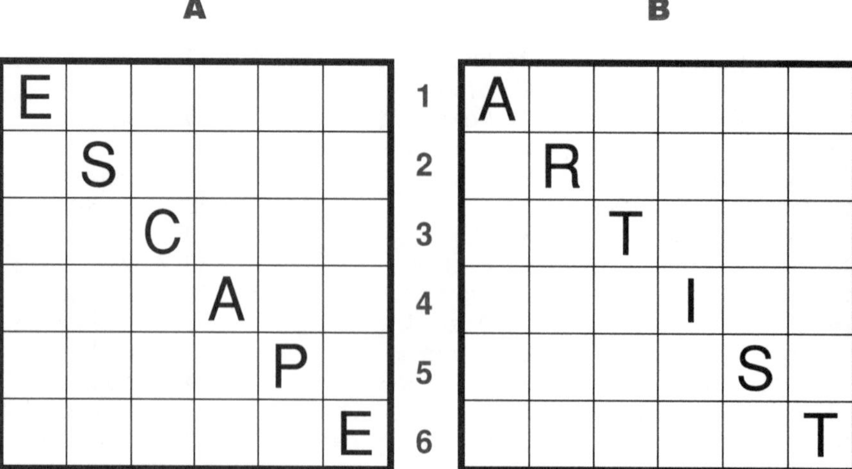

BULL'S-EYE 20 QUESTIONS #4

Here's your last shot at the bull's-eye. The answer to each of the 20 questions in this puzzle is one of the 26 words in the bull's-eye target. Each answer scores a "hit," which you may cross off in the target since no answer word is used more than once. When all the clues have been answered, the six unused words can be rearranged to form a quotation by humorist Robert Byrne.

ANSWERS, PAGE 127

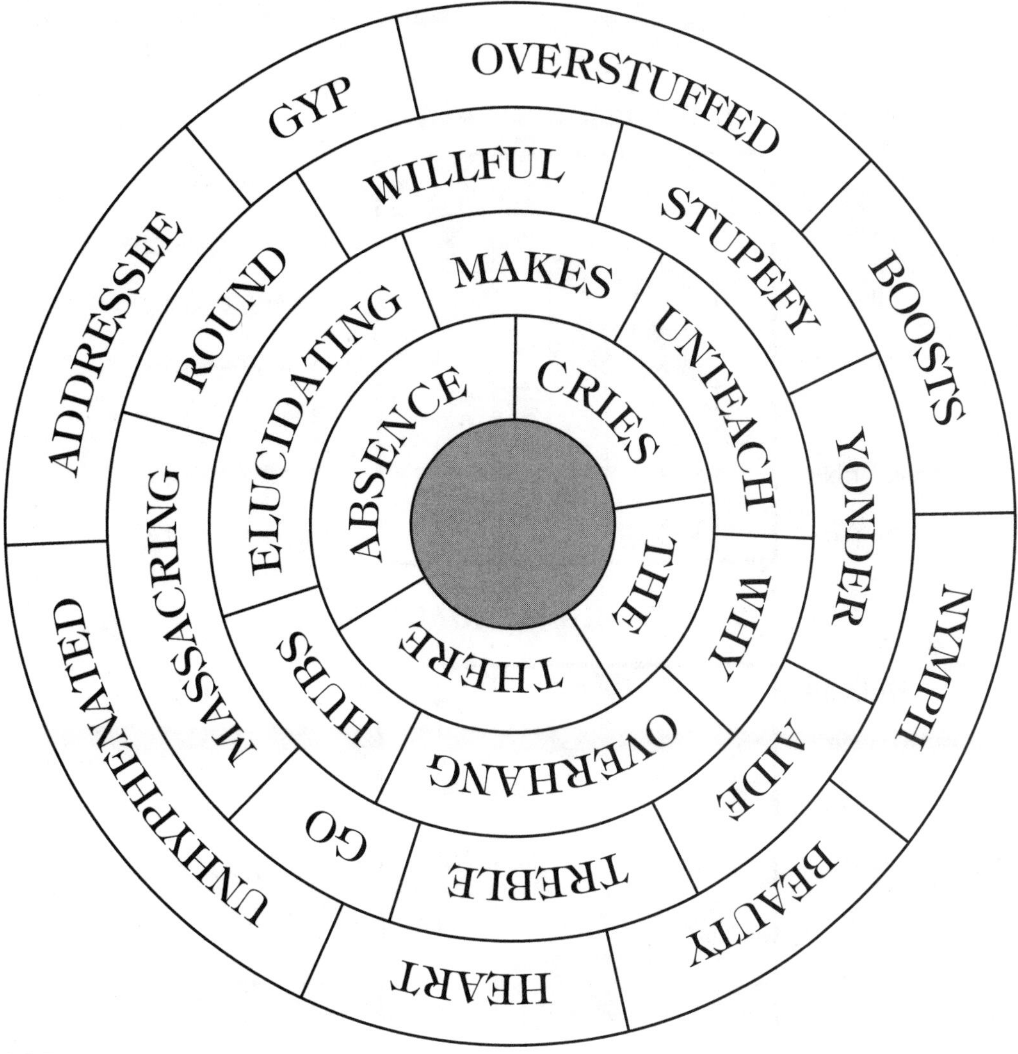

WHICH WORD ...

1. would be pronounced the same without its first two letters?
2. contains the name of a state, reading every other letter?
3. would become a phrase meaning "loyal," if the letter U were inserted before every E?
4. is an anagram of a President's name?
5. consists of a word meaning "clear" inside "dinnertime activity"?
6. would become its own opposite if you removed its first letter?
7. can be broken into two consecutive men's names, which, said one after the other, sound like an article of apparel?
8. is self-descriptive?
9. has more syllables than it has vowels?
10. would, if written in lower-case script, have strokes below the line on all its letters?
11. is an acronym, of sorts, for the speed limit in Manhattan?
12. would become a sign of the zodiac if you changed its first letter?
13. represents (assuming A =1, B = 2, etc.) the year that World War II ended?
14. contains four consecutive letters of the alphabet, in order, in a row?
15. completes this sentence in a punny way: "Horace will have to ___ lower the top of the door by 12 inches."
16. would become a synonym of itself if you inserted a T somewhere within it?
17. would become a new word if its last syllable were put first?
18. could represent OTTAWA in a cryptogram?
19. contains three doubled letters?
20. has no letters in common with any of the other six remaining words?

WRY SANDWICHES #3

Rearrange the letters of each word on the left below, and add two or three letters in the middle, to form a seven-letter word answering the clue on the right. The words on the left are the outside letters, or "bread," of the seven-letter "sandwich." The letters you add are the "filler" and will appear consecutively in the shaded squares inside. For example, given the word ASTER and the clue "Weird," you would answer STRANGE, with the letters NG appearing in shaded squares. When a puzzle is completed, read the shaded letters in order, line by line, to spell a daffynition of the puzzle's title. Note: In puzzle #3, as an extra challenge, determining which squares should be shaded is left to you. **ANSWERS, PAGE 128**

1. PULLMAN TICKET

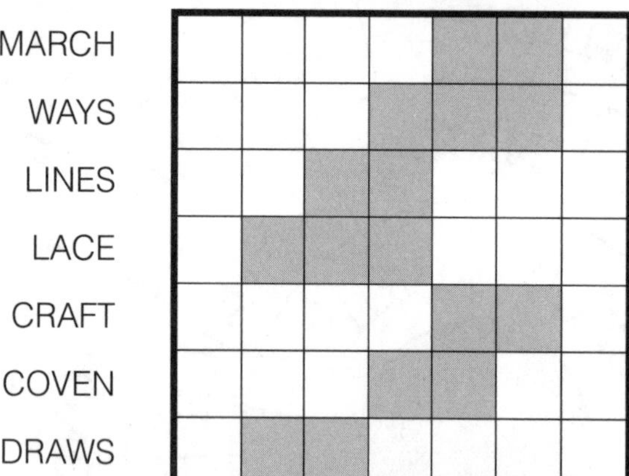

MARCH	Formal room
WAYS	Dark-complected
LINES	Driving or fishing permit
LACE	A, an, or the
CRAFT	Rush-hour bother
COVEN	Curving inward
DRAWS	Kitchen chief

2. JOGGING MANUAL

DELTS	German pastry
VOICE	Plan, in an underhanded way
RYES	Doctor's needle
TAPIR	Brandy flavor
SINE	Gigantic
GIVE	Important wine data
TALCS	Fine glassware

3. RECTANGLE?

WELT	Engage Hulk Hogan in a fight
PASTA	Cooking implement
COUPS	One who's armed and dangerous?
USER	Come up, as a submarine
TYRE	San Francisco sight
BLOKE	The Washington Monument, e.g.
PERE	Western settler

X-WORD PUZZLE

The answer to each clue in this cryptic crossword is a six-letter word, and it is to be entered in the diagram in the shape of a *cross*. We have filled in the answer to number 1, HUMBUG, as an example. The word starts in the box corresponding to its clue number, proceeds from upper left to lower right, and crosses upper right to lower left. Words will not otherwise be formed in the diagram.

Each cryptic clue, as usual, contains a definition or direct reference to the answer, *and* a second description of the answer through wordplay. For the example filled in, HUM is "To sing," BUG is "To annoy," and "So says Scrooge" suggests the whole, HUMBUG. Other words may or may not break so neatly into two equal parts! Answers include one uncommon word (#4) and a variant spelling (#16). **ANSWER, PAGE 128**

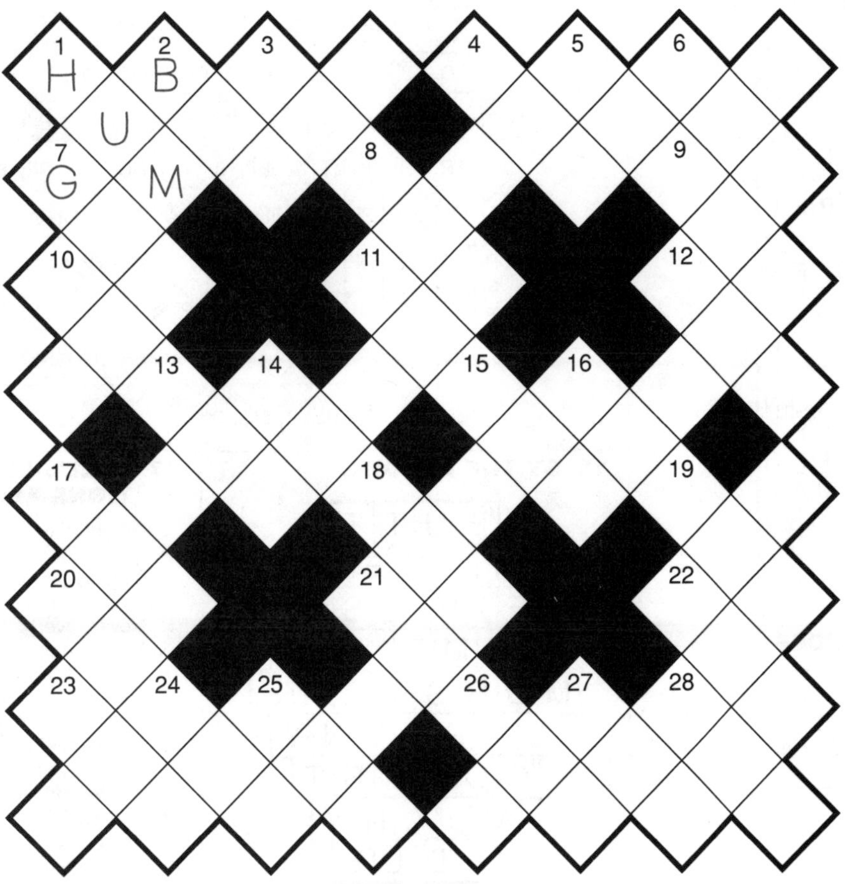

CLUES

1 "To sing? To annoy!" So says Scrooge

2 The lower part of banner's front and back reading, e.g., "Don't Tread on Me"

3 Tidy bite misses tail ends of morsel

4 Twice Tom returns a tropical bird

5 Male is female—he's been tagged "unsuitable person"

6 The monks have chickens for barbecuing, I hear

7 Ma sang rock 'n' roll to the meter reader

8 Physician way out around Connecticut

9 TV program shown in nurseries

10 Resort city is rebuilding saunas

11 Poor Clara's knave

12 Burn $ to start company (in the end I will leave rich!)

13 First tennis player put head of racket into chop

14 Wrongly revile the woman who covers her face

15 Reverse a pastry's layers

16 Anaesthetic for the ear infection

17 Oddly, Peter Lorre's first bird

18 Finland's mostly away from the ocean

19 Sailor with a light brown plaid

20 Note from the landlord?

21 Left in a tossed salad east of Fort Worth

22 From northeast a cardinal approached

23 Beat for the leading parts in Rock Hudson's young Thomas Hardy movie

24 Athletic girl's vault gets a "zero" at the athletic center

25 Fragrant medicine for a lamb's injury

26 Non-expert in Malay manners

27 After April 30th, hel-l-lp!

28 Listener enters thirsty and cheerless

ANSWERS

9 PUZZLETOWN ZOO

Camel	Donkey	Hare	Mole
Cat	Ermine	Hedgehog	Monkey
Coney	Gnu	Hog	Rat
Dog	Goat	Mink	Skunk

Goa (the name of a Tibetan gazelle) is also acceptable.

10 LEFT AND RIGHT #1

SUM	MIT
REB	UTS
TRA	UMA
TEL	LER
DIA	DEM
YEL	PED
TRO	OPS
SLI	VER
WEI	MAR
DOR	MER
NIA	CIN
ELO	PES
CIT	RON
YAW	NED
LAT	TER
ANI	MAL
DEB	RIS
SUI	TOR
NET	HER

11 MARKET SLICES

1. Kellogg's
2. Duracell
3. Pillsbury
4. Schick
5. Progresso
6. Smucker's
7. Beefeater's
8. Charmin
9. Tropicana
10. Pringles
11. Brillo
12. *Newsweek*
13. Hershey's
14. Campbell's
15. Salem
16. Trident
17. Drano
18. Wheaties

12 THE SPIRAL #1

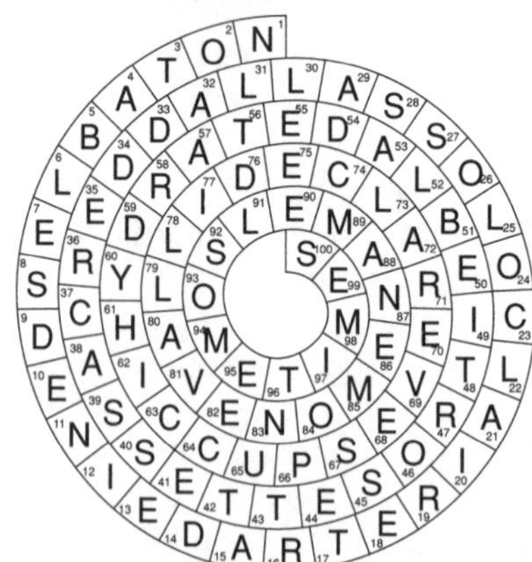

14 ON WITH THEIR HEADS!

1. B	6. H	11. R	16. M
2. L	7. E	12. J	17. F
3. O	8. A	13. N	18. T
4. C	9. D	14. G	19. I
5. K	10. S	15. Q	20. P

13 TWO BY TWO

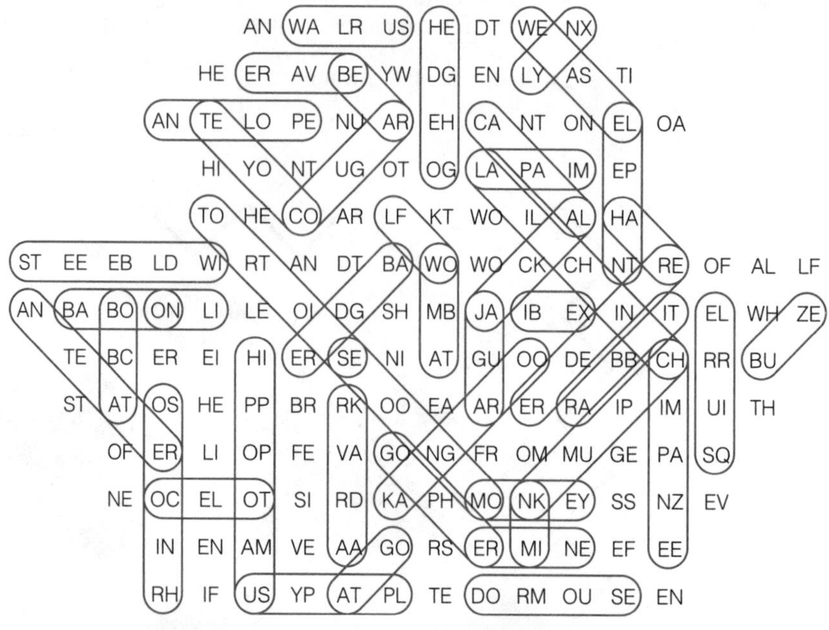

16 BY THE ARROWS

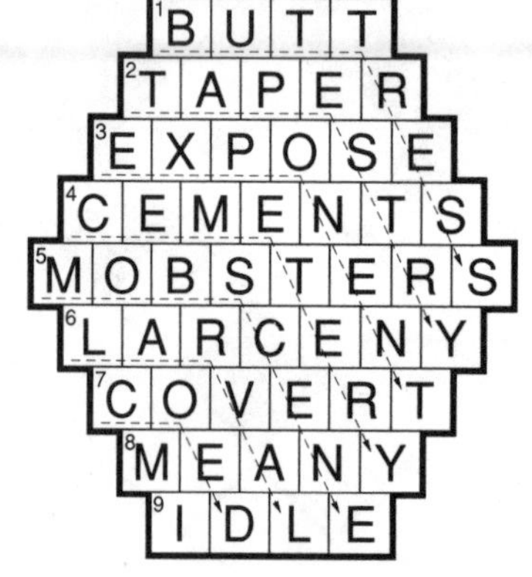

16 TWIST-A-RHYME

1. STONE, SEWN, GROWN, THRONE
2. CURSE, WORSE, VERSE, TERSE
3. NUDE, LEWD, CRUDE, STEWED
4. REIGNS, PANES, VEINS, PLAINS
5. GANDER, SLANDER, CANDOR, DANDER
6. BRUISE, LOSE, SHOES, VIEWS

17 BULL'S-EYE 20 QUESTIONS #1

1. Heighten (eight, ten)
2. Aunt (tuna)
3. Outstay (stout)
4. Dynamo (Monday)
5. Never (ever)
6. Murder (red rum)
7. Misery (Missouri)
8. Stonewall (stall!)
9. Trespass (spa, tress)
10. Child (children)
11. Chintz
12. HIAWATHA
13. Bets (*E.T.*)
14. Sauna (stunt, skunk)
15. Wintry (win, try)
16. Flue (flu, flew)
17. Happenchance
18. Elating (gelatin)
19. Mainland (Massachusetts, Indiana, Louisiana, North Dakota)
20. Backward (question 6)

"Few great men could pass personnel."—Paul Goodman

18 LINK ACROSTICS #1

1. JUST DESSERTS

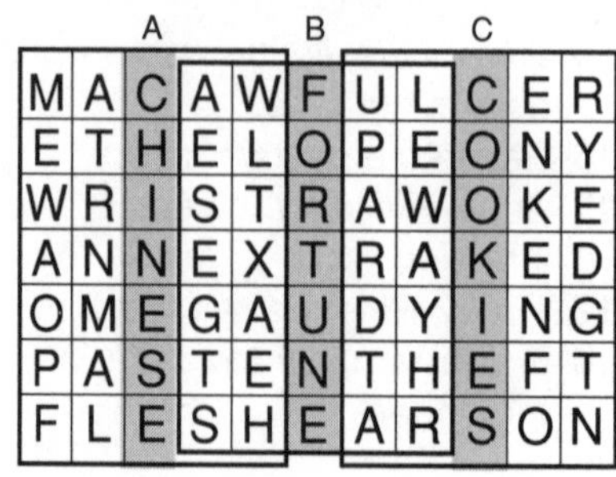

2. THEY NEED THEIR SPACE

		A			B			C		
N	E	H	R	U	M	B	A	C	O	N
A	B	O	D	E	I	G	N	O	M	E
A	Z	U	R	E	S	I	N	N	E	R
N	A	S	A	L	S	O	P	T	I	C
L	A	T	H	E	I	S	T	R	U	M
P	O	O	C	H	O	I	R	O	N	Y
J	U	N	T	A	N	G	O	L	L	Y

ANSWERS

19 SQUARE ROUTES #1

H	S	I	F	E	E	L	I	F
S	A	B	L	A	N	K	E	T
A	F	T	E	R	I	X	H	G
W	E	C	C	T	C	G	S	N
F	A	A	H	H	I	N	T	I
R	S	T	A	N	D	A	R	D
A	O	N	I	P	E	G	I	A
M	G	O	R	S	M	O	K	E
E	L	C	S	U	M	M	E	R

20 3-D WORD HUNT #1

Our list of relatively common words: ABATE, ABIDE, ACHED, ACRID, ACTOR, APRON, ATONE, BATCH, BATON, BIDED, BIRCH, BORON, BOTCH, CACHE, CHEAP, CHIDE, CHIME, CHIMP, CHIRP, CRIME, CRIMP, CRONE, DINED, INANE, NABOB, NOTCH, PRIDE, PRIME, PRIMP, PRONE, ROBIN, ROBOT, ROTOR, TEACH, TENET, TENON, TENOR, and TORCH. Our less common words: ACNED, HIDED, NATCH, NONET, ORIBI, and TABOR.

22 AT THE SCENE OF THE CRIME

1. 5:45
2. Saturday, the only day the produce store was open after 5:00
3. Jane's
4. Bates Ave.
5. Two
6. Yes
7. Three
8. No
9. Eight
10. V.L.
11. A falling potted plant
12. Woman
13. Crawfordtown Produce
14. Myrtle St.
15. Grapes
16. F472
17. It was parked in a 4-6 P.M. "No Parking Zone"
18. Left rear tire
19. Her purse was being stolen
20. No
21. b and e

Scoring: Count one point for each correct answer to questions #1-20, and two points for each correct identification in #21.

Ratings:
20 and up: Lieutenant Columbo
16-19: Old Hawk-Eyes
10-15: Sharp Observer
5-9: Inspector Clouseau
0-4: Amnesiac

22 SWAP SHOP

1. Youth, storm
2. Exact, tonic
3. Grate, oiled
4. React, shove
5. Align, prone
6. Inner, graft
7. Blond, spoil
8. Guilt, dense
9. Budge, shale
10. Snoop, bawdy
11. Rough, peony
12. Quota, stein
13. Eight, quilt
14. Manor, judge
15. Swept, elate
16. Flute, skunk
17. World, shout

23 CROSS-O #1

1. STATE: Florida, Oregon, Texas, Hawaii
2. JOINT: Ankle, Elbow, Shoulder, Knuckle
3. GODDESS: Diana, Venus, Minerva, Aurora
4. GENERAL: Pershing, Custer, Patton, Grant
5. SPICE: Oregano, Paprika, Ginger, Nutmeg
6. MAGAZINE: *Forbes*, *Vogue*, *Glamour*, *Ebony*
7. SAINT: Bernard, Nicholas, Peter, Louis
8. COLLEGE: Brown, Purdue, Tufts, Stanford

24 PETAL PUSHERS #1

25 LINK-LETTERS

1. It Has Three Parts

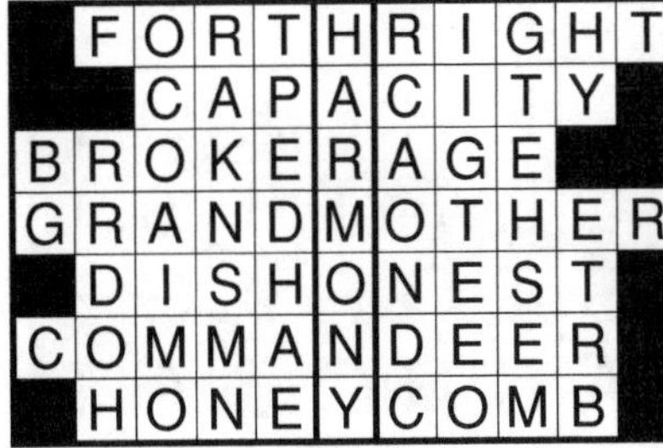

FORTHRIGHT
CAPACITY
BROKERAGE
GRANDMOTHER
DISHONEST
COMMANDEER
HONEYCOMB

2. A Dollar a Kiss?

SWEEPSTAKES
NIGHTMARE
PANTALOONS
LANDSCAPE
BOOKPLATE
BULLETIN
DIVERGENT

3. Beauty Spot

ENTERPRISE
CASTANETS
GINGHAM
LITERALLY
PARAMOUNT
DISCONTENT
MAINSTREAM

28 PAPER CLIPS

1. Celebrity gossip column
2. Comic strip (*Little Orphan Annie*)
3. Sports/basketball story
4. Bridge column
5. TV listings
6. Editorial
7. Weather forecast
8. Horseracing results
9. Horoscope
10. Advice column
11. Crossword puzzle
12. Fashion story
13. Radio listings
14. Classified ad
15. Stock market listings
16. News/election story
17. Lottery results
18. Movie listings

27 PICTUREGRAM

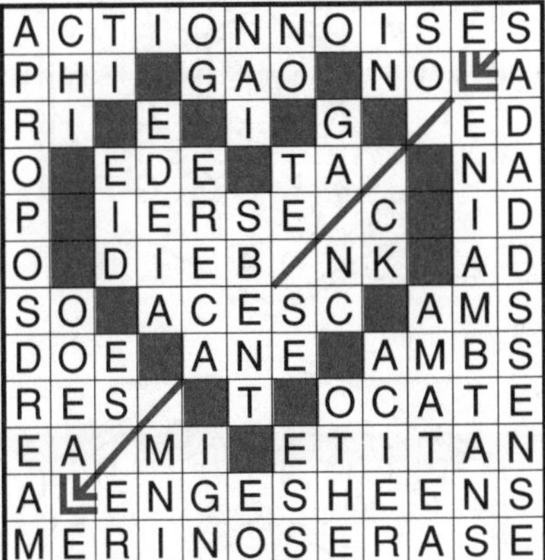

A	C	T	I	O	N	N	O	I	S	E	S
P	H	I		G	A	O		N	O		A
R	I		E		I		G			E	D
O		E	D	E		T	A			N	A
P		I	E	R	S	E		C		I	D
O		D	I	E	B		N	K		A	D
S	O		A	C	E	S	C		A	M	S
D	O	E		A	N	E		A	M	B	S
R	E	S			T		O	C	A	T	E
E	A		M	I		E	T	I	T	A	N
A		E	N	G	E	S	H	E	E	N	S
M	E	R	I	N	O	S	E	R	A	S	E

31 QUIET, PLEASE!

1. Aisle (between the shelves)
2. Czar (picture of Peter the Great)
3. Gnome
4. Gnu
5. Hour (on the clock)
6. Knee (wrestler's)
7. Knickknack (the palm tree, e.g.)
8. Knife
9. Knight (on *Chess Life*)
10. Knob (on the door)
11. Knot (in the librarian's hair)
12. Knuckle
13. Llama
14. Mnemonic ("I before E," etc.)
15. Psalm
16. Pseudonym (Mark Twain)
17. Pterodactyl
18. Tchaikovsky (composer of *The 1812 Overture*)
19. Wrestler
20. Wrinkles
21. Wristwatch
22. Writer (Twain again)

ANSWERS

26 HONEYCOMBS

1.

2.

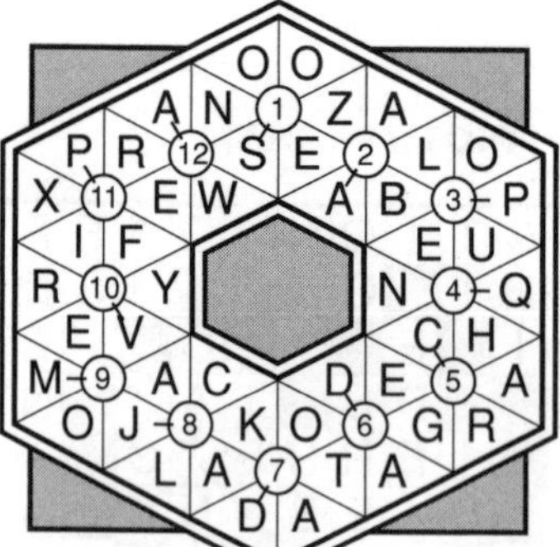

3.

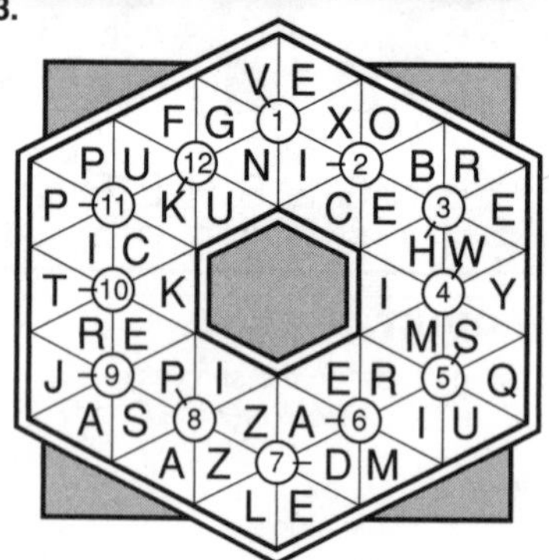

36 UNITED NATIONS

1. Brazil, Israel, Greece
2. Uganda, Jordan, Kuwait
3. Sweden, Canada, Mexico
4. France, Cyprus, Turkey
5. Poland, Angola, Norway

36 MIND YOUR P'S AND Q'S

1. Queer/quaint/quizzical
2. Quick
3. Quarry
4. Quiet/quiescent
5. Quill
6. Quandary
7. Quintet
8. Quest
9. Quarrelsome
10. Quail
11. Queue
12. Quilt

40 LETTER CARRIERS

1. DA (cedar)
2. MC (march)
3. TD (timid)
4. TV (stove)
5. IQ (pique)
6. UN (chunk)
7. LP (clump)
8. AM (camel)
9. CB (scrub)
10. VP (vapor)
11. ID (ideal)
12. PS (pushy)

30 WRY SANDWICHES #1

1. QUADRUPLETS

C	H	I	F	F	O	N
T	O	U	R	I	S	M
E	N	C	R	Y	P	T
S	Y	R	I	N	G	E
R	O	U	T	I	N	E
E	P	S	I	L	O	N
A	U	D	I	T	O	R

2. SKYWRITING

S	M	A	S	H	U	P
S	U	S	P	E	C	T
E	V	E	N	I	N	G
B	R	O	A	D	E	N
G	O	D	S	E	N	D
C	A	N	T	E	E	N
S	I	N	C	E	R	E

3. HUSH MONEY

P	E	R	F	E	C	T
L	E	F	T	I	S	T
S	T	O	R	A	G	E
A	C	R	O	B	A	T
A	B	Y	S	M	A	L
T	E	R	M	I	T	E
V	E	T	E	R	A	N

34 EQUATION ANALYSIS TEST #1

a. Letters of the Alphabet
b. Wonders of the Ancient World
c. Arabian Nights
d. Signs of the Zodiac
e. Cards in a Deck (with the Jokers)
f. Planets in the Solar System
g. Piano Keys
h. Stripes on the American Flag
i. Degrees Fahrenheit at which Water Freezes
j. Holes on a Golf Course
k. Degrees in a Right Angle
l. Dollars for Passing "Go" in Monopoly
m. Sides on a Stop Sign
n. Blind Mice (See How They Run!)
o. Quarts in a Gallon
p. Hours in a Day
q. Wheel on a Unicycle
r. Digits in a ZIP Code
s. Heinz Varieties
t. Players on a Football Team
u. Words that a Picture is Worth
v. Days in February in a Leap Year
w. Squares on a Chessboard (or Checkerboard)
x. Days and Nights of the Great Flood

Based on an idea by Morgan Worthy in Aha! A Puzzle Approach to Creative Thinking.

35 OH, OH!

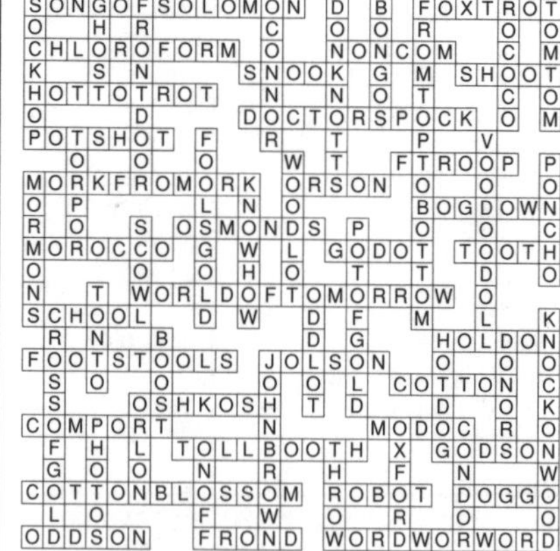

32 HALF AND HALF #1

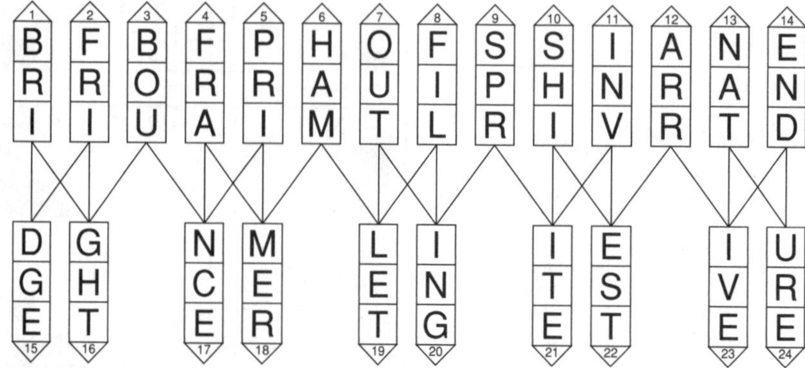

ANSWERS

33 WORDS AND NUMBERS

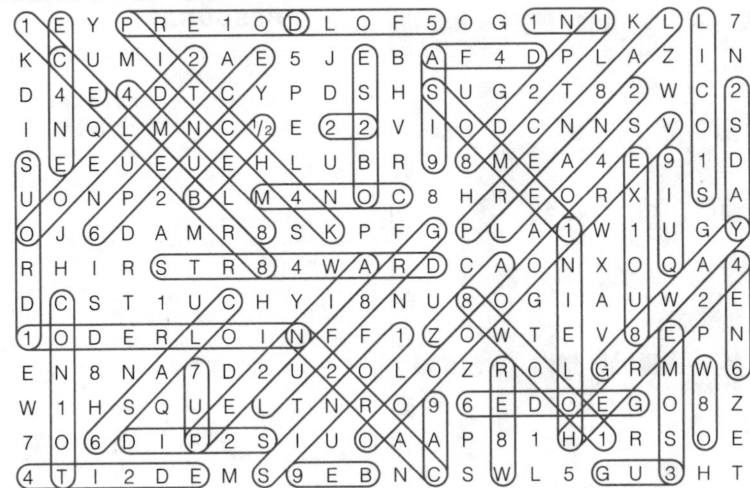

AF 4 D
ASI 9
BE 1/2
BE 9
CA 9
CAR 2 N
CELEBR 8
CLAS 6
CON 4 M
CON 10 T
EN 4 CE
EX 10 U 8
5 FOLD
4 EN 6
4 MUL 8
4 TI 2 DE
G 8 WAY
GEODE 6
GR 8 FUL
GU 3
HERE 2 4
HOLE IN 1
100 W 8
LEAN 2
OB 2 SE
1 CE
PE 2 NIA
PITCH 4 K
PREN 8 AL
PRE 10 D
QUI 9
7 UP
6 PENCE
SOME 1
S 10 CIL
STR 8 4 WARD
S 2 PID
10 DERLOIN
10 NIS
3 SOME
2 DLEOO
2 SDAY
2 2
UN 1
UP 2 D 8
VER 1,000,000
W 8 ER
W 80
1 DROUS
Z 8 A

37 DIG THIS!

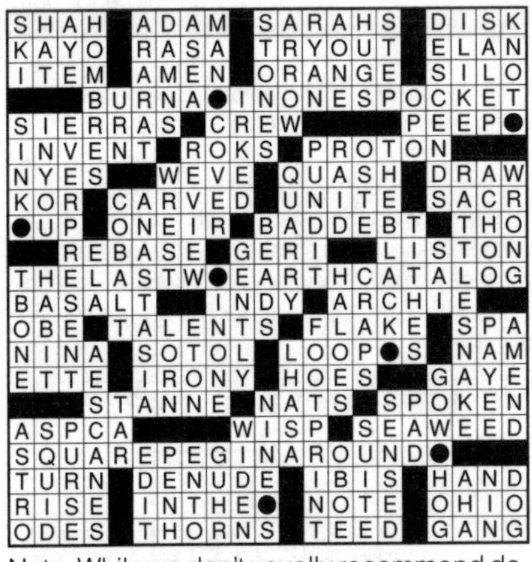

Note: While we don't usually recommend defacing the pages in a book, we point out that the answer to this puzzle could be made literal by poking "holes" through the paper with the point of your pencil.

39 "B" HIVE #1

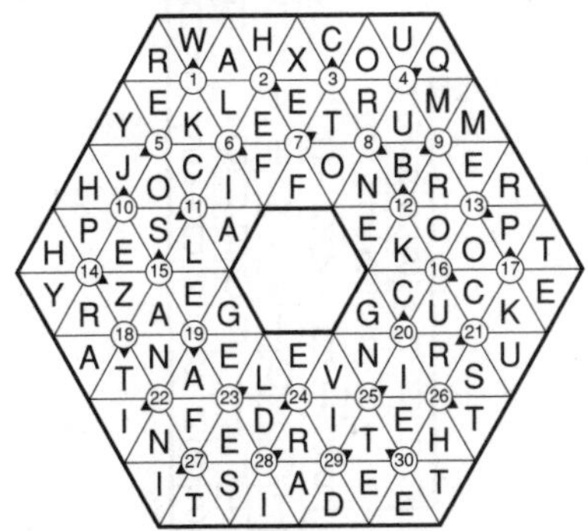

41 RHYME AND REASON #1

1. Straw (wars + T)
2. Camel (acme + L)
3. Stunk (tusk + N)
4. Sweater (waters + E)
5. Friend (diner + F)
6. Pencils (splice + N)
7. Eights (sight + E)
8. Heart (hare + T)
9. Spread (dares + P)
10. Saturn (runts + A)
11. Barge (grab + E)
12. Wrote (wore + T)
13. Twirl (wilt + R)
14. Doubt (bout + D)
15. Joker (jerk + O)
16. Hoarse (shore +A)
17. Treason (tenors + A)
18. Cache (each + C)
19. Break (rake + B)
20. Shield (slide + H)
21. Yearning (engrain + Y)
22. Drawl (ward + L)
23. Bride (bier + D)
24. Chair (arch + I)
25. Snore (nose + R)
26. Sailor (roils +A)
27. Plain (pail + N)
28. Cherry (cryer + H)

The couplet by Ogden Nash:
If called by a panther,
Don't anther.

40 PUNS AND TWISTS

The words were:

1. Thistle
2. Aftermath
3. Cellulite
4. Shudder
5. Buccaneer
6. Foresighted
7. Schnapps
8. Bowstring
9. Affiliate
10. Withdrawals
11. Meteor
12. License
13. Sunstruck
14. Antifreeze

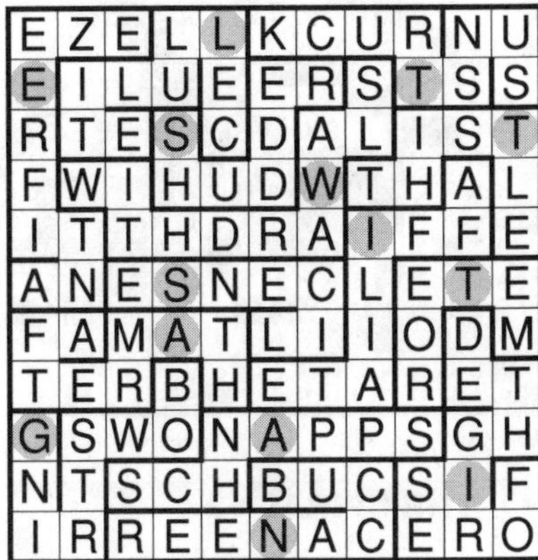

The song title: "Let's Twist Again"

38 THE TREASURE OF SILVER ISLAND

All the information you needed to find the buried treasure was indeed condensed on that single sheet of paper (clue 1), but did you check both sides? Clue 3's unusual phrasing of "in turn" hinted at turning the page. Clue 4 indicated that the solution was "completely on the square"—that is, on the square-shaped crossword ("Dig This!") on the preceding page. If those clues were a bit cryptic, clue 6 broadly suggested you try a puzzle nearby.

The "signs of digging" (clue 5) were the holes you were to make by solving the crossword. Several clues in that puzzle called for answers containing the word "hole" (BLACK HOLE, PEEPHOLE, etc.), and wherever that word belonged in the crossword grid, you were to poke a hole through the paper—seven holes in all. (See the note below the answer grid for "Dig This!" at left.) When you then examined the treasure map, the "signs of digging" revealed treasure at seven locations (clue 2): Lookout Point, Ancient Burial Mounds, Waterfall, Well, Cave, Buzzard's Peak, and Footbridge.

45 PROVERBS AND CONVERBS

1. Absence makes the heart grow fonder.
2. All work and no play makes Jack a dull boy.
3. You can't teach an old dog new tricks.
4. Too many cooks spoil the broth.
5. Curiosity killed the cat.
6. Nothing ventured, nothing gained.
7. You can't take it with you.
8. Nice guys finish last.
9. He who hesitates is lost.

ANSWERS

42 KREUZWORTRÄTSEL

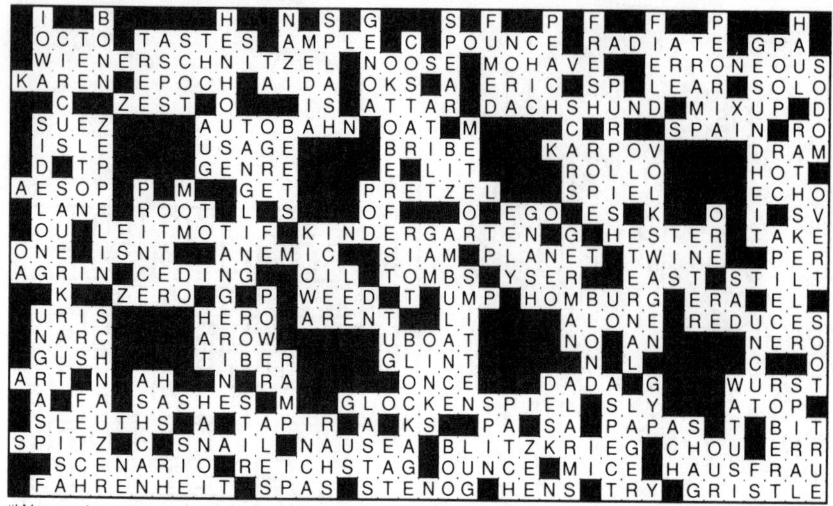

"We ought to learn from the cows one thing: ruminating": Friedrich Wilhelm Nietzsche

44 THE SPIRAL #2

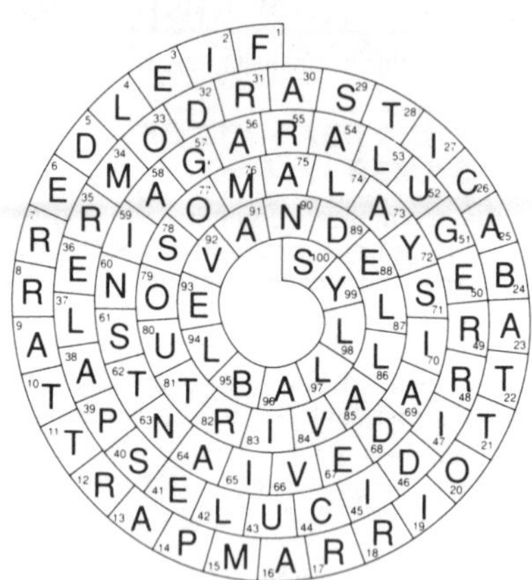

54 TRANSPLANTED CAPITALS

1. Georgia
2. Virginia
3. Texas
4. New Jersey
5. New York
6. Illinois
7. Ohio
8. California
9. Indiana
10. New Hampshire
11. Kansas
12. Idaho

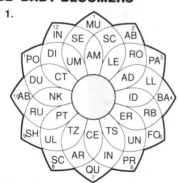

47 A TO Z #1

1. F, plowed
2. J, wastebasket
3. R, yardman
4. S, nun
5. Q, very
6. P, buckle
7. K, quantum
8. B, medium
9. Z, country
10. L, raise
11. N, innings
12. W, luckily
13. D, zany
14. C, helmet
15. M, gander
16. H, xenon
17. T, decamp
18. A, tsetse
19. V, fjords
20. U, ounce
21. X, jacks
22. O, skycap
23. E, arming
24. I, kibbutz
25. Y, eon
26. G, underexpose

52 BABY BLOOMERS

1.

2.

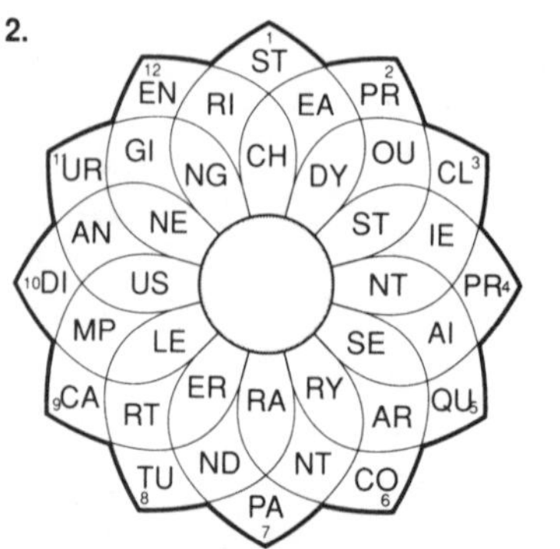

46 CAN YOU THINK UNDER PRESSURE?

1. The letter X should be crossed out in the first sentence.
2. The word "gaiety" should be circled.
3. The stack contains 25 cubes.
4. The square should be left empty.
5. The blank should contain your correct age.
6. 10¢, 10¢, 5¢, 1¢.
7. The space should contain the word DOG.
8. The next space should be empty.
9. The next space should contain NO.
10. GOLF should appear in the next space.
11. The next blank should be empty.
12. True.
13. Thursday.
14. MADAM, MEDIUM, MOM, MUM, MUSEUM. Many other answers are possible.
15. Uncle.
16. The square should contain a check.
17. 2:36.
18. ICE should be written at the bottom of the page.
19. Eleven.
20. I QUIT should appear at the end of the sentence.

Scoring: Count 1 point for each correct answer. The maximum score is 20 points.

Ratings: 20 points—Ace. You work exceptionally well in situations requiring rapid and tricky brainwork. Unfortunately, this skill has no positive correlation with income. 18-19 points—Excellent, indeed. You maintain a cool head and sharp wits when others are losing theirs. 16-17 points—Very good. You can fill out an IRS 1040 on time without the help of H & R Block. 14-15 points—Good. You can slip tab A into slot A. 10-13 points—Fair. But sometimes you are confused by tricky instructions and sometimes even by not-so-tricky instructions. Under 10 points—Try another quiz.

48 LEFT AND RIGHT #2

ANSWERS

49 PICTURE PROVERB

A. DISH
B. FLUTE
C. BEADS
D. ICEBERG
E. CANNON
F. MITTENS
G. SATYR
H. CANTEEN
I. EYES
J. STOOL
K. SANTA
L. SHIP

It is an easy conscience, and not an easy bed, that brings the most restful sleep.

50 CROSS-ANAGRAMS #1

1A

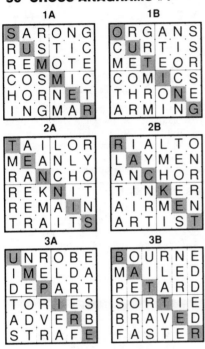

S	A	R	O	N	G
R	U	S	T	I	C
R	E	M	O	T	E
C	O	S	M	I	C
H	O	R	N	E	T
I	N	G	M	A	R

1B

O	R	G	A	N	S
C	U	R	T	I	S
M	E	T	E	O	R
C	O	M	I	C	S
T	H	R	O	N	E
A	R	M	I	N	G

2A

T	A	I	L	O	R
M	E	A	N	L	Y
R	A	N	C	H	O
R	E	K	N	I	T
R	E	M	A	I	N
T	R	A	I	T	S

2B

R	I	A	L	T	O
L	A	Y	M	E	N
A	N	C	H	O	R
T	I	N	K	E	R
A	I	R	M	E	N
A	R	T	I	S	T

3A

U	N	R	O	B	E
I	M	E	L	D	A
D	E	P	A	R	T
T	O	R	I	E	S
A	D	V	E	R	B
S	T	R	A	F	E

3B

B	O	U	R	N	E
M	A	I	L	E	D
P	E	T	A	R	D
S	O	R	T	I	E
B	R	A	V	E	D
F	A	S	T	E	R

56 TO CATCH A THIEF

When the dots are connected correctly, beginning with the letter J, they show a profile of the thief and form a letter chain revealing his boastful message: JULES CROOK, FIVE MILLION DOLLARS IN PRECIOUS GEMS, DIAMOND HEAD, HAWAII. Based on this self-incriminating evidence, Mr. Crook was apprehended by the Hawaii Five-O squad, held briefly in custody, and then released upon his own recognizance. At his trial, Mr. Crook was convicted and "drew" a stiff sentence: 1,000 hours of community service at the Honolulu School for Remedial Art. A made-for-TV movie of Mr. Crook's case is in the works and is tentatively titled *Jewels and Gem.*

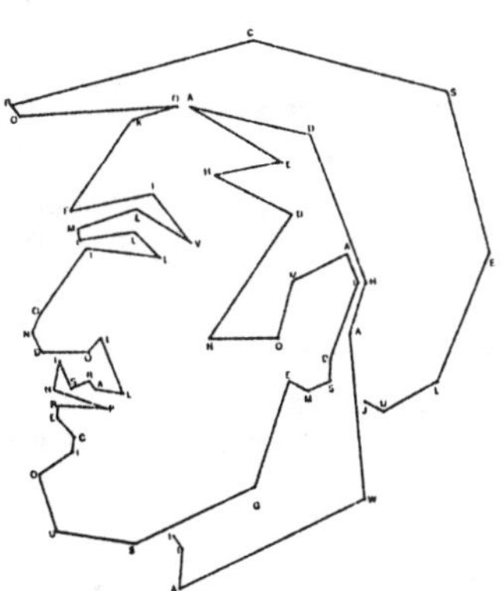

51 BULL'S-EYE 20 QUESTIONS #2

1. Rebelliously
2. Terrific (terrible)
3. Ventriloquism
4. Effete
5. Saturday (sturdy)
6. Overgenerous (verge, onerous)
7. Basic (sick bay)
8. Mute (mate, mete, mite, mote)
9. Go (went)
10. Hijinks
11. Indiscreetly (nicety)
12. Knight (think)
13. Filibuster (fill a bus to)
14. Cablegram (cab, leg, ram)
15. Looped (poodle)
16. Committee
17. Corps
18. Truce (truth)
19. Aspirate (spirate, pirate, irate, rate, ate: "spirate" means "voiceless" or "breathed," according to *Webster's Second*)
20. And

"When in doubt, wear red."—Bill Blass

53 SQUARE ROUTES #2

1 F	2 T	3 G	A	4 R	5 D	6 E	N	R
I	C	U	7 C	A	B	I	N	8 E
N	I	A	R	9 T	A	E	A	D
G	N	I	10 N	T	11 H	G	I	12 L
E	O	O	N	L	13 L	14 G	15 N	U
R	16 T	U	E	E	E	E	I	O
E	O	A	V	G	R	17 A	A	18 H
19 F	A	E	20 L	V	I	R	R	21 S
22 S	L	E	E	23 P	24 F	25 P	26 B	M

58 PETAL PUSHERS #2

57 SYLLASTEPS #1

A.

STA	BIL	IZ	ING
DIC	TION	AR	Y
WIG	GLE	WAG	GLE
DAN	DE	LI	ON
CON	GRAT	U	LATE
DI	VER	SI	FY
IM	PRAC	TI	CAL
DIS	AS	SEM	BLE

B.

DIC	TA	TOR	SHIP
STA	TION	MAS	TER
SANC	TU	AR	IES
PHO	TO	COP	Y
DEF	ER	EN	TIAL
TAX	I	DER	MIST
GE	RA	NI	UM
SAT	IS	FAC	TION

60 STORIES FROM THE SAFARI

The hunter made 11 identifiable errors:

1. "Wrestling with a tiger" (it was a leopard)
2. "Armed with only a knife" (the hunter had a pistol)
3. "The attack occurred around noon" (the sun was low in the sky)
4. "Two miles from ... Bukwimba" (it was two kilometers)
5. "I was all alone" (he had an aide)
6. "I left the canteen back at camp" (the hunter had it with him)
7. "A pride of lions could be seen" (no lions were nearby)
8. "The gun wasn't loaded" (the shot could be seen)
9. "Wrestled the tiger to the pavement" (the road was unpaved)
10. "You can still see the scar where he gashed me" (the hunter already had the scar at the time of the attack)
11. "His head mounted on the wall behind me" (the head is not of the animal that attacked)

64 READING BETWEEN THE LINES

1. *Doctor Zhivago/The Good Earth*
2. *Lord of the Flies/Myra Breckenridge*
3. *Animal Farm/Vanity Fair*
4. *Brave New World/Robinson Crusoe*
5. *Huckleberry Finn/Of Human Bondage*
6. *Don Quixote/Steppenwolf*
7. *An American Tragedy/War and Remembrance*
8. *Beowulf/Ulysses*
9. *A Bell for Adano/The Caine Mutiny*
10. *Atlas Shrugged/Les Misérables*
11. *Catch-22/Kon-Tiki*
12. *Jane Eyre/Moby Dick*
13. *Brideshead Revisited/The Canterbury Tales*
14. *So Big/Trilby*
15. *A Passage to India/Great Expectations*

ANSWERS

61 SPIDER'S WEB

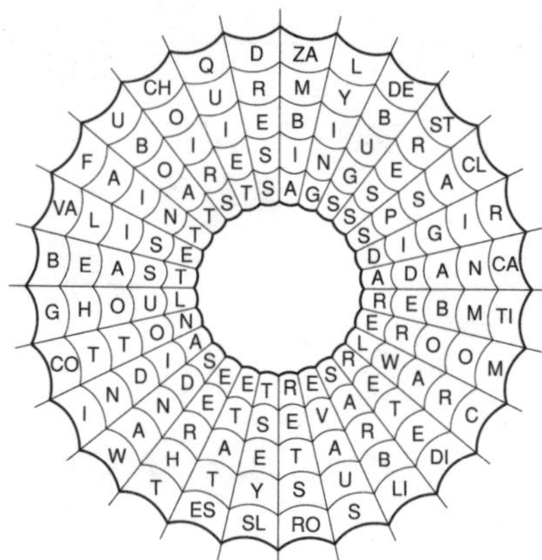

1. Crawl
2. India
3. Faint
4. Timber
5. Rigid
6. Cotton
7. Roster
8. Choirs
9. Suave
10. Lying
11. Three
12. Libras
13. Stress
14. Ghoul
15. Dress
16. Moore
17. Quiet
18. Estate
19. Valise
20. Canada
21. Slyest
22. Dieter
23. Wands
24. Clasps
25. U-boat
26. Zambia
27. Beast
28. Debugs

The letters in the second and fourth rings spell: "My brain, more busy than the labouring spider, weaves tedious snares."

65 FOUR-IN-ONE CROSSWORD

H	A	G		C	A	B	S	B	A	D		A	S	P
E	R	A		U	T	A	H	O	W	E		T	H	O
M	E	G	A	D	O	S	E	M	A	B		H	A	S
	A	L	F		L	I	D	B	R	A	V	E	R	Y
B	R	I	T	T	L	E	A		D	R	A	N	K	
R	U	N	O	N	S	G	E	N		K	N	I	F	E
A	G	E	N	T	U	I	N	E	T	S	N	A	I	L
	S	P	Y	A	L	E	N	T	F	I	A	N	N	S
	T	E	E	S	N	D	S	I	T	B	O	A	S	
D	R	E	N	C	H	S	W	A	F	E	R	V	O	R
Y	A	K		O	A	R	Y	H	A	N	S	O	L	O
E	T	A		U	S	A	B	A	R	N		C	O	B
R	E	B	I	R	T	H	A	W	A	Y	G	A	M	E
	G	O	O	S	E		J	E	D		O	D	O	R
	Y	O	U				A	D	S		D	O	N	T

"A genuine talent finds its way."—Goethe

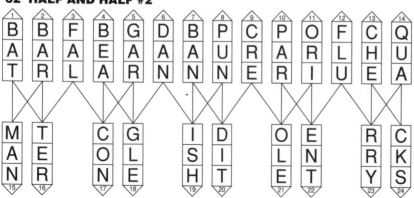

63 BUILDING BLOCKS

1.

O	R	C	H	E	S	T	R	A
P	R	O	G	N	O	S	I	S
W	O	M	E	N	F	O	L	K
A	M	P	L	I	T	U	D	E
H	O	U	S	E	W	I	F	E
M	A	T	R	I	A	R	C	H
T	H	E	O	C	R	A	C	Y
D	A	R	E	D	E	V	I	L

2.

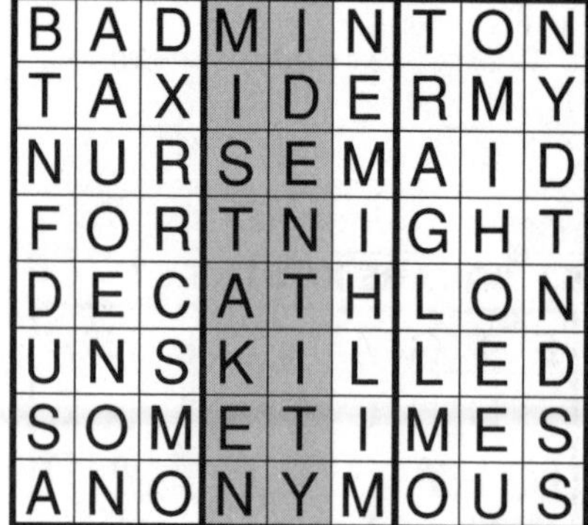

B	A	D	M	I	N	T	O	N
T	A	X	I	D	E	R	M	Y
N	U	R	S	E	M	A	I	D
F	O	R	T	N	I	G	H	T
D	E	C	A	T	H	L	O	N
U	N	S	K	I	L	L	E	D
S	O	M	E	T	I	M	E	S
A	N	O	N	Y	M	O	U	S

3.

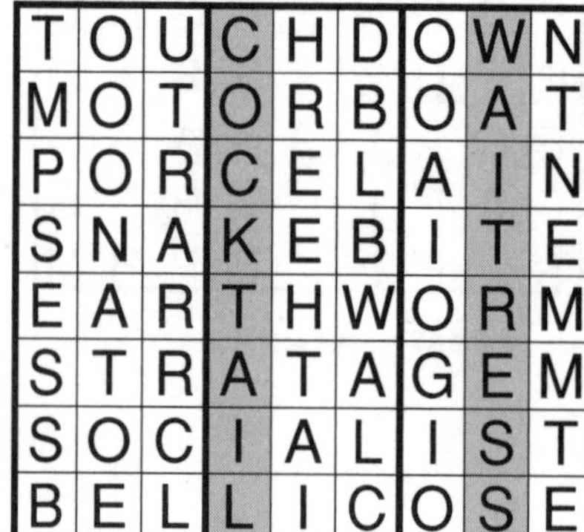

T	O	U	C	H	D	O	W	N
M	O	T	O	R	B	O	A	T
P	O	R	C	E	L	A	I	N
S	N	A	K	E	B	I	T	E
E	A	R	T	H	W	O	R	M
S	T	R	A	T	A	G	E	M
S	O	C	I	A	L	I	S	T
B	E	L	L	I	C	O	S	E

66 ROUND AND ROUND

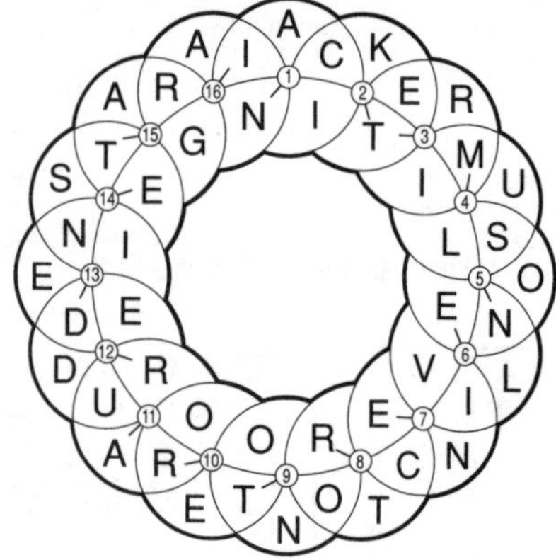

1. Niacin
2. Ticket
3. Termite
4. Muslim
5. Nelson
6. Enliven
7. Evince
8. Rector
9. Toronto
10. Rooter
11. Aurora
12. Rudder
13. Denied
14. Einsteins
15. Target
16. Ingrain

66 OY, A QUIZ!

1. Ahoy
2. Bolshoi
3. Corduroy
4. Doughboy
5. Kilroy
6. St. Croix
7. Convoy
8. *Playboy*
9. Portnoy
10. Decoy
11. Illinois
12. Tolstoy
13. Life buoy
14. Iroquois
15. Viceroy
16. Savoy
17. Cowboy
18. Killjoy
19. Envoy
20. Hoi polloi

68 THROUGH-THE-HOUSE TREASURE HUNT

Starting puzzle Northwest corner of bedroom carpet
Bedroom puzzle Under lampshade by davenport
Lampshade puzzle Left fringe of dining room curtains
Dining room puzzle Bathroom sink
Bathroom puzzle Under mat on front steps
Front steps puzzle Lower right desk drawer
Desk puzzle Look inside yogurt carton in fridge
Refrigerator puzzle Pocket of raincoat in closet
Closet puzzle Congratulations! You have solved the last puzzle. The treasure is behind the encyclopedias.

Thanks to Henry Hook for several of the puzzles and ideas.

62 HALF AND HALF #2

1. BAT
2. BAR
3. FAL
4. BEA
5. GAR
6. DAN
7. BAN
8. PUN
9. CRE
10. PAR
11. ORI
12. FLU
13. CHE
14. QUA
15. MAN
16. TER
17. CON
18. GLE
19. ISH
20. DIT
21. OLE
22. ENT
23. RRY
24. CKS

75 TELESCOPES

#1 The objects pictured are:

1. Rabbit
2. Lips
3. Crab
4. Lyre
5. Italy
6. Seal
7. Reel
8. Rabbi
9. Ellipse

The telescope:
CRABBITALYREELLIPSEAL

#2 The objects pictured are:

1. Chest
2. Owl
3. Train
4. Torch
5. Rainbow
6. Error
7. Bowler
8. Orchestra

The telescope:
TORCHESTRAINBOWLERROR

ANSWERS

67 CONNECT-A-WORD

1 SHORT	2 HAND	3 SPRING	4 CHICKEN	5 FEED
6 FALL	7 OVER	8 TIME	9 OUT	10 BOX
11 FLAT	12 HEAD		13 GO	
14 FOOT	15 LIGHT	16 YEAR	17 ROUND	18 HOUSE
19 HOLD	20 UP	21 END	22 TABLE	23 TOP
	24 LIFT		25 SETTING	26 OFF
27 CHECK	28 BACK	29 GROUND	30 FIRE	31 SIDE
32 BOOK	33 DROP	34 IN	35 PLACE	36 KICK

74 THE SPIRAL #3

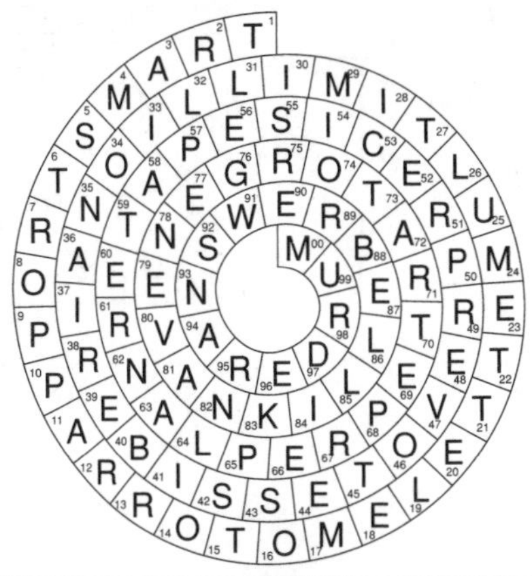

70 WRY SANDWICHES #2

1. BASEBALL UMPIRE

I	M	P	A	N	E	L
E	X	P	L	O	I	T
R	O	B	E	R	T	S
G	O	N	D	O	L	A
A	S	O	C	I	A	L
S	U	M	M	O	N	S
R	E	D	S	K	I	N

2. CASINO CHIPS

S	C	H	O	L	A	R
S	T	R	A	N	G	E
P	R	E	F	A	C	E
S	H	O	R	T	E	N
S	H	E	B	A	N	G
L	E	T	T	U	C	E
D	I	V	O	R	C	E

3. EGOTISTICAL

H	A	Y	S	E	E	D
L	E	I	S	U	R	E
A	M	O	N	G	S	T
T	E	R	M	I	T	E
S	O	L	O	I	S	T
T	W	I	N	K	L	E
A	T	H	L	E	T	E

71 TRIMMING THE TREE

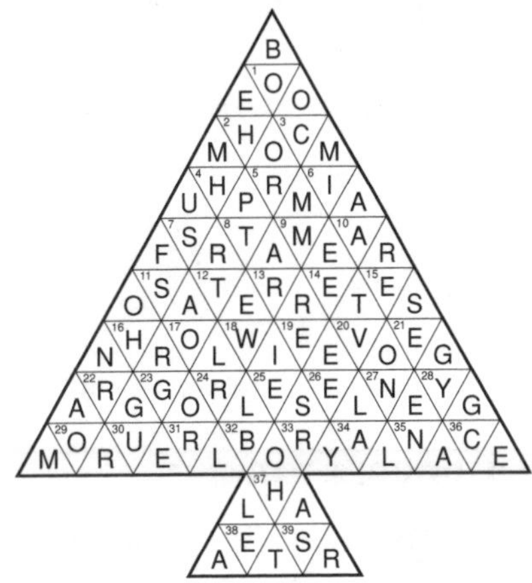

The answer message: "... Oh, Christmas tree, how evergreen your branches!"

72 ALPHABOXES

R	E	G	I	M	E	N
S	C	H	O	L	A	R
N	I	T	P	I	C	K
P	I	Q	U	A	N	T
A	N	A	L	Y	S	T
I	N	D	E	X	E	D
P	O	P	O	V	E	R
S	U	B	Z	E	R	O
D	I	V	O	R	C	E
G	L	I	M	P	S	E
B	A	R	O	Q	U	E
P	R	E	T	Z	E	L
L	O	C	K	J	A	W
L	A	U	N	D	R	Y
H	A	M	S	T	E	R
S	I	Z	A	B	L	E
B	E	J	E	W	E	L
R	E	F	U	G	E	E
B	O	W	L	F	U	L
A	S	K	A	N	C	E
A	M	N	E	S	I	A
S	N	O	R	K	E	L
V	U	L	T	U	R	E
G	A	S	O	H	O	L
A	N	Y	B	O	D	Y
T	A	X	I	C	A	B

76 LINK-ACROSTICS #2

1. CAN YOU TOP THIS?

		A			B			C		
H	U	M	A	N	K	L	E	P	E	R
S	Q	U	I	D	E	A	L	I	K	E
G	U	S	T	O	T	E	M	C	E	E
M	E	T	A	L	C	O	A	K	E	N
C	R	A	N	E	H	R	U	L	E	R
M	A	R	C	O	U	C	H	E	C	K
M	E	D	A	L	P	H	A	S	T	Y

2. WELL, WHAT DO YOU KNOW?

		A			B			C		
K	I	T	T	Y	P	O	S	C	A	R
H	A	R	P	O	U	C	H	O	I	R
Q	U	I	T	O	R	S	O	N	A	R
E	L	V	E	S	S	E	X	T	R	A
A	M	I	G	O	U	G	E	E	S	E
B	E	A	C	H	I	N	A	S	T	Y
V	I	L	L	A	T	I	N	T	R	O

77 SPLIT ENDS #1

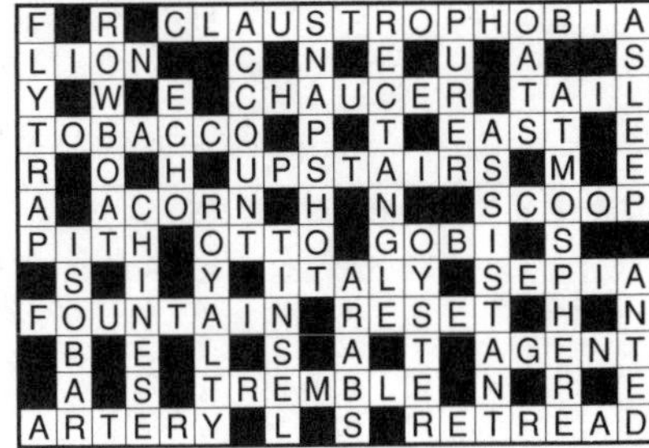

The clue parts for each answer are as follows: 7 = 5 + 2; 13 = 4 + 9; 21 = 13 + 8; 29 = 23 + 6; 35 = 19 + 16; 38 = 26 + 12; 42 = 39 + 3; 45 = 15 + 30; 50 = 18 + 32; 58 = 44 + 14; 59 = 49 + 10; 61 = 34 + 27; 62 = 33 + 29; 63 = 17 + 46; 65 = 64 + 1; 73 = 51 + 22; 75 = 50 + 25; 76 = 31 + 45; 80 = 7 + 73; 81 = 28 + 53; 84 = 24 + 60; 85 = 11 + 74; 88 = 68 + 20; 89 = 54 + 35; 92 = 21 + 71; 94 = 37 + 57; 98 = 58 + 40; 99 = 56 + 43; 102 = 36 + 66; 103 = 42 + 61; 106 = 47 + 59; 110 = 38 + 72; 113 = 65 + 48; 116 = 41 + 75; 118 = 63 + 55; 121 = 52 + 69; 132 = 62 + 70; 143 = 67 + 76.

ANSWERS

73 SUPER SEVEN SEARCH

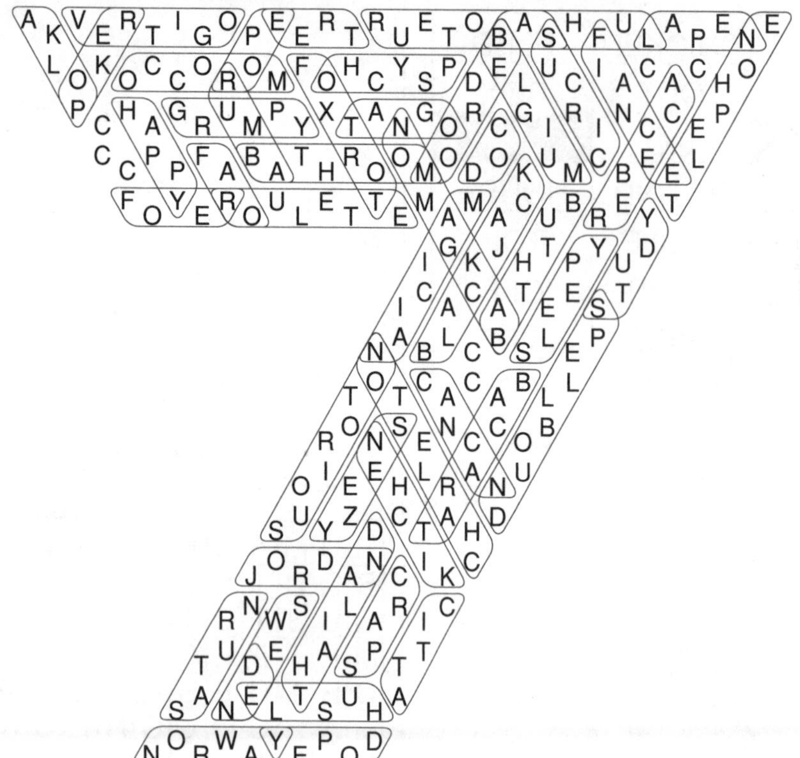

The leftover letters form the "seven seas" (C's)!

78 SPINOFFS

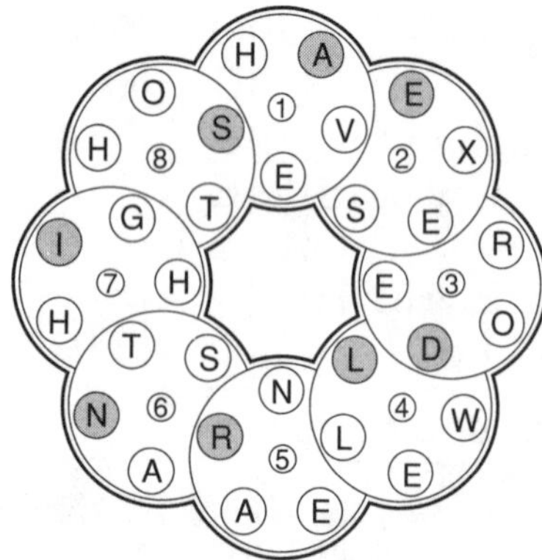

The Bonus Clue answer: ISLANDER/SLANDER

78 EX TERMINATIONS

1. Reflex
2. Apex
3. Pyrex
4. Unisex
5. Hex
6. Perplex
7. Duplex
8. Vertex
9. Index
10. Latex
11. Convex
12. Memorex
13. Annex
14. Windex
15. Complex
16. Timex
17. Telex
18. Cortex

79 WORD DERBY

All the answer words contain names of musical instruments:

1. Conun*drum*
2. *Viol*ation
3. Am*bassa*dor
4. Funi*cello*
5. *Fiddle*sticks
6. Matter*horn*
7. H*oboe*s
8. M*organ*
9. Abso*lute*
10. *Harp*oon

The results of the race are: 1st–O (30 lengths); 2nd–A (29); 3rd–I (26); 4th–E (25); 5th–U (21).

80 DOUBLE PARKING

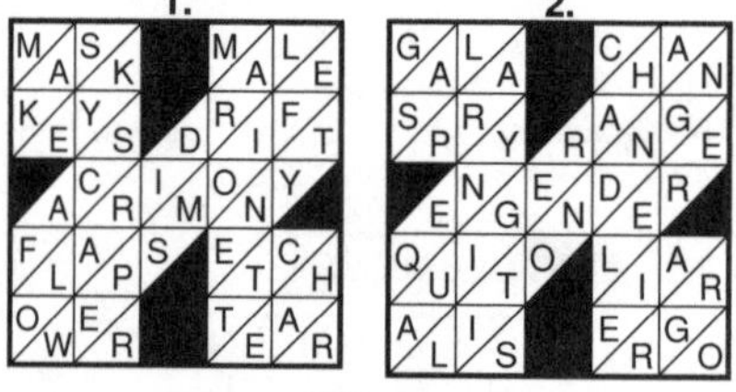

80 CONFUSABLES

1. The other way around
2. Stala*c*tites, with a *c*, hang from the *c*eiling (stala*g*mites, with a *g*, rise from the *g*round)
3. Warp (woof is the filler thread)
4. Bronze (brass is copper and zinc)
5. Apogee, highest; perigee, lowest
6. Ophthalmologist (an optometrist examines for and prescribes correctional lenses, and an optician grinds the glass for them—whew!)
7. Lower
8. Right to left
9. Plato was a student of Socrates
10. *Monitor*, Union; *Merrimac*, Confederate
11. Alaska was first
12. Right (left is port)

88 WORD MAZE

1. Cod
2. Carp
3. Pike
4. Shad
5. Sole
6. Tuna
7. Scrod
8. Shark
9. Trout
10. Turtle
11. Piranha
12. Mackerel

Other less common answers include: ACARA; HARP (seal); ORCA; SAMA; and SCAD.

81 "B" HIVE #2

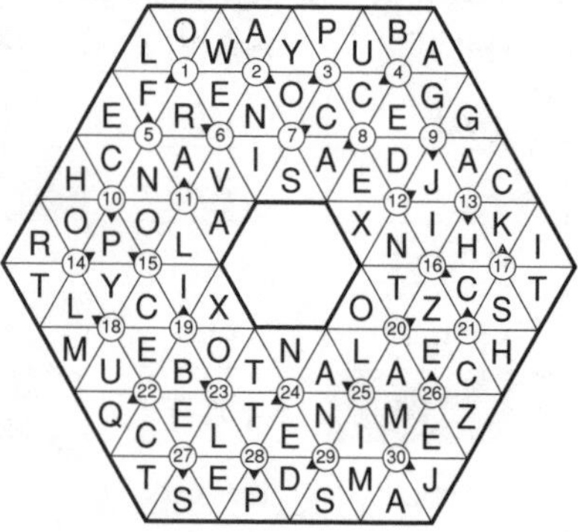

82 CARTOON REBUSES

1. Woody Woodpecker (wood-E-wood-peck-er)
2. Connie Stevens (con-east-evens)
3. Studebaker (stewed-uh-baker)
4. Billy Graham (Bill-league-Ram)
5. Thurgood Marshall (thir-good-marshal)
6. *Goodbye, Mr. Chips* (good buy-missed 'er-chips)
7. Slide rule (sly-drool)
8. Champagne (sham-pain)
9. Mike Schmidt (mike-sh-mitt)
10. Shoshone (show-show-knee)
11. Khartoum (car-tomb)
12. Goldilocks (goal-D-locks)
13. Hopscotch (hops-Koch)
14. "The Birth of the Blues" (the-berth of the Blues)

84 FLOWER CROSS

87 CROSS-O #2

1. FRUIT: Cherry, Banana, Orange, Kumquat
2. JEWEL: Diamond, Emerald, Topaz, Amethyst
3. HAIRDO: Beehive, Poodle, Pageboy, Marcel
4. METAL: Cobalt, Yttrium, Silver, Nickel
5. INVENTOR: Whitney, Edison, Marconi, Morse
6. SITCOM: *F Troop, Alice, Roseanne, Cheers*
7. CURRENCY: Ruble, Dollar, Drachma, Pound
8. DESSERT: Eclair, Sherbet, Pudding, Jell-O

ANSWERS

85 SYLLASTEPS #2

A.

AS	TON	ISH	MENT
PA	TRON	IZ	ING
TAP	I	O	CA
YEL	LOW	HAM	MER
CO	PEN	HA	GEN
TEM	PER	A	TURE
FOR	TY	NI	NER
STREP	TO	COC	CUS

B.

LIT	TLE	BIG	HORN
CAT	ER	PIL	LAR
MA	TRI	AR	CHY
OR	THO	DOX	Y
COM	MU	NI	QUE
TRAM	PO	LIN	IST
EN	THU	SI	AST
IL	LUS	TRA	TION

86 EQUATION ANALYSIS TEST #2

a. 36 = Inches in a Yard
b. 6 = Wives of Henry the Eighth
c. 212 = Degrees at which Water Boils
d. 3 = Points for a Field Goal in Football
e. 20 = Years that Rip Van Winkle Slept
f. 101 = Dalmatians
g. 60 = Seconds in a Minute
h. 7 = Hills of Rome
i. 56 = Signers of the Declaration of Independence
j. 5 = Fingers on the Hand
k. 40 = Thieves (with Ali Baba)
l. 30 = Days Hath September, April, June, and November
m 1 = Day at a Time
n. 10 = Amendments in the Bill of Rights
o. 435 = Members of the House of Representatives
p. 16 = Ounces in a Pound
q. 31 = Ice Cream Flavors at Baskin-Robbins
r. 50 = Cents in a Half Dollar
s. 2 = Turtle Doves (and a Partridge in a Pear Tree)
t. 4 = Horsemen of the Apocalypse
u. 13 = Cards in a Suit
v. 8 = Parts of Speech in the English Language
w 20,000 = Leagues Under the Sea
x. 9 = Innings in a Baseball Game

88 A LITTLE OFF THE TOP

1. Preach, reach, each
2. Twitch, witch, itch
3. Whoops, hoops, oops
4. Strain, train, rain
5. Clever, lever, ever
6. Pledge, ledge, edge
7. Gramps, ramps, amps

89 BULL'S-EYE 20 QUESTIONS #3

1. Aggregate
2. Shorts (Stroh's)
3. Evacuate (vacate)
4. Sometimes (sum + times)
5. Henchmen
6. Drano (*Dr. No*)
7. Pygmy
8. Thorn (north)
9. Faceful (faithful)
10. Queue
11. Unoriental
12. Read
13. Bartender (barter, after dropping end)
14. Suitcase
15. Male (female)
16. Maximized (M + M + D + X + I + I)
17. Toboggan (to bargain)
18. One (bone, cone, done, gone, hone, lone, none, pone, tone, zone)
19. Revolver
20. Outside

"Moral victories don't count."—Savielly Tartakower

90 WORLD TOUR

1. Warsaw, Sydney, Manila
2. Athens, Munich, Bombay
3. Bogota, Moscow, Prague
4. London, Ottawa, Naples
5. Taipei, Odessa, Dublin
6. Ankara, Beirut, Lisbon

90 THE THREE R'S

1. Reporter
2. Terrier
3. Narrator
4. Treasurer
5. Mirror
6. Rearward
7. Barrier
8. Reorder
9. Corridor
10. Raspberry
11. Derrière
12. Sorcerer
13. Retriever
14. Irregular
15. Worrywart

92 3-D WORD HUNT #2

Here are the 44 relatively common words we found: ABATE, ABOVE, AREAS, ASTER, BARER, BARGE, BOOST, DIRER, DIRGE, DIVER, DIVOT, EGRET, GRATE, GREEN, IRATE, LASTS, LOOTS, PAPAL, PAPAS, PASTA, PASTE, PEEVE, RABID, RARER, RATER, RIDGE, RIVER, RIVET, SALVE, SALVO, SOLOS, SOLVE, STARE, STATE, STEAL, STEEP, STOOL, STOVE, TABOO, UNDID, UPEND, VERGE, VIVID, and VOTER.

A few of the less common words we found (not an exhaustive list) are: AREAL, EASTS, PASTS, PUPAE, PUPAS, RAREE, SOOTS, STATS, STERE, TATER, and TOTER.

91 A TO Z #2

1. S, ocean
2. Q, retreat
3. E, quell
4. K, India
5. J, plot
6. A, despair
7. Z, X-rayed
8. N, squeak
9. H, unattractive
10. O, Norway
11. B, Huxley
12. W, caves
13. Y, ennui
14. G, kibitz
15. R, walkie-talkie
16. M, agonize
17. F, myself
18. X, boudoir
19. U, Jazz
20. C, zero
21. I, loosely
22. P, toast
23. L, Vader
24. V, gondola
25. T, Fuehrer
26. D, yogurt

93 SKELETON

M	A	I	D	E	N		F	R	I	G	H	T	E	N
O			O		O		O			U		U		E
R	E	S	T		R		W	H	I	Z		R		E
A		A		S	M	I	L	E		Z	O	N	E	D
L		V			A			L		L			O	
S	T	E	E	P	L	E		P	R	E	S	E	N	T
	W			I		A			E			R		A
G	O	W	N	S		S	P	I	C	E		G		V
L		H		T	O	T	E		K		H	O	L	E
A		O		O			A		O		I			R
D	E	A	D	L	O	C	K		N	A	T	I	O	N

95 LETTER "S" PICTURE TEST

The letter "S" word pairs are:

1. Sale, ale
2. Schick (razor), chick
3. Scoop, coop
4. Shay, hay
5. Shoe, hoe
6. Shooter, hooter (owl)
7. Shovel, hovel
8. Sink, ink
9. Sledge, ledge
10. Snail, nail
11. Soil, oil
12. Spine (on book), pine
13. Spot, pot
14. Stable, table
15. Stack (of hay), tack
16. Stool, tool
17. Stopper, topper (hat)
18. Strap, trap
19. Swine, wine

ANSWERS

94 HALF AND HALF #3

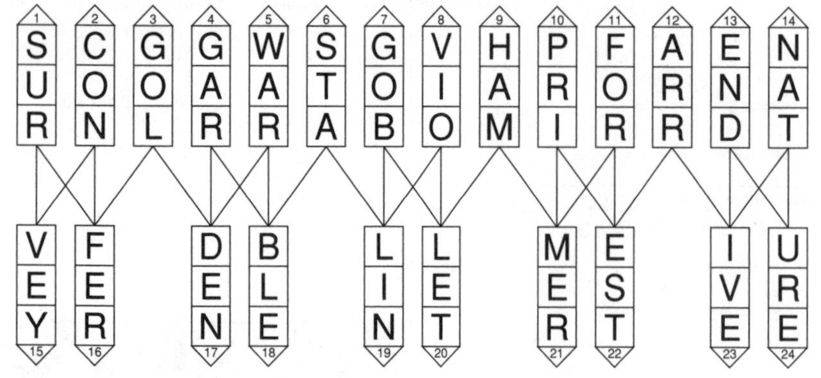

96 PUZZLE POTPOURRI

1. New Math

2. Target Word

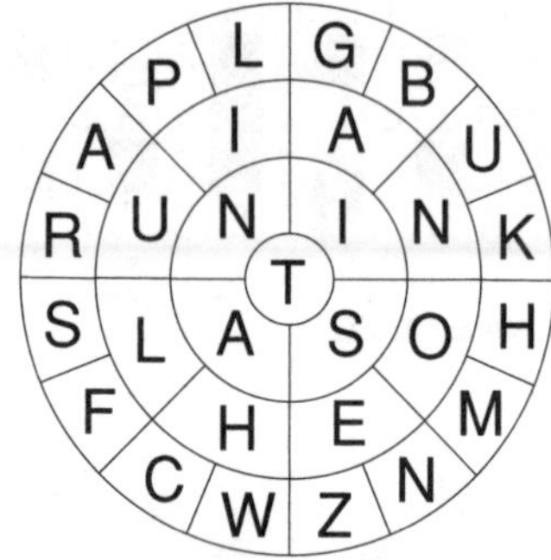

3. Change of Clothes

1. Dress	5. Shawl	9. Sarong
2. Scarf	6. Bonnet	10. Sweater
3. Cloak	7. Bikini	11. Trousers
4. Glove	8. Jacket	12. Stocking

4. Six-Packs

a. 6×6−6÷6=5	e. 6×6+6+6=48
b. 6+6÷6+6=8	f. 6+6×6−6=66
c. 6÷6+6+6=13	g. 6+6+6×6=108
d. 6÷6+6×6=42	h. 6×6−6×6=180

5. Mischmasch

Here are our answers (yours may differ):

1. Windmill	7. Bathtub
2. Submarine	8. Vodka
3. Leprechaun	9. Hypotenuse
4. Prohibit	10. Saxophone
5. Technology	11. Daydream
6. Fingernail	12. Jodhpurs

6. Solitaire Jotto

1. Light 2. Mouse 3. Swami

104 MEASURE FOR MEASURE

1. n, television	11. b, telescope
2. g, computer	12. r, stock price
3. c, shoes	13. j, radio wavelength
4. p, engine	14. i, noise
5. f, gold	15. q, soft drink
6. l, medicine	16. h, pencil
7. d, film	17. a, air conditioner
8. m, pants	18. k, typing
9. o, photograph	
10. e, light bulb	

98 LEFT AND RIGHT #3

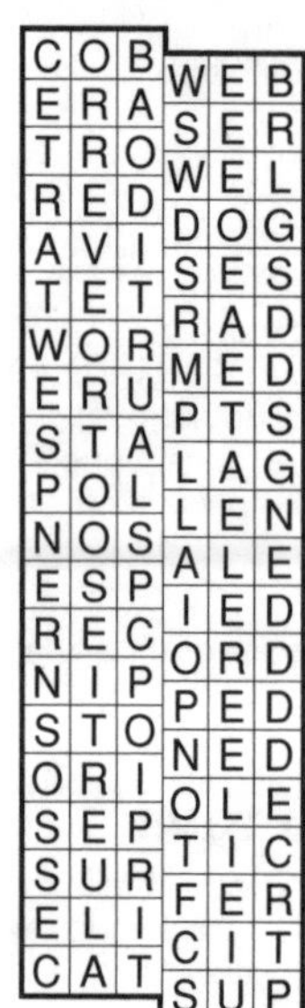

99 QUIZ-ACROSTIC

1. Sneezing	11. Hawaii
2. June	12. Monkees
3. Truman	13. Yellow
4. Norway	14. Edward
5. Oldsmobile	15. Fathom
6. Twiggy	16. *Us*
7. Edgar	17. Remarque
8. Accordion	18. Denmark
9. Venus	19. Liberty
10. Butter	20. Iron

A tombstone in Belturbet, Ireland, says: "Here lies the body of John Mound, lost at sea and never found."

110 SIT FOR A SPELL

Our list of relatively common words totals 51 points. Other answers may be possible.

1-Point Words: accede, accost, cannon, cannot, cocoon, comma, commode, common, corrode, cotton, dollop, doorman, loess, loose, loosest, lotto, mamma (or momma), manna, moose, morocco, motto, noose, oddest, oppose, ottoman, posse, proceed, process, processor, proof, roost, sloop, stood, stool, stoop (35).

2-Point Words: access, foolproof, footloose, footstool, poolroom, possess, possessor, toolroom (8 x 2 = 16).

100 ILLUSTRATED HONEYCOMB

101 SQUARE ROUTES #3

102 THE SPIRAL #4

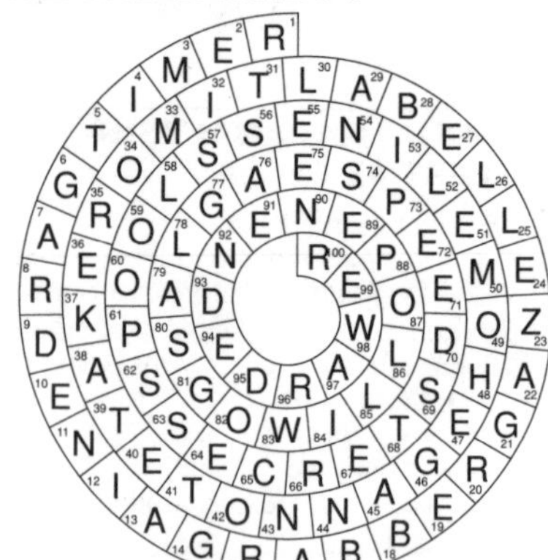

106 PETAL PUSHERS #3

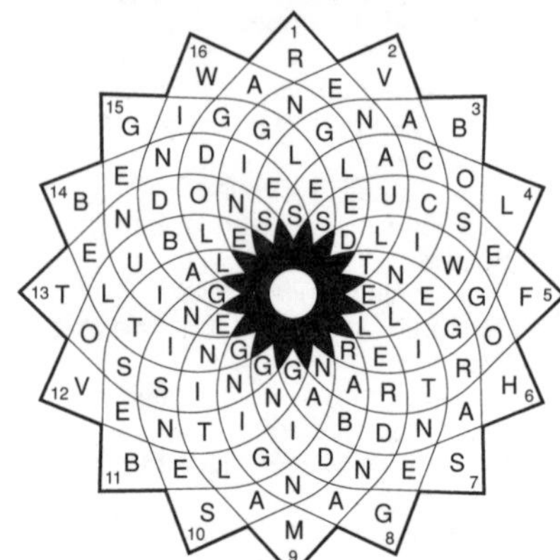

ANSWERS

104 AT THE SCENE OF THE ACCIDENT

1. 6:45 PM (the theater ticket booth has just opened) 2. Monday (the video store was open at 6:45 on all other days) 3. 3 4. No 5. LKD 5 6. Utah 7. 1986 (oops!) 8. 3 9. "No Left Turn 4:00 to 8:00 PM" 10. No 11. DISNEY WORLD 12. Leaking gas, while bystander was smoking a cigarette 13. *Rocky VII* 14. A fall from his ladder 15. E (next letter in "Special Matinee") 16. "Hair Today" barbershop 17. Second 18. Man running with a gasoline can 19. "Caution People Working" 20. 6X 21. The boy was riding a girl's bike (note the absence of a crossbar) 22–24. b, e, f 25. Eyewitness "e" has grown a moustache.

Scoring: Count 1 point for each answer (maximum score: 25)

Ratings:

21 and up:	Sherlock Holmes
16-20:	Dr. Watson
10-15:	Keen observer
5-9:	Forgetful witness
0-4:	Duh ... what accident?

105 RHYME AND REASON #2

1. Swept (pest + W)
2. Baker (bark + E)
3. Plaids (sapid + L)
4. Cater (race + T)
5. Rhine (hire + N)
6. Stitch (chits +T)
7. Shriek (hiker + S)
8. Guessed (segued + S)
9. Shaking (asking + H)
10. Whitest (theist + W)
11. Smash (hams + S)
12. Fleas (safe + L)
13. Sleighs (Gishes + L)
14. Stank (ants +K)
15. Tepee (Pete + E)
16. Groan (rang + O)
17. Anchor (ranch + O)
18. Pastor (ports + A)
19. Preach (parch + E)
20. Third (dirt + H)
21. Dancer (cadre + N)
22. Flavor (flora + V)
23. Prime (ripe + M)
24. Boast (stab + O)
25. Royalty (Taylor + Y)
26. Score (rocs + E)
27. Wrinkle (winker + L)
28. Sleuth (lutes + H)

The quotation by Oscar Wilde: "Only the shallow know themselves."

111 SPLIT ENDS #2

T	█	S	█	█	G	L	O	B	E	T	R	O	T	T	E	R	S
H	O	T	E	L	█	U	█	█	X	█	A	█	E	█	I	█	A
A	█	U	█	A	R	C	T	I	C	█	I	█	L	E	G	A	L
N	U	D	E	S	█	R	█	█	H	I	N	G	E	█	H	█	T
K	█	█	█	S	I	E	S	T	A	█	F	█	P	A	T	T	Y
S	P	R	A	I	N	█	I	█	N	E	A	T	H	█	E	█	█
G	█	O	█	E	G	G	N	O	G	█	L	█	O	P	E	R	A
I	R	O	N	█	E	█	K	R	E	M	L	I	N	█	N	█	L
V	█	S	█	A	█	T	█	A	█	O	█	D	E	B	T	█	M
I	N	T	E	G	E	R	█	T	H	R	E	E	█	O	H	I	O
N	█	E	█	E	█	A	█	O	█	O	█	A	█	R	█	█	S
G	I	R	L	S	█	P	H	R	E	N	O	L	O	G	I	S	T

107 INSIDE AND OUT

L	O	A	F	I	N	G	N	E	E
E	I	R	F	S	E	L	I	A	D
S	T	O	I	N	T	M	A	H	S
U	O	D	I	I	O	N	M	I	N
C	X	O	A	T	Y	D	O	E	O
	E	M	N	T	N	E	T	X	
W	N	E	I	C	E	N	I	P	L
O	D	A	R	E	N	I	R	E	A
S	U	J	T	H	R	E	R	G	N
T	O	M	E	I	R	D	A	D	A
I	S	I	D	N	A	N	O	I	T

Answer words (with definitions in parentheses): 1. Affinity (liking) 2. Singleton (one) 3. Oriole (bird) 4. Maine (part of New England) 5. Shade (darkness) 6. Custodian (clean-up man) 7. Oxen (farm animals) 8. Domino (a political theory) 9. Extent (room) 10. Meadow (field) 11. Alpine (Swiss) 12. Just (fair) 13. Hindi (Indian language) 14. Errand (quick trip) 15. Radio (receiver) 16. Isometric (kind of exercises) 17. Tangerine (color)

Quotation: Loafing needs no explanation and is its own excuse.—Christopher Morley

112 CROSS-ANAGRAMS #2

1A

M	O	B	B	E	D
C	A	N	D	O	R
R	E	S	I	G	N
L	I	N	K	E	D
A	I	S	L	E	S
I	N	T	E	N	D

1B

B	O	M	B	E	D
D	A	C	R	O	N
S	I	N	G	E	R
K	I	N	D	L	E
L	A	S	S	I	E
I	N	D	E	N	T

2A

D	E	A	C	O	N
G	E	R	M	A	N
R	E	S	C	U	E
A	R	R	E	S	T
O	C	C	U	R	S
S	I	L	E	N	T

2B

C	A	N	O	E	D
M	A	N	G	E	R
S	E	C	U	R	E
S	A	R	T	R	E
C	R	O	C	U	S
I	N	L	E	T	S

3A

E	L	P	A	S	O
E	S	P	R	I	T
U	P	C	A	S	T
I	S	R	A	E	L
S	E	R	A	P	H
R	U	S	T	L	E

3B

A	S	L	O	P	E
P	R	I	E	S	T
C	A	T	S	U	P
S	E	R	I	A	L
P	H	R	A	S	E
R	E	S	U	L	T

The clue parts for each answer are as follows: 9 = 6 + 3; 15 = 5 + 10; 26 = 14 + 12; 29 = 9 + 20; 32 = 31 + 1; 33 = 7 + 26; 43 = 28 + 15; 44 = 2 + 42; 46 = 16 + 30; 52 = 19 + 33; 58 = 13 + 45; 60 = 39 + 21; 61 = 23 + 38; 65 = 57 + 8; 68 = 36 + 32; 70 = 52 + 18; 71 = 67 + 4; 74 = 25 + 49; 75 = 40 + 35; 79 = 62 + 17; 83 = 56 + 27; 84 = 60 + 24; 85 = 44 + 41; 88 = 77 + 11; 96 = 22 + 74; 98 = 34 + 64; 99 = 70 + 29; 100 = 63 + 37; 102 = 54 + 48; 104 = 46 + 58; 108 = 55 + 53; 109 = 43 + 66; 115 = 65 + 50; 118 = 47 + 71; 120 = 69 + 51; 129 = 68 + 61; 132 = 59 + 73; 148 = 76 + 72; 153 = 78 + 75.

108 SCRAPBOOK MIXUP

1. *The Sunday Guardian* (Trinidad and Tobago). Roti, barra, doubles, black pudding, souse, pelau, and coconut water are "local foods" of the Caribbean.
2. *Metro Manila Times.* Movie listings included both Filipino and English titles.
3. *The Lititz* (Pa.) *Record-Express.* Only a small-town newspaper would list local school menus.
4. *The* (Montreal) *Gazette.* Only the Canadian newspaper would list snow conditions for both Quebec City and New England and use the British spelling of "centre."
5. (London) *Daily Mirror.* The style in which the date is expressed, 28-1-84, would rule out the U.S., and the cool January climate would rule out South Africa, Australia, the Philippines, and Trinidad and Tobago. (Canada is eliminated by #4, and Ireland by #7.)
6. *Los Angeles Herald Examiner.* Radio stations with call letters starting with K are located only in the United States and normally only west of the Mississippi River.
7. *Irish Independent.* The advertised airfares could be offered only from Dublin. The shamrock also suggests Ireland.
8. *The New York Times.* Broadway is in New York City.
9. *The Australian.* Only a country south of the equator would have a "Summer Spectrum" TV series in January. "ABC" stands for Australian Broadcasting Corporation. (South Africa is ruled out in #10.)
10. *The* (Johannesburg) *Star.* Only the South African newspaper would be likely to list exchange rates for Zambia, Malawi, and Zimbabwe, but not South Africa itself.

113 BULL'S-EYE 20 QUESTIONS #4

1. Why (Y)
2. Unteach (Utah)
3. Treble (true blue)
4. Hubs (Bush)
5. Elucidating (lucid, eating)
6. There (here)
7. Beauty (Beau, Ty; bow-tie)
8. Unhyphenated
9. Massacring
10. Gyp
11. Nymph (N.Y. m.p.h)
12. Cries (Aries)
13. Aide (1945)
14. Overstuffed (r, s, t, u)
15. Stupefy (stoop if I)
16. Round (rotund)
17. Overhang (hangover)
18. Boosts
19. Addressee
20. Willful

"Absence makes the heart go yonder."—Robert Byrne

ANSWERS

19 SQUARE ROUTES #1 WORD LIST

1. Hatch
2. Safe
3. Fish
4. Earth
5. Leg
6. File
7. Blanket
8. Exchange
9. After
10. Wash
11. Chair
12. Strike
13. Frame
14. Race
15. Standard
16. Night
17. Pin
18. Gang
19. Moth
20. Smoke
21. Medicine
22. Contact
23. Summer
24. Muscle
25. Reading

53 SQUARE ROUTES #2 WORD LIST

1. Finger
2. Turtle
3. Garden
4. Rattle
5. Dial
6. End
7. Cabin
8. Eagle
9. Train
10. Note
11. Hen
12. Lightning
13. Level
14. Gear
15. Nerve
16. Tonic
17. Arm
18. High
19. Fountain
20. Leaf
21. Shoulder
22. Sleep
23. Plate
24. Fire
25. Pigeon
26. Brain

101 SQUARE ROUTES #3 WORD LIST

1. Spread
2. Amuses
3. Terrapins
4. Stream
5. Sent
6. Escallop
7. Nation
8. Alarming
9. Glean
10. Early
11. Mash
12. Heart
13. Disperse
14. Pole
15. Sparse
16. Raiment
17. Pickets
18. Rise
19. Taste
20. Night
21. Sidearm
22. Unsoiled
23. Tsar
24. Idler
25. Seeing
26. Esprit
27. Gulp

68 TREASURE HUNT HINTS

Starting puzzle Columns 4 and 6, reading down, will tell you the location of the next clue.

Bedroom puzzle Start in the lower right corner of the square (letter U), and read counterclockwise in a spiral.

Lampshade puzzle The numbers in parentheses are not library call numbers, but indications of letters to be taken from the titles. For example, the 1st, 9th, 6th, and 7th letters of *Lord of the Rings* are L-E-F-T.

Dining room puzzle Add and subtract the letters in the names of the objects pictured, then read the result *backwards*.

Bathroom puzzle The answers to the clues are: TRUMP, FONTS, ANTED, and SNORE. Put the letters in the new order indicated, beginning with the U in TRUMP and N in SNORE.

Front steps puzzle Insert the letters under each column, in an order for you to determine, in the squares directly above them.

Desk puzzle Rearrange the ten groups of letters (without rearranging letters within groups) to spell the hiding place of the next clue. The first two words in the message are LOOK INSIDE.

Refrigerator puzzle Perform the arithmetic as given, and keep a running total after each step. Then, using the subtotals, let 1 = A, 2 = B, etc. The letter values will spell the location of the next clue.

Closet puzzle A simple-substitution cryptogram. Knowing that this is the last clue of the hunt should help you figure out what the first word is likely to be. Additional help: The word THE appears three times.

114 WRY SANDWICHES #3

1. PULLMAN TICKET

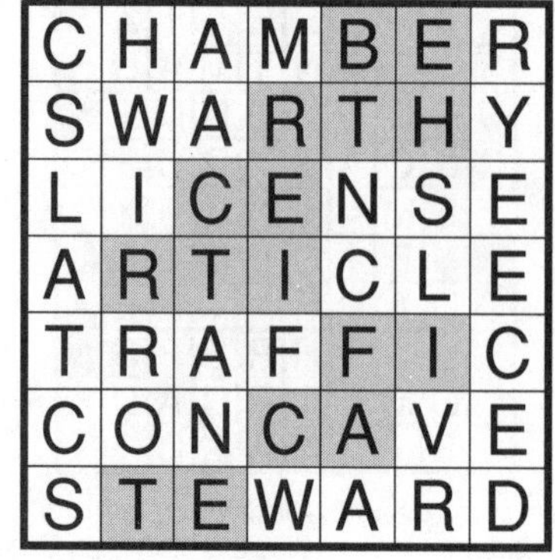

2. JOGGING MANUAL

S	T	R	U	D	E	L
C	O	N	N	I	V	E
S	Y	R	I	N	G	E
A	P	R	I	C	O	T
I	M	M	E	N	S	E
V	I	N	T	A	G	E
C	R	Y	S	T	A	L

3. RECTANGLE?

W	R	E	S	T	L	E
S	P	A	T	U	L	A
O	C	T	O	P	U	S
S	U	R	F	A	C	E
T	R	O	L	L	E	Y
O	B	E	L	I	S	K
P	I	O	N	E	E	R

93 SKELETON WORD LIST

3-letter Words: HIT, EON, TWO, DOT

4-letter Words: GLAD, SAVE, FOWL, WHIZ, REST, PEAK, EAST, TURN, TOTE, NEED, HOSE, ERGO, HELP, WHOA

5-letter Words: SPICE, SMILE, ZONED, GOWNS

6-letter Words: RECKON, MAIDEN, PISTOL, MORALS, TAVERN, NATION, NORMAL, GUZZLE

7-letter Words: STEEPLE, PRESENT

8-letter Words: FRIGHTEN, DEADLOCK

73 SUPER SEVEN WORD LIST

1. Seven Rooms in a House: Attic; Bathroom; Bedroom; Den; Foyer; Kitchen; Study

2. Seven Hitchcock Films: *Notorious; Psycho; Rebecca; Rope; Saboteur; Spellbound; Vertigo*

3. Seven Dances: Cancan; Charleston; Foxtrot; Hustle; Polka; Rumba; Tango

4. Seven Gambling Games: Baccarat; Backgammon; Blackjack; Craps; Faro; Poker; Roulette

5. Seven Countries That Have Kings: Belgium; Jordan; Morocco; Nepal; Norway; Sweden; Thailand

6. Seven Things That Have Rings: Bathtub; Circus; Fiancee; Magician; Saturn; Telephone; Tree

7. Seven Dwarfs (mystery category): Bashful; Doc; Dopey; Grumpy; Happy; Sleepy; Sneezy

115 X-WORD PUZZLE

1 Humbug (hum + bug)
2 Bottom (b + motto)
3 Tidbit (tidy – y + bite – e)
4 Motmot (Tom + Tom)
5 Misfit (M + is + F + it)
6 Friars (fryers)
7 Gasman (ma sang)
8 Doctor (door + CT)
9 Series (nurSERIES)
10 Nassau (saunas)
11 Rascal (Clara's)
12 Scorch (S + co. + rich – i)
13 Server (sever + r)
14 Veiler (revile)
15 Strata (a tart's)
16 Aether (the ear)
17 Petrel (Peter + L)
18 Inland (fINLAND)
19 Tartan (tar + tan)
20 Letter (two meanings)
21 Dallas (salad + l)
22 Neared (NE + a + red)
23 Rhythm (*R*ock *H*udson's *y*oung *T*homas *H*ardy *m*ovie)
24 Tomboy (tomb + O + Y)
25 Balsam (a lamb's)
26 Layman (maLAY MANners)
27 Mayday (two meanings)
28 Dreary (dry + ear)